WITHIN

HEALING THROUGH SACRED FEMININE ARCHETYPES - AWAKEN THE GODDESS WITHIN

COURTNEY HANSON

BALBOA.PRESS
A DIVISION OF HAY HOUSE

Copyright © 2021 Courtney Hanson.

All rights reserved. No part of this book may be used or reproduced by any means, graphic, electronic, or mechanical, including photocopying, recording, taping or by any information storage retrieval system without the written permission of the author except in the case of brief quotations embodied in critical articles and reviews.

Balboa Press books may be ordered through booksellers or by contacting:

Balboa Press
A Division of Hay House
1663 Liberty Drive
Bloomington, IN 47403
www.balboapress.com
844-682-1282

Because of the dynamic nature of the Internet, any web addresses or links contained in this book may have changed since publication and may no longer be valid. The views expressed in this work are solely those of the author and do not necessarily reflect the views of the publisher, and the publisher hereby disclaims any responsibility for them.

The author of this book does not dispense medical advice or prescribe the use of any technique as a form of treatment for physical, emotional, or medical problems without the advice of a physician, either directly or indirectly. The intent of the author is only to offer information of a general nature to help you in your quest for emotional and spiritual well-being. In the event you use any of the information in this book for yourself, which is your constitutional right, the author and the publisher assume no responsibility for your actions.

Any people depicted in stock imagery provided by Getty Images are models, and such images are being used for illustrative purposes only.
Certain stock imagery © Getty Images.

Print information available on the last page.

ISBN: 978-1-9822-7551-8 (sc)
ISBN: 978-1-9822-7553-2 (hc)
ISBN: 978-1-9822-7552-5 (e)

Library of Congress Control Number: 2021920587

Balboa Press rev. date: 10/19/2021

I felt a deep call to share my story after one of the toughest seasons of my life. A true rock bottom if you will. I was desperate to find my purpose and I knew, deep down in my soul, that I was just meant for more. The work in healing made me the woman I always dreamed of becoming. For so long I continued down a path of self-sabotage and self-hate, no matter how much I did the external work - I had to go deep within. I had to walk through some very deep shadows in order to be the light house glowing in the midst of the deep, dark ocean. I know now, this was all part of my dharma.

With a desperation to experience true joy I went fearlessly into my healing. I wanted to create a legacy for my children and help women all over to gain the vision and perseverance to live the life they always have dreamed of but maybe lacked the tools or know how to obtain. This is dedicated to all the goddesses ready to step into their divine purpose in which they were destined for.

To my children & husband whom have taught me the definition of unconditional love and given strength through critical moments that I never thought was possible; My grandmother who gave me a foundation of life-long immunity from harsh conditions and showed me what true resilience means.

My intention for you is to gain confidence and knowledge in just how beautifully created you are. There is only one of you and you are here for a reason. Your soul is magnificent, and you can truly do amazing things in this lifetime if you choose too. When the mind, body, and soul become in sync and begin to work together the mountains become tangible and life slowly begins to unravel into this miraculous state of being. Cheers to taking a step in this direction and believing in yourself. You are meant to do great things. Within this book my blessing to you is the empowerment of archetypes and to teach you that the answer has always been within.

With love & gratitude,

Courtney

Contents

The Awakening 1
The Ego 31
Algal 43
The Inner Child 49
Inner Child Meditation 61
The Maiden 81
The Mother 93
The Huntress – Warrioress 121
The Wise Woman – Crone 135
The Wild Woman – Mystic 155
The Lover 195
The Queen 213
The Sage 233
The Healer 261
The Creatrix 273
The Enchantress 291
The Priestess 319
About the Author 335

The Awakening

As I took the last sip of my sixth bottle of wine, I lay crying on a hotel floor screaming on my knees, angry with God, angry with myself, angry with the world. Why couldn't I just pass out and not wake up? Why was it so hard to peacefully go out in this world and stop causing harm to those around me? I cried, I screamed, I yelled a lot of fucks and felt like I was crawling outside of my body and just wanted to escape.

Nothing could take this dis-ease away. I had given up.

I could feel myself fading away, and the sense of powerlessness that came with it was brutal. No matter what I did or how hard I tried to help myself, nothing seemed like enough anymore. It didn't seem possible for things to get any worse than they already were but yet somehow every day they would worsen just a little more with each minute that passed - until one day when everything shattered into catastrophe.

Little did I know my life was about to change forever.

I had just given up on life. I felt my body go limp and the pain become unbearable, then after a moment of stillness everything changed in an instant- like waves crashing against rocks changing their shape from smooth to jagged as they wash ashore. Suddenly it was not just me that laid there waiting for death but someone aside me...someone who loved me unconditionally.

That is when I heard her voice speak again "I'm here."

It all made sense now; Laying on the floor ready to end it all I felt a sense of warmth and comfort. I smelt the god-awful overwhelming scent of passion - the perfume my grandmother wore. It was an embrace that I had never experienced before- like suddenly time slowed down, my mind calmed, the world around me ceased to exist for just one moment in time.

I've only had one other encounter with the spirit world, and it was when I was about ten. One day while biking, my leg got caught in the chain which made me stumble and fall right in the middle of the street– an older woman and a younger girl appeared out of nowhere - I can remember the details of them so vividly. The older woman was in her forties with shoulder length chestnut brown hair, pale skin and a smile that lit up your soul like the grand finale at a Fourth of July show. The younger girl had long, wavy dirty dish water hair and piercing brown eyes that made you want to reach out for a hug with the warmth and embrace. They had items around their shoulders... chains, ropes, almost like a lasso.

They unhooked me to freedom and whispered "go home" before disappearing down the street. I looked up to say thank you and they had disappeared. Panicked, I ran inside to tell my grandmother and father what happened only to find out they both saw spirits often, so they didn't act surprised or shocked by their appearance. It scared me so much that afterwards I subconsciously turned off whatever gift or power led them to finding me, until the age of thirty-three. On my knees in the Holiday Inn something triggered memories again from childhood and everything came flooding back into my conscious mind.

My grandmother was always my peace within the storm. When my mother left at the age of two to chase her own personal happily ever after, my dad and I moved in with my grandmother so she could be the mother role model I needed so desperately in my life.

She would play dress up with me, wash my hair until it squeaked clean in the sink, snuggle me and read books, drive me to school, style my wild lioness curls, match my clothing to my American girl dolls - she was my world. She did all of this while working full time in the corporate world at a company called Fluke.

I used to stand in awe of her color coordinated closet with pencil skirts and blazers - all the bold color palettes with matching stacked boxes of heels.

Her outfits were immaculate. The matching earrings down to the pumps. My grandmother was anything but ordinary. She was extraordinary. If she wanted something in life - she got it.

When I was eleven, I walked home from school just like any other day and she was sitting on the front porch step with my dad. The scene felt off - I knew they were about to tell me something, but I just assumed it was about my mom. At the time there was constant drama with our visitation or just not seeing her at all. I had just begun visits with her for the first time in years and just thought she had gone away again, and they were going to give me the speech on how much they loved me, and it wasn't my fault. They invited me to sit on the porch steps with them and told me she was diagnosed with lung cancer. It was aggressive. Up to this point, I had never experienced death, I didn't really understand the concept. My assumption was she was sick, and she would get better.

As she began to fight her cancer, my world was turned upside down. I would flush away all of the cigarette boxes that she had hidden throughout the house, but she just found better hiding spots. My stepdad would sneak by our house when we were gone and bring her cigarettes since everyone refused to buy them for her. She was feisty and like I said this woman got what she wanted. She knew she was dying and was going to enjoy all she loved in her last days. Cigarettes being one of those things. Her body became yellow as chemo and radiation took over her life; this strong woman who used to be able to do anything began to disintegrate before my very eyes. It was only months before she became bed ridden. My dad took care of her, but it got to the point hospice had to be called in, she wasn't herself anymore. There were IV's in her bedroom pumping her full of morphine and fluids, she began to not be able to eat foods, she was dying.

My everything was about to leave me. She was sixty-four. She had a lot of life left to live.

I felt this overwhelming sense of loss with no goodbye when my grandmother passed. She ended up having to go into the hospital for her last weeks and I was getting ready to leave for camp with my school. It was September 22nd, 1998, and we went for our daily visit to the hospital to see her. I was telling her how excited I was for camp with school being back in - I had just started the 6th grade. Mrs. Roppo's class was going over the ferry and all my best friends would be there. She told me to go have fun at camp and she would see me when I got back. The pain was beginning to overtake her, and she knew she was getting ready to cross, but she never let me know she was hurting. She never complained.

We received a phone call as soon as we got home to turn around and come back to the hospital - my grandmother was fading fast. My dad warned me on the drive over that she was in her last hours. We walked into the hospital and to the left was her room.

Everything happened so fast and was such a blur. As soon as the double doors opened the nurse ran down the hall to meet us - the words I never wanted to hear came out… "I'm sorry you're too late she just passed".

My body went limp, and I ran as fast as I could to her room not believing the nurse. My hugs could bring her back - I just knew it. Everything around me no longer existed at that moment. I ran in and hugged her lifeless body - I couldn't breathe. I kept screaming "bring her back" - Her best friend PJ was there holding her hand through her crossing.

My dad had me escorted out of the hospital room by the nurses because I was inconsolable. My emotions were never validated – they were unacceptable and drama. I sat sobbing in a ball by myself on the hospital room floor. I remember the cold white linoleum with grey lines. The nurses tried to console me, but nothing would fix that my person just left me. My world was about to drastically change.

July 10th

Dear Grandma,

I can't even find the words to tell you how dearly I miss you, how I wonder daily what my life would be if you were still here and didn't leave this earth so soon. I know you would have saved me from so many situations. You were my safety, my sounding board, my person. I thank you for all you did for me. All you sacrificed for me. Not a day goes by something doesn't remind me of you or something doesn't make me wonder about you. I wish you could have met my children; I wish you were there when I was pregnant with my son and so young and scared. I had no idea what the fuck I was doing but somehow felt a security in knowing someone would love me like you did - my child. My husband's favorite drink is Dr. Pepper, I knew there was some connection of you signaling "he's the one" when he told me that. I miss our talks so much - I did pass along to my kids "find something to get excited about every night before bed for the next day. Wake up in wonder of what good news may happen." I still think this is the best advice anyone has ever given me. I try to do it myself but fail from time to time. I am so sorry with how you were treated toward the end. You were so sick, and I am sure so scared, but you never showed it. You are still the strongest woman I have ever known, and I have met a lot of women on my journey thus far. I don't know how you did it all. I never once saw you cry or be sad, you smiled and persevered through every situation. I am sorry I didn't get to say goodbye to you. I remember it like yesterday.

I had just started seeing my mom for visits and I didn't understand the concept of death. I thought you would be here forever. I was leaving with dad from the hospital and his phone rang. They said you were fading fast, so we rushed to the hospital, but we were too late. I'll never forget seeing PJ's face as you held her hand. You told her to tell me you loved me, but I didn't get to say it back. I curled up on the white cold linoleum tile in the hall of the hospital while shut out of the room - I wanted to hold you forever. I ran in the room once more to hold you and was told that was enough and it was time to go. I felt like I couldn't breathe even writing it down I can feel that piece of me that died that day. It still hurts so bad. I never went on my camping trip because after your funeral we left your house - my home. We moved to Illinois with dad's new girlfriend, Phyllis. I knew no one, everyone made fun of me and all I wanted was to tell you - to talk to you. You always had the answer. I don't even think you have a tombstone, I tried to visit you last year in Seattle and no one would tell me where you were. You deserved to be honored, you deserved flowers, you got nothing and sacrificed everything for your family. The day you died I promised to be strong, I promised to never feel that pain again because it wasn't allowed. I was just supposed to forget you. You weren't talked about; I saw you in my dreams for a while which let me know your presence was still there. As an adult dad would tell me stories of how much you hated him or how he was your meal ticket. He said you were a workaholic and never around, so you tried to make up for it with me. I have never listened - I saw first-hand all you did for him, for me. You paid the bills, allowed him to have breaks while playing the essential mom role I was missing.

I wish I could thank you as an adult I have no idea how you managed. I am sorry I've let you down, I know you would be rolling over in your grave about half of what I've chosen to do in life. When I think of childhood, I think of you. When I think of the stableness in my life it was you. When you left, I had no one to talk to - no one to tell my secrets to - no one to tell me it was going to be okay. Your' legend was erased so fast. Within a month I was in a new school with no friends, a new state, a new house, a new "mom", new stepbrothers - I remember shortly after we moved Phyllis's x husband thought we were gone. My dad had run to the store, and I was home alone. He broke into our house, and I was so scared.

I ran to the fourth-floor bathroom and while I was on the phone with 911, I remember you saying, "stay here". He ran out spooked because a pot fell off the counter randomly -

I know that was you. I wish often I had an eighth of the strength you had - you met any situation head on, and I just crumbled. You were a true Libra; I knew when my sons were both Libras it was another sign of strength - another sign of you. My first borns due date was the day you passed; I knew that was you with me. Signs have always been all around me that you were guiding me - I just didn't know how to see them. I never realized until I met Julianne (my therapist) This woman is changing my life - I wish you two could have met. Your personalities are so much alike. We are working with how much life changed when you left. How much I never received the permission to miss you openly, how I never got to cry for you, they played Amazing Grace at your funeral because you were the definition of grace. That was your song on the hard days. Since your funeral if I hear the song, I change the station or remove myself from the room. It hurts so bad because it's the closest thing I have left of you. The fucked-up part of it all - Julianne wants me to listen to this very song while writing to you. I can still feel you like you're here with me through every verse that plays. You defined who I am at a core level. I believe in so much because of you - I know angels exist and know I am guided even through my darkest times because of your presence. Do you remember when you started losing hair and taught me how to do your makeup when you couldn't lift your arms. I became a makeup artist. You were the most glamorous woman I had ever met. I am pretty sure you made the slogan "put on some lip stick and handle it." God, I miss you...I will honor you by being the woman you shaped me into being. I was just so lost along the way. I lost myself - I've always just tried to make everyone happy, for everyone to like me... Then I became a mother. That was my identity. I haven't been Courtney in so many years. I promise to get your tombstone and honor your memory. I promise to create that woman that you envisioned for me as an adult. Most importantly I promise to not shut you out. When I smell your perfume I'll smile, when I hear Amazing Grace, I'll blast it, and when I think of you, I'll feel it. You are worth that and so much more.

I'll pick up traditions with my children I have let die out because they are painful and remind me of you and I will stop numbing out when things get hard. I will be the woman you were to me to my children.

I thank you for showing me that. I guess this is my goodbye - the one I never got to say to you. Every time I am at Edmonds beach I drive by our house and just cry; I wish I could have brought my family there to feel the love you poured into every inch of it. Thank you from the bottom of my heart for shaping and molding me when no one else wanted too. I never lacked love or feeling like a normal child because of you.

Love you forever and always,
Courtney

WITHIN

Dear Poohster,

I wish I could have told you the truth and said goodbye, but I didn't want you to worry - I was trying to protect you. I asked Phyllis to take care of your dad and you, and she promised she would. I look down and smile at all our times together. What I would give for a little Dr. Pepper, Reese's and some Murder She Wrote. I want you to smile - you were always my light and that's why I showed you so much strength. I know you needed me just as I needed you. I was never upset you wanted visits with your mom over sitting in a hospital - I wanted you two to have a relationship desperately. I wish she was better to you, I tried everything. I would have set things up very differently if I knew what your future was to hold. For this dear girl I am sorry. I want you to remember me - you're an empath, stop shutting it off. I always told you this was your gift. Life is hard but you can do hard things - you're a Hurley and that's what we do - persevere. I'm your guide and have never left your side. I am in no pain and can dance and play bingo whenever I damn well please now. I want you to know and remember everyone has something, don't let that steal your sunshine. Find a reason to be excited every day and stop hiding from the world. What they think of you is none of your business. You get ready, put your best foot forward and always work like you're working for God. We all have a history and are meant to learn lessons. You're stubborn my dear girl so it takes you a bit longer. I am not disappointed but my heart hurts that you are aching. I know you went through the dark to help so many people heal in the future. Your pain will have a purpose, it will not go unnoticed. I want you to let go - stop holding on so tight to things that maybe just aren't meant to be. There are special plans for you, it's just not your turn to see them yet. I want you to carry on our Christmas traditions with your children, keep my memory alive. Show them my pictures and tell them our best of times. I bet your daughter would love American Girl dolls just like you did. I know you sold them all and wanted to hand them down to your future kids, but it was the right thing to do for your situation at the time. Love is so hard. I want you to know pain will not kill you - it softens you to grow stronger but Pooh, you have to stop running

Plant your seeds, water them vigorously and grow. It's time. You have nothing to lose and everything to gain –

COURTNEY HANSON

it's time to fly Courtney. Be proud of who you are despite your past and what you've seen and done. Guilt and shame lead nowhere productive – forgive yourself, you are not a bad person, you are worthy of love. You were always my princess, and you need to put back on your tiara. Sit at an ocean and remember how small you are but what a difference one wave can create. You are that wave – learn to ebb and flow with the Universe directing you. I will never stop loving you – I am always here looking down on you and smiling. A tombstone doesn't define my connection with you – my spirit does and that is something which will live on forever. You know I am blunt and to the point but before we say goodbye, I want you to do something for me. Have fun and enjoy life, it's gone before you know it. Stop staying home so much and feeling guilt for feeling joy. Go for adventures, smell fresh air, live excited to open your eyes upon rising. I love you to heaven and back.

Make me proud – I am watching,
Grandma

For years I let the outside noise determine who I was. The outside beliefs. The self-pity. The constant moves. The perceptions, which were not mine, but adopted over the experiences I had in life. I learned from a very young age to smile and be strong – crying fixed nothing. Emotions were in the way. Being raised by a man, who was damaged himself, I knew very little of feminine energy and only lived within the masculine. This mentality of playing the victim followed me everywhere, until one day it was just too much. I was the shadow Maiden - the damsel in distress. For a long time, I thought there was only one path for me. To be this victim role and accept whatever life threw my way, or to try my best not to get hurt by anything that happens along the journey - but then sitting in a conference one of the speakers said something that was the starting point of my mindset shift "You have two options in life – to be the patient or become the Doctor".

It's not like life suddenly became perfect that second but in realizing my own worth outside what others told me about myself-I realized how wrong they were: Healing doesn't mean the damage never existed. It means the damage no longer controls your life. Growing up with shame and guilt is a difficult thing to deal with, especially when you feel as if it's something that can never be fixed. We all make mistakes in life; some are just bigger than others. Shame makes these moments seem even worse because we have nowhere else to turn for help but ourselves--we must look within. It may sound complicated, but this type of trauma often begins much earlier on in our lives-when we were children without any understanding of what was happening around us.

The fear associated with childhood memories can manifest itself into adulthood behaviors which cause an immense amount of pain for those who care about us the most: family members, friends, and relationships.

When I looked for outside sources to fix my shame, it only amplified. I thought that if someone else could find the way out of this guilt-filled hole with me then everything would be okay again. But as soon as they left and went back into their own lives, all those feelings came flooding right back in because now there was no one left to sit with but myself. Living in self-shame is very difficult when you are constantly looking for external sources to help alleviate your burdens - but what happens if those people eventually leave? All these negative emotions come rushing back. It's a vicious cycle which can't be broken unless we start taking care of ourselves. It wasn't until I began to do trauma and shadow work that memories started coming back for me. My subconscious locked my childhood in this safe little box and placed a dead bolt on it for safe keeping.

It had been the birth of my youngest child, when something snapped inside of me. I'd never experienced a sense of depression so deep; for months after his birth, loneliness became more than just how I felt when I was alone - It was the feeling of being in a room full of people, but no one was there. I wanted to be the best mom but also couldn't pull myself together enough even just for playing with my children. I didn't want friends because when they weren't there, it was too much of a commitment and became overwhelming. They would ask me what's wrong or if everything is okay? And all that did was make me cry more because those questions felt like an inquisition on why I'm not happy, which led back into wanting to feel anything at any cost so numbing out sounded good again instead of feeling nothing at all anymore - It seemed easier than facing the world head-on without running. It was this dark cycle I just couldn't shake.

My husband had left for a promotion at work shortly after my son, who had spent weeks in the NICU came home from hospital life and with all his fire academy training he wasn't able to be around for that first six-month period. I wanted to support his dream, I wanted to be a super woman, a super wife but the depression kept sinking in deeper.

Suddenly our picture-perfect family became like strangers living under one roof. It was this pattern I just couldn't break; when things should have been the happiest months of my life with this beautiful new baby - every day, they only got worse. I went to my post-partum checkups and marked all the right boxes. I told them that I was doing just fine but in reality, it felt like an act of self-preservation for me so that they wouldn't know how bad things were really getting. My occupation at the time was being a mommy blogger and Etsy expert. I provided insights on parenting - what if the truth came out about my mental state? What would people say? Little did I know that self-medicating with alcohol would slowly turn into an addiction.

It started off as a few glasses of wine at night and then it became more frequent until I was drinking every day to escape the pain in my life. In today's society wine every night is normal right? That's the story line I continued to tell myself for months.

After a while, the hangovers stopped bothering me because all they felt like were just another reminder of how bad things had gotten for me after starting this habit – the hangovers felt like an appropriate punishment – but in reality, these were warning signs telling me something needed to change before it got worse than ever imagined. When everything seemed so tough going on inside my head from depression and anxiety coupled with being put down by everyone around including myself – what better way could there be than escaping?

I would scroll social media and be blinded by the perfect families, husbands, kids. I was always jealous of what they had because it wasn't me. It didn't matter though I would still find ways to complain about everything and anything that goes wrong in this world just so people will feel sorry for me... I was never satisfied with myself, or the cards handed to me - even when there were plenty of other things going well in my life. Deep down inside I wanted nothing more than someone else's happiness instead of sitting with my own feelings. From a young age I always felt like the black sheep. I was different and never understood why. After a few months of my husband being gone I got lonely. Like really, REALLY lonely. He was focused on his job and had no idea what was going on with me, which is probably why he missed the signs that something else might be wrong in our relationship (or at least one reason). - but then boom an old fling resurfaced from years ago.

I felt like I was just going through the motions, not feeling anything. That all changed when he resurfaced – I felt excitement, I felt something for the first time in a long time. It was like your first roller coaster ride right before the plunging drop – the adrenaline made me feel alive again. I started getting ready for the first time in a year, working out, it felt scandalous, but it was an emotion I was capable of feeling. Before I knew it, I had done the very thing I swore I would never do. I had an affair. I come from a long line of cheaters and promised myself too never be like them. I was the Susie home maker, I was the glue, I was the ultimate sacrificing wife and mom - or so I thought.

I turned out to be just like them. We're the family that found out about other siblings on ancestory.com - whoopsie daisies. The dis in function.

The things that made me judge other women and make them feel bad about themselves, when in reality it was happening right in my own home.

There were so many lies being told but eventually they caught up with me; then everyone knew my business because people like a good scandal in a small town don't they?

On the outside I was a successful and happy person. I helped others with their problems, but that changed when my guilt and shame took over me. I was trying to live two lives - I was out of control. I felt dirty and disgusting all the time, like my reflection in the mirror wasn't even me anymore but a shadow of what had once been myself. My drinking amplified because I couldn't deal with who I had become, hating every aspect of myself from head-to-toe as if looking into a broken mirror reflecting nothing but shame.

Every day my hate grew deeper and deeper. No one could understand why everything had gone downhill so fast for me. My friends and family began to fade away, but none of it made any difference in this nightmare life I now lived on repeat as if trapped inside an eternal hell hole. Darkness dwelled around every corner waiting patiently. Like all of the demons from your worst nightmares coming back into haunt you. I knew my husband was going to leave me and it would be as if history were repeating itself.

I tried desperately to get help, but nothing seemed to work - western medicine failed me. I went to my doctor and explained the truth of what was going on in my head. It was ugly word vomit everywhere and the doctor looked at me and replied, "I think anyone would be on the verge of a melt down with the dynamics of your life right now".

Validation – YES. Meds to numb out even deeper – YES.

She decided that Prozac might be a good idea, but she also suggested Xanax for when I find myself feeling uncontrollably anxious. This fun little cocktail had a reverse effect on my body, especially since my wine consumption was still two bottles a night on the meds. My moods began to rapidly shift from happy-go lucky to dark depressing anger with no warning whatsoever - it just happened! I started losing track of days, I was manic, I was checked out, I couldn't get out of bed most days. A few weeks after being on the medication my husband and I began to argue about the affair, and I decided I would leave. I was in no condition to drive and so my husband tried to take the keys away from me. I bit his arm trying to get him to release his hand away from the ignition. The police were called and guess who went to jail? The night I was arrested for domestic violence my life spiraled out-of-control.

The last time anything bad happened to me, it went from a minor setback into total disaster and rehabilitation took months. CPS had been called because my children were home, I was incapable of working in my mental state, my family had sided with my husband. When I needed someone the most no one was around. I was left with myself. I had tried fighting and that didn't work out so hot for me, so I leaned into option b. – Flee.

On Thanksgiving my husband left for work, and I began drinking heavily around noon. I became in a frantic state that I needed to leave the situation, I came up with this plan to fly to Seattle early the next morning before he came home for work. My father-in-law with his sweet soul tried to come to my house and diffuse the situation but my decision had been made - I was leaving my husband and starting over.

At 4 a.m. I woke up and began drinking more wine to ease the hang over from the night before, my friend picked me up and drove the kids and I to the airport. Angels carried me this day with divine intervention – I had hit the point of not knowing what to do anymore.

It was as if my soul had evacuated my body. I was in autopilot. My husband and I were at war, while I was at the airport, he shut down our bank accounts,

I had absolutely no money, a phone that was being tracked, and felt my every move was being watched.

As I went to pay for our luggage my card declined, and I just began to sob at the flight attendants' station. I couldn't be strong anymore; I had hit my breaking point and out of all places at the airport. "I am so embarrassed; I think I am going through a divorce, and I have these tickets but no way to check our luggage."

My oldest tugged on my sweater. "Mama let's just spend Christmas in Hawaii." I looked at him with tears welling heavier by the minute in my eyes and told him "I am sorry buddy; I promise this will be better soon." My daughter had been over petting a service dog of a couple leaving their families in California for Thanksgiving. She is quit the conversationalist and makes friends wherever she goes. This couple had overheard the situation that was happening and upgraded our tickets to Hawaii. I couldn't hold back anymore and burst out crying and told them "I have no way of paying this back, thank you. How can I repay this?"

They replied, "You don't – just get through this." The baggage claim worker came over and gave me $40 cash and told me "Don't worry about the bags, you may load your flight it has been taken care of for you."

As we buckled in for take-off - I felt I could exhale for the first time all morning. I ordered more wine and tried to plan what I would do when we unloaded the plane in Seattle. I had $40, tickets for a layover to Hawaii, and three children who needed me to be strong. When the plane unloaded the flight attended asked me to stay on board. I was terrified, my palms were sweating, and I had no idea what was going to happen next. The captain called my children to the cock pit and showed them all the controls of the aircraft. The flight attendant whispered, "don't worry, we're going to help you." The captain came toward me and said "follow me" we all unloaded the plane together and walked to an ATM where he withdrew $200 and then introduced me to a woman named Kim. Kim walked us through the SeaTac airport and gave us food vouchers and showed me where the kids could play in the cafeteria while I figured out what I was going to do. I looked at her with eyes full of emptiness and sincerely asked "am I going to be okay".

"Of course, you are, this happens more often than you think, that's why we are here." They wished me well and we exchanged phone numbers in case anything happened. I decided to not go to Hawaii and my uncle picked us up from the airport.

I spent the next two weeks at my aunt and uncles regaining my thoughts, allowing myself space, and giving my children time with no conflict. I purchased a car while in Seattle, got my own phone plan, and was able to have honest conversations with my husband for the first time in a long time. I realized I deeply loved him but didn't know that balance of where I could have space to heal while still being married. I agreed to fly home and we both made a promise to make Christmas special for our kids. Later that month, the charges were dropped from my arrest. I just felt there wasn't any point in piling up more mistakes onto an already unbalanced scale, so I just let myself fall down that hole again like before with no concern for where I'd land.

What happened in that jail cell was triggers? All sorts of triggers I would never understand until I embarked on my healing journey. My ego was raging. "This can't happen to you; people are going to ruin you." "Everyone hates you" "Your family has turned against you; they are on Cameron's side" "You're going to be homeless and alone"

"Your children are scarred what kind of mother are you?" "You were never meant to be married or be a mom, you need to leave before you do to them what your mom did to you." They wouldn't stop. The voices got louder and louder. The little me inside was screaming, terrified, crying out for help but the adult me just tuned it out and shut it down. My husband and I decided to stop drinking all together and this lasted for about six months, and we were slowly beginning to heal. Then we went out to Sushi and decided to drink.

All the thoughts, the depression, the anxiety, it came back as if it never went away. I couldn't stop drinking. I was hiding it in the closet, in the shelves, I was pretending to be sober when everyone knew I was clearly not. I saw everything begin to spiral again so I woke up at 3 a.m. and decided I couldn't live this way any longer. The therapist was not helping, the meds were not helping, I was hopeless.

I called a friend to watch my kids and said Cameron and I just needed some time apart and it was urgent I leave before he came home from work.

My intention was to book a hotel room, drink myself into oblivion, stop caring about anything at all-just wanting the pain of abandonment out of my body with as much alcohol as it took for that happening. I was preparing to fall asleep and not wake up. I kissed my children goodbye and told them how deeply I loved them and how I would always be with them. The entire drive I cried in hysterics white knuckling the steering wheel trying to convince myself I was doing what was best for everyone around me. All I did was cause damage – I believed this was the most selfless act I could do in order to protect them and have them live happy and healthy lives. This was the only way I saw to break the family cycle – to eliminate the last one who would pass down the trauma.

I knew my husband would be tracking my phone and calling the police for well fare checks as I checked into the hotel, so I texted who I needed to text, saw who I needed to see and then locked myself in the room to begin drinking into oblivion. The police came and I explained I was getting a divorce and that I left to just recollect myself. After hours passed where nothing happened but more drinking in an empty hotel room without any other human being around except one, the one I knew just wouldn't go away - I realized what this really meant: I was stuck with me. I had to face myself.

On the 4th of July I woke up and knew it was time to stop. I have personally never been through a detox or even known that a detox off alcohol was a thing but let me tell you that if anything was going to kill me, it was that detox.

I laid crying, panicking, shaking, throwing up blood for almost five days. I saw no light at the end of the tunnel and still had no way to make sense of my divine moment in the hotel room. My brother-in-law had found someone who specialized in trauma therapy, and I agreed to go because I simply had no shits left to give. I thought a trauma therapist was a little extreme and tried to explain I had never experienced trauma, but everyone who knew me continued to urge me into going. I had no options it was do this or lose my children. I thought it would be like every other therapist "how do you feel about that" "let's explore these feelings." Ummm. No thank you, I like these feelers in that little box they safely reside in. We found out a day before I was supposed to meet her our funding fell through. Our finances were a disaster. Our family was falling apart. I was at a place of sheer surrender.

I was broken and just began to write. I had not picked up a journal in a very long time but through these months it seemed to be the only thing that listened to me. A safe space in the midst of pure chaos.

July 9th

I am powerless. Now the funding isn't coming into place and I am so afraid. I know I can do this alone I never want to feel like this again, but I am so desperate to process with someone that isn't family. Trying to stay in the moment and enjoy every second with my children while I have it. Last night we stayed up talking and I found out all the damage I had caused and felt like I had a mental breakdown. I have really ruined everything. I want to push everyone away. I want to blame, and I feel like no one gets me. Like they think I don't have feelings because of my actions. I have a problem to live in a solution by and fix but I am not an animal that I am being made out to be. I found out my family called CPS not the police and I am so hurt. I won't say anything, but I still feel so much pain that everyone's boundaries are set but I get none. I am trying to stay busy, to not react and do the right thing but I want to burst into tears at any given time. I have no access to my husband's phone as he has changed the code, but he has full access to me at any given time. I want to change and live a happy life. What the fuck is a happy life? How are people happy? This is a nightmare. Someone just wake me up. Everyone can keep secrets from me, and I would never know. But my life…my life is the main event for everyone to sit and gossip about. I guess it all doesn't matter. I am doing this for myself to be free once and for all. It sure would be nice to feel like I could trust just one person. I have truly hit a bottom I never thought could happen. I am exhausted constantly trying to prove myself. I feel like my insides have been turned out like I am just standing here butt ass naked for the world to see. I am slowly killing myself trying to tear down these walls I have built up so high. Who am I? I am doing everything the opposite as to what I want to do, and everything just feels like a storm in my soul right now.

—Courtney

July 10th

I got ready this morning for the first time in over two months. It is still so hard to look at myself in the mirror. I had to straighten my hair reading a book, but I did it. I figure maybe I should stop looking like I stuck my finger in a socket. My eyes are already swollen enough from all the crying. I get to talk to a therapist today. I feel like a Mount St. Helens of words may just come exploding out of my mouth like word vomit. I am really struggling with what everyone's saying about me. It feels like walls caving in all around me. I want to text and tell everyone sorry, but the counselor told me to wait so now I feel like I am putting the weight of everyone on Cameron which hurts me so deeply. I wish there was a way to make him understand I am sorry for who I am, for how I am. I don't know what is wrong with me. I don't want to be like this. I wish I could have stopped it; I wish I could remember but the more he tells me the more it scares me to death. My insides physically hurt from all of this. My head gets clear, and I feel good for a few minutes and then BOOM train incoming fast. Words make me freeze inside. Yesterday my chest was hurting so bad I thought I was having a legit heart attack. I keep telling myself each day it will get a little better but each day I just feel like I am gasping for air drowning. I wish my family knew the damage in which they have caused. I wish they knew all I ever wanted was to feel accepted and loved by them. Now I am repeating the same cycle with my family. I hate myself. As far as my husbands concerned, I am not sure he will ever touch me again. He is an amazing man and person, so he is helping to save my life but as far as intimacy goes... I am not sure we will ever get back to where we were. Now I am crying and haven't even started the day. Off to therapy - talk soon.

– Courtney

COURTNEY HANSON

July 15th

I am so confused with where my life is taking me right now. Cameron and I had such a good weekend, everything felt like it was going to be okay and then I had a super emotional week at therapy, and everything went to shit. I am trying so hard to open up to him but nothing I give is enough. Everything I feel is wrong and I am having to face these issues I didn't even know were issues from childhood. I walked into Julianne's office explaining all I had done and was honest beyond honest and she looked me dead in the eye and said "Why do you feel guilty? What are you afraid of?" IM AFRAID OF EVERYTHING are you kidding me, what kind of question is this? I am the bad one here can't you see... She looked at me with tears almost welling in her eyes and said "Courtney you have been through a lot of traumas. Let's start at when this all started. When your grandmother died." Oh shit. No, no, no. Not this topic, I don't even remember half of it. I was only 12. This has nothing to do with my post-partum. She gave me a smirk like she knew something I didn't and said "This started a long time ago. You had a very traumatic childhood and the post-partum maybe triggered it, but it is not the problem here." I started sobbing. Ugly embarrassing crying and do you know the only thing I could say... "Can you fix me?" Like I was a broken toy being brought back to Target. Can we trade it in for something that works? I feel so alone right now. I feel like everyone is against me and at any time everything could take a turn for the worse. I guess I'll at least give this weird letter shit a try. I just want to feel good enough. I want a magic wand right now I feel like I am living in one big double standard. My brain won't shut up it's going five billion miles an hour at all times.

Just. Make. It. Stop.

-Courtney

Now, I could share my entire journal with you but for all educational purposes I was desperate and felt broken in to a million shattered pieces. It was as if the universe had been holding me up just long enough for my spiritual awakening to happen. As I started doing this work everything on the spiritual path aligned and before I knew it, all of these things were happening at once: there are no coincidences in life after all. I became fearless in my pursuit to help other women on their healing journey. I went back to school and completely changed careers and lives at the age of thirty-three. I had been on this quest to find myself and kept hitting dead ends. I knew my soul's contract was to create, but I didn't realize a part of that creation process was in creating myself. I wasn't broken - nor did I need fixing. I was wounded and needed healing. Everything that made up who I am was within me all along.

A good therapist can help you work through the past and make sense of it. But when I was going through my own formative years, shadow work not only helped me heal but also changed what I saw in myself for the better. It woke up something inside that told me to believe in who I am enough so that others could see it too. I never knew how much darkness had been weighing on my shoulders until shadow work came into my life. The two together were able to change everything about me - even right down to the cellular level where all cells are nurtured by love instead of despair as they had been before; nothing is off limits anymore. I had discovered duality. There was power within my shadows. The reality was that life was not all "love and light".

From a young age we fear the dark, this dates back to cave man days when we were always on the lookout for predators and had to be in a fight or flight response for our safety. Darkness is one of the most terrifying things to human beings. It is something that humans have developed a primal fear for through evolution due to how important vision has been throughout history. When our eyes are at full power, we can see everything around us and feel safe in what's familiar. However, when it gets dark, that comfort vanishes because all sense-of sight-is gone. When darkness sets in on a person, they become more cautious about their surroundings; every sound becomes amplified even if there was nothing but silence before. The mind begins to play tricks on us.

The history of dark meditation dates back to Taoism. Obsessed with understanding the human mind, ancient philosophers would seek refuge in caves and other places that were darker than average. Their time spent there helped them experience higher states of consciousness while also celebrating yin-the divine feminine aspect as life. Our subconscious and conscious are really miraculous. Let's take a minute to break down what that means before we move on with my personal story. I want to share some science with you before we go any further, as it'll help provide context - The conscious mind is your thoughts, memories, feelings. It's what you're aware of at any given moment in time. Now here comes the kicker: Our consciousness only has access to certain types of memories. Our subconscious mind is like a reservoir of feelings, thoughts, urges and awareness. It does not discriminate between past memories that are traumatic or positive ones; it holds on to all the trauma as if they were going out of style. The bad news about this type of storage system is when we run into stressful situations similar to those from our past- such as being bullied in high school for example - then these old wounds open up and cause us pain again.

We have two major nervous systems: the sympathetic (our fight or flight) which gears you up for action while the para-sympathetic (rest and digest) brings your body back down so you can be more present with what's happening now rather than reacting impulsively and acting out embarrassingly just because someone bumped into you.

With all the adrenaline rushing through your bloodstream, it's easy to understand that we are in a fight or flight state. This is not only because our muscles tighten and those around us can feel how tense we become but also when we activate this sympathetic nervous system there will be three different responses happening: freeze, anger/rage (fight), and startle response with an understanding for safety which would lead someone into fleeing (flight).

As human beings with both impulses such as running away from danger versus fighting against it; however, one thing does remain constant-the physical effects caused by stress hormones on the body during these differing moments. When faced with a stressful situation the brain activates what is known as "sympathetic arousal" where our nerves activate and send epinephrine through the autonomic nerve, they tell the adrenal gland to pump it out into your blood stream so now you can be ready if needed no matter what situation arises. When you were a child, your body had this amazing power of shaking away any negative thoughts or emotions that came up during traumatic moments in life. We would throw ourselves on the ground, shake and clench our fist, yell, one way or another it was coming out at a physical level. When we reach adulthood though these methods may seem unpractical if not impossible in certain situations (such as grocery stores). So, what do adults end up doing? We hold it all in and go into the "freeze" part of our bodies. Our psoas muscle is the connective tissue linking our upper and lower bodies together. It's one of those "invisible" muscles that we often mistake for just another part of us, but it keeps us safe by storing chemicals released from trauma in this area as well. When trauma occurs, it is stored in the unconscious mind for safe keeping and can be released at a later time. Trauma that we experience during our waking hours are usually stored away into the subconscious memory as to not disrupt us while going about daily life- but when traumatic memories occur, they stay with you until processed by your conscious self - so for "safe" keeping our physical bodies hold on to the trauma.

When you experience an event that leaves a lasting impression, it is encoded into your synapses. This can lead to limiting beliefs and fear conditioning being hardwired because the information will be there every time you think about something similar happening in life. Glutamate bonds are difficult to dissolve, but they do eventually disappear when other new connections turn up or our brains get reorganized by the healing process of neuroplasticity. The difference between before someone begins their journey towards "healing from a cellular level" and after doing so might even show up on x-rays as different brain structures based off changes in synaptic density. Amazing right? Okay - back to the story...

I found myself in intense therapy sessions day after day that lasted for several months with my therapist. I wrote over a hundred letters to her, and some days felt like she was crazy while other times I believed the same of me. I've spent years trying to reconstruct my sense of reality. I felt like a wet rag that could never be wrung out, always dripping with the need for attention and approval from everyone around me. My therapist helped me take apart these beliefs one by one until I was able to start believing in myself again. I had been acting as if everything revolved around other people's needs because it was easier than facing the intense feelings inside of myself.

I've been looking to heal my inner demons for a long time, and I thought that meant finding out how they work. But what if healing means knowing, understanding, accepting? What if it's not about things which "expose" us but rather ourselves; instead of being ashamed or afraid we would take them as challenges in life because at the end there will be something gained from overcoming our own weaknesses- knowledge. Knowledge is power. Knowledge is divine wisdom. I wasn't the victim. I was a fucking warrior. I was the wild woman.

I've never felt more alive than when I was doing what my soul needed me to do. It seemed as if Source had dismantled and then remade me piece by piece, sign by sign.

After one of my podcast interviews, which featured a woman discussing the art of receiving instead of always chasing, it became clear to me that I was masculine energy. I was the chaser. The subject matter really resonated with me. After being raised religious I never really thought about energy or science. It was just something that had to be believed without question. I was intrigued by the idea of energy and how it affects our bodies, but I struggled to let go of my old ideas. Reiki helped me understand that we are all connected through a vast field that is ever-changing – changing us as well. It wasn't until I became a Reiki Master that I truly understood we are all composed of energy. Society has long associated masculine energy with strong, powerful males. This is the same kind of power that can be seen in other aggressive creatures—elephants and lions are both typically considered to have a very male-like strength. Feminine energy might seem like it corresponds closely with what we think of as "womanly" qualities, but these two energies exist within every person regardless of gender or sex. Both men and women have masculine and feminine energy in their bodies. The dominant energy does not necessarily correlate with the person's sex, but instead reflects which of these energies has been cultivated more fully throughout one's life. The duality of one coin. The left to the right. Masculine energy is knowledge whereas Feminine energy is knowing.

The essence of feminine energy is all about turning nothing into something. She embodies the frequency of that which she wishes to experience and then attracts it like a moth to a flame because her worldview goes outside what we typically think as possible, making fantasies reality just by believing they are true with every fiber in her being. She is a woman who does not suppress her emotions but instead recognizes them as message-bearing messengers. She listens to the lessons they provide and understands that feelings are like an ever-changing tapestry, with each feeling being valuable in its own way. The feminine energy also perceives time differently than masculine; whereas linear thinking sees every event occupying one space on the timeline simultaneously, circular motion means everything moves through their own cycles of existence--interconnected yet distinct from other events happening at different points in time. She does not need to chase because she is a magnet – what she wants will flow to her with ease. When a woman discovers her creative abilities, she is able to tap into the wisdom of her higher self. These new paths are not only possible, but they can be created with ease when tapped in with feminine energy. Her intuition guides these creations and leads them down fruitful pathways without effort required because it follows natural rhythms, death then rebirth. She knows when to let go of what is no longer serving in order to make space for new projects or ideas. She needs expression through creativity and prioritizes nurturing herself. Her operation system is from the heart center.

The masculine energy is structured, with a strong focus on rules and logic. These qualities lend themselves to stability and predictability while also making the energy more difficult to read emotionally. He is the protector and guide for people to follow. He can sense danger from a great distance, but he also knows that his loved ones are just as vulnerable in need of protection too. The masculine will fight tooth-and-nail against anything or anyone who might try to hurt him or those close by. In order to achieve their goals, they're direct with commands and always on point when it comes down to what needs done next - there's no confusion involved here either. This all stems back into one crucial trait: masculinity thrives off plans and clarity; well laid out guidelines that stem not only from logic...but experience too. It's this nature which makes them masters at planning things far ahead of time, so nothing slips through the cracks.

If they want to get to C, they will always conquer A and B first. Linear. The masculine energy is just like a straight line, it never changes and always completes the task. It follows every step of its plan without blinking an eye or faltering in pace.

Women are taught to be strong, but when we lean too far into that masculine energy the pendulum swings in a direction of negativity. We come across as intense and easily pissed off which can make it difficult for others to connect with us on an emotional level. This often leads women who experience this phenomenon feeling the need to always do, trouble relaxing or sitting still because their need is so great while simultaneously being unable to receive help or support because they feel like there's things only they can do themselves. That drive for perfection means many times these women fall into a chase and hustle mentality. They feel like failures if they are not always doing. The art of receiving appears lazy.

Divine Feminine Energy helped guide me through life's lessons until finally reaching that moment of understanding where all the pieces of who you are come together in one glorious burst of light – dissipating into a trillion tiny particles again waiting for their next assignment on this grand journey called life. I had never really considered myself to be a masculine energy – but I am the chaser. I never stop until I get what I am "hustling" for. I was raised by a man that was sexist and any feminism was not allowed. I had learned from a young age to suit up, show up and take care of your shit. You speak when spoken to.

When she talked about receiving instead of chasing my whole world opened up. I always thought I had to be someone else, and in order for that to happen I would have to change who I was. However, after my interview it occurred to me that what was needed most wasn't a personality transplant but rather embracing my true spirit – awakening the Goddess within. I began to practice embodiment of each divine archetype and study all I could find on this topic. As I read through passage after passage and article after article, my eyes widened, and it felt hard to swallow. Why are we not being taught about these archetypes? The way that they relate is fascinating but something this powerful should be more well-known! Nowadays people seem obsessed with everything new or trending on social media, which often does nothing but distract them from what's really going on in life. One of the things you will learn in this book isn't just how some women feel when experiencing a certain archetype – it will reveal different aspects of each personality type including their shadows (or hidden traits). It will allow you embodiment of your power.

Through the practice of divine feminine energy, I've been able to manifest my lifelong dreams, travel more and pursue opportunities in speaking gigs and video projects that align with what I believe. My customized healing modalities have helped hundreds of women step into their divine power and birthright. It allows you to experience new ways to heal yourself on all levels: physically, emotionally, mentally and spiritually. I used to be ashamed of the very thing that I now know is my superpower.

These archetypes I am about to share with you have opened up my gifts of Claircognizance, past lives have become clearer and easier for me to explore with each passing day. I realized the very thing I was searching for outside of myself to bring me joy was within me. I was her. I was the collective. I was Source. I was the very being I searched for all along; a part of me that had never left my side and it took such an exhausting journey to realize her presence. For so long, we were separated from our true selves through outside noise, but the answer is through our heart center, through love, through realizing we are soulful beings just having a human experience. The first time I had an idea for this book, it came to me in a meditation. Within the quiet of my mind's eye, there was writing on a page that said "Within".

It kept coming up and no matter how much I tried pushing it away or focusing elsewhere – the text just kept appearing. On signs, through the radio, on social media. Then one morning as soon as I turned off the water from taking a shower-I knew what this meant: A simplistic and accessible way for women to heal. For women to embody their divine feminine energy in the sacred space of their homes. I had been working on the archetypes through feminine energy as a yoga workshop and realized this needed to be a book. It was the worst timing for me to write a book as I had a billion other projects going, but I had this strong intuition I couldn't shake that someone needed this.

If just one person is allowed healing through these pages, through my story, I know it was worth every late night.

The Ego

The ego is a powerful part of who we are. It's always looking for ways to bolster its identity and sway the way that others see it. Some people have an outwardly confident, "I'm better than you" attitude while other people think they need someone else as their savior because deep down inside they can't save themselves from whatever pain or disappointment life throws at them. The danger in these two sides is not realizing your true self which then leaves us vulnerable to emotional attachment with our physical form and what stories inevitably come along with it; good or bad, happy or sad, etc…

The ego has a strong influence on shaping who we believe ourselves to be throughout our lives. The ego is that special little friend the guru's say must "die", but I disagree because the ego can be good or bad depending on how you use it; whether positively for self-development, or negatively to manipulate others.

The ego is not good or bad it just is.

The Law of Polarity: Everything is dual; everything has poles; everything has its pair of opposites; like and unlike are the same; opposites are identical in nature, but different in degree; extremes meet.

Like any other aspect in the Law of Polarity there is light and there is darkness. Sometimes, we are so afraid of what others might say or think that we end up doing nothing. The pressure to be accepted by society and the fear of being judged can cause many people not to take risks and live a safer life than they would otherwise have chosen for themselves. This is because it's easier to let other people's beliefs control your own actions rather than taking responsibility for them yourself - but when you do this, all you're really giving away is your freedom. In life, we find it difficult to make decisions because of fear. The ego is a menacing yet jaded entity that feeds on our insecurities and fears. When we allow the ego to rule us, it forces its will upon us as if trying to break down any hope for relief from mental anguish or sorrowful memories of past failures.

The Ego has two options: To become victorious or become the victim. It doesn't care which you choose. Either way the ego is being fed and nourished.

The ego is never satisfied, and we are always trying to find something that will fill the void. It begins with this sense of identity which develops our veil onto the world, the perceptions and beliefs that begin to be developed when we are children. This all starts from comparisons made between yourself and others or your ancestors where these limiting beliefs start taking shape in our mind. Sometimes when you're amid a difficult time, it can seem like there's no way out. But what if I told you that your deepest self is already awake and helping guide you? What if we are not just those thoughts our ego tells us...

The first step in distinguishing between ego and authenticity is to take the time for contemplation. Our ego is a protection mechanism.

It keeps us shielded from vulnerability but what this does is prevents us from being authentic. The ego is the part of you that tries to "protect" you, but often it prevents us from connecting with life itself.

It's not good for people who are in a state of their unhealthy ego because they have an intense energy that is always trying to prove something or be "enough". When we're within this toxic mindset it is impossible to be operating from a state of authenticity.

All the conflicts we experience in life stem from ego. We cultivate a personality to feel better about ourselves, but this is not what will make us happy or successful. In western society we are all about building these big self-esteems from a young age. We all get trophies, we all pass, we build and build and build these perceptions and beliefs that we're all winners, we are superior. What this is doing is creating an inferior complex when we do not measure up to these societal expectations. We go into the real world and experience loss, disappointment, and sadness but our ego has no way to handle this other than to prevent or protect. We are pushing self-esteem so heavily when we are all parts of source, parts of God, we each are freaking miracles with our own set of gifts. The answer is within authenticity- within humbleness in knowing we are all a connected consciousness.

The ego is our intellect in the material state and what we want. The ego, or self-image created by society's perceptions of us, can be a fragile thing. It requires constant upkeep to maintain its strength through possessions that affirm what it believes about itself (in other words "I have").

Who am I?

Every person has an "ego story" - a personal narrative that can be used to make sense of their own experiences. The human brain struggles with the idea of vastness and needs something more practical, so it reduces chaotic events into relatable narratives where there are heroes and villains; good guys who always triumph against all odds. What's in every fairy tale? That's right: heroines or heroes taking on challenges bravely while defeating villainous forces for themselves, others they care about, and society as whole when necessary.

Once upon a time there was an island where all the feelings lived together. One day, the sea became angry, and the island was in danger of drowning. The waves crashed bigger and bigger with every moment that passed. Every feeling was terrified, but Love began building a boat to escape. Every feeling boarded the boat but one feeling refused. Love got down quickly to ensure the feeling arrived safely in the boat. The feeling was Ego.

Love tried and tried but Ego was not budging. "I'll be fine, the sea will never take me". Love pursued vigorously to talk sense into Ego, but Ego refused to board the boat. The water was rising at a quick pace, and everyone was begging Love to leave him alone and come to safety in the boat, but she refused. In the end Love sends everyone to safety and dies with Ego on the island in hopes to change his mind.

Authentic love is not an exchange or transaction but a feeling of admiration for another person and wanting to contribute what you have without expecting anything in return. Egoistic, possessive love involves ownership which means that it can't be authentic because we're always compromising ourselves when we compromise the other's happiness.

We make decisions from two places. Love or fear. It is that simple.

Fear is nothing more than false evidence appearing real. Fear is one thing but giving into other people's negativity is something else entirely—and the decision to realize it's time to let go is when magic begins to unfold.

Write down five examples of when you didn't act on something you wanted for your life based on what others thought or said.

1.
_____
_____
_____
_____

2.
_____
_____
_____
_____

3.
_____
_____
_____
_____

4.
_____
_____
_____
_____

5.
_____
_____
_____
_____

Now, I want you to sit and think about the people who you "think" or know are talking negative about you? Go ahead take a few minutes. It's hard to know what someone else is thinking. But here's the deal - we are all mirrors. What someone else is doing towards you is simply a projection of what they are experiencing internally. Maybe there's something going on in their life that causes them unhappiness and maybe the best way for them to feel better about themselves is by causing pain to others, even if they don't intend this.

When you train yourself to look at the bad things that happen in your life, for what they are and not as a reflection of who you are, it can help you act out of empathy instead of revenge or fight-or-flight. It becomes easier than just feeling anger towards people when they say something about us which is only them talking about themselves.

You know that feeling when you feel unstoppable and like everything is aligning for the better? That's your spirit giving you a message. You just need to trust it. There are so many times where we shy away from our passions because of fear or insecurity, but if these feelings tell us anything, it's that this might be exactly what we're looking for in life.

According to the Disease Control and Prevention (CDC) the average life expectancy is 78.6 years. (For this were going to round it up to 79 years.)

SEVENTY-NINE YEARS
692,040 hours on this earth.
28,835 days on this earth.
947 months on this earth.

Imagine a world where every day is like your' last. Imagine the purest form of joy, and all those things you want to experience in this life; amazing people, adventures down unknown paths that were previously closed off for years on end due to fear or guilt--fear no more. Now's not the time to be living with regrets about what could have been. There are so many opportunities out there waiting patiently for you. The Universe is on standby just waiting for you to create what is already yours.

> *The Universe is not going to give you what you want –*
> *The Universe is going to give you what you are.*

If you feel a source of negativity around something that is just lingering on you or a person that every single time you around them, you just walk away completely drained – you need to remove it immediately. Trust your intuition and don't think of it as forever, but just for right now. The people or activities that energize you and leave you feeling good are the people who are going to be your tribe and allow you to be in a state of "good" to attract more "good".

We place so much value in the word "toxic". It's thrown around like candy out of a pinata - someone pisses you off, boom, their a toxic person. Let's break down the definition of what toxic means.

Toxic: Poisonous or very harmful to one for being pervasive and insidious.

No human being should be labeled as inherently good or bad, and it is important to take into consideration the individual's past experiences before labeling them with a toxic label. Toxicity often comes from insecurities that are not dealt with internally over time; this can lead someone to act out destructively without taking responsibility for their actions.

Toxic behavior is using emotional manipulation tactics such as blaming others when they have done something wrong themselves, hiding jealousy by playing nice on the surface but still harboring resentment deep down inside of them, and trying desperately to control every little thing around them while refusing help from anyone else because they have convinced themselves that no one cares about their well-being.

The artist Marina Abramovic says that "the moment we begin to believe in our own greatness, that we kill our ability to be truly creative." She is speaking on the toxic ego. The way self-absorption ruins any progress it had made by being stuck up and not accepting anything else but its glory. I spent hours upon hours researching the how behind coming into consciousness, how to delve into humbleness and true alignment with your highest self. Almost every article, every show, every scholar, ever yogi, every book came back to these basic principles.

Passion is the fuel for our fire, but when it burns out, we're left with nothing. <u>Purposeful people live and die by their dharma - they wake up every day knowing that everything they do will be a part of something bigger than themselves</u>. When you let go of how things happen naturally, all those worries are swept away because everything in life happens as it should-and being guided this way allows us to align with our highest selves.

"It is impossible to learn that which one thinks one already knows"

The more we are sure of, the less open our minds become. We stop growing and learning when we refuse to give ourselves space for new ideas or information. Pick up a book on something you know nothing about and watch how quickly your perspective changes--it reminds us just how much there is left out there waiting for discovery with every second that passes by! The average millionaire reads at least two books per month; challenge yourself and begin craving the wealth of knowledge.

Sharing too much about your projects can block what the universe wants to manifest for you. Too often, we end up talking openly about our manifestations with other people and in turn create a projection of ourselves onto someone or something outside of us- which creates blocks before they happen.

Allow yourself time with creative work by taking care not to project your own ideas into anything else until after the manifestation has happened. Stop searching for outside validation and learn to seek the harmony from within. The only part of ourselves which is being "validated" through the praise of atta girls is our ego.

In her new book, "The Imposter Syndrome," Dr. Julie de Azevedo Hanks contends that one reason we feel so unmotivated when others see our work before it's finished is because they're typically not in the right frame of mind to give constructive feedback on your project and are therefore more likely to just point out flaws than offer any solutions or encouragement.

Dr. Julie DeAzevedo-Hanks has a theory about why we lose motivation after sharing projects with other people ahead of time: It could be due either subconsciously or consciously as an attempt at self-preservation from criticism for incomplete work—or even worse judging by someone's else's standards.

The subconscious and conscious minds are two different beings that do not realize they exist. Close your eyes, imagine you're cutting a lemon to make some fresh squeezed juice for yourself. You can visualize the crisp pulps of each slice, the yellow color; how it feels in your hands when trying to cut through with a knife; and finally tasting all those natural flavors explode on your tongue after slicing into perfect slivers.

Are you salivating?

THIS is your subconscious thinking it's getting a lemon just because we are reading the words on this paper.

When we share our projects and get praise before completion, it's like giving ourselves a mini orgasm. We feel good about what we're doing; that is until afterwards when the reality of the situation sets in. What usually happens after an intense feeling? You need to recharge your batteries - by napping or eating something sugary for example! And you do this without even realizing at a conscious level.

When people receive positive feedback while working on their projects early on in its development cycle, they are experiencing moments akin to sexual climaxes with themselves subconsciously taking away from your drive and motivation.

We all need to start living in the moment. Begin by spending some time every day connecting with Mother Earth; her wisdom can teach you about your place and importance on this planet. When we become too caught up our material success, we forget how fortunate it is that there are three-thousand-year-old trees around us! Stand at the sea's shoreline or under a tall oak tree and feel small again- listen as thunder crashes against ancient rocks beneath feet planted firmly into the dirt. With courage cut through any haze of doubt-- live life fully present no matter what discomfort may come from doing so.

In the book The Death and Life of Philosophy, author Robert Greene talks about how there are two types of time: dead time - when people wait around being passive until their next opportunity to act. This is contrasted with alive time where individuals learn or experience something new as they continue acting in order to better themselves. During periods of failure, it's common for egos to pick out a spot during this type of dead time space and stay put waiting until its future arises again instead of continuing learning from earlier mistakes. In order for life not just be wasted away at these moments we should start thinking circularly rather than linearly - cycling through stages so that nothing gets stagnant. We ebb and we flow, but we are in a constant state of movement as The Newton Law of Motion explains.

The Newton Law of Motion: In the first law, an object will not change its motion unless a force acts on it. In the second law, the force on an object is equal to its mass times its acceleration. In the third law, when two objects interact, they apply forces to each other of equal magnitude and opposite direction.

To become humbler, learn how to be still. Learning the art of listening and not asking all the questions is key here. When you tap into mindfulness and pure presence in the present moment, there are answers that can only come from within yourself. Being still can be the hardest thing in an age of rampant distraction. Meditation is how we come to this mindfulness state - to stay grounded and calm.

When it comes to spiritual growth, we all need grounding. Grounding meditation is essential because it grounds your energy on earth and connects you with the forces of life like an electrical ground wire does for power outlets. With this grounded connection, you are able to experience yourself in a way that no one else can understand but you-you are able to connect to your highest self. This allows you to be in touch with your power and energy. When grounded, we are more aware of our surroundings which can help prevent a case of impulsivity from manifesting (as seen when one gets emotional). We feel safer too, since grounding helps us control how we use both intellect and emotion in the physical world. Grounding has been around since the beginning of time because humans have always felt drawn towards reconnection - it is needed now more than ever where technology disconnects people even further from their roots. You've felt the pressure of your stress and anxiety building up, sometimes to an uncomfortable degree. That's why grounding is so beneficial-it helps relieve that tension in different ways like through your grounding cord or by touching the ground with bare feet if possible. Grounding allows for releasing excess energies before they accumulate too much when there are many things pulling on us energetically, which can happen from time to time. Grounding can also be used as an escape from anxiety, anger, or boredom. Meditation provides relief by helping you find peace within the moment so that you are not dependent on external noise to fill the void. When we meditate, we must focus on breath which forces us into the right here and right now.

Everything is energy.
Your thought begins it.
Your emotion amplifies it.
Your actions increase the momentum.

When we serve those in need, it offers a great opportunity to be humble and regenerate our sense of self. Serving others is a way for us to tap into humility and remember who we are. The act also provides the chance to reconnect with the collective and come back to our roots that we are all interconnected.

When people think about their ego and soul, they often find themselves feeling torn between the two. Our souls are designed to help us tap into our spirituality. To do this we must strengthen ourselves through experience in physical life by embracing who we really are--our egos which include all these experiences- as well as spiritual growth or enlightenment for when it comes time to return back home from a lifetime here on Earth where there is no more division between self and source.

Before we enter the physical realm, our souls' contract with each other to learn specific lessons. Therefore they're paired up when entering this thing called life on Earth. In order for them to help themselves grow in any way possible and fulfill their contracts-they need emotions. That's where your ego comes into play: it provides you with all that icky suffering needed just so the soul can regain its wisdom. We must walk through the experiences. The not so sexy side of spirituality which can't be bypassed. We are spiritual beings having a human experience and do not get to pick when that human experience is over or when our lessons have been learned. The ego is a tricky creature that allows for pain to happen, but eventually the soul must decide when it's time to end the suffering and accept the lesson inherent in it.

There's no master or slave here - only energy which flows. Pain brings us closer together by first tearing us apart; we all make mistakes with our lives because there are imperfections within this human shell of ours. Awareness helps awaken each one of these souls as they remember their perfect origin from before life began, bringing us back to pure love.

The ego and soul are yet another fine example of duality. If our ego "dies" we have no reason left to be in this human form. We have then learned all our lessons which our soul contracted here to grow from.

The more we understand the different ways in which people do spirituality and what they believe, the closer to divine perfection our own spiritual journey becomes.

Algal

Alcohol seems like a harmless substance to most people. They drink it and party with friends without thinking about the consequences of alcohol consumption. However, when one considers that all aspects of life are interconnected, they will be able to see how drinking has effects on their spiritual side as well. Alcohol is mass produced by industrial-sized companies for profit maximization purposes, but this doesn't mean we shouldn't consider its impact spiritually too! Alcohol companies like to use our subconscious minds against us. They know that one of the most powerful things about this is that we don't really realize it's happening, so they are able to trick you into buying their product and joining society without too much resistance because essentially your mind is doing all the work for them before any thought process has even come in contact with reality. The moment you realize that there are so many paths up a mountain is when your personal discovery of spirituality begins. There's no one way or right answer for everyone; instead, it all comes down to how each person embraces their life with meaning and appreciation as well as honoring themselves. The etymology of the word alcohol comes from Arabic meaning algal' which is a demon or spirit in ancient Indian beliefs that produces intoxication. Aka (body eating spirit.) Brutal right?

Alcohol has the power to extract an entity's soul essence. It is used in alchemy for extracting essences of essential oils and sterilizing medical instruments. When consumed into the body it extracts a person's very soul which then makes them more susceptible to other entities that are most commonly low frequencies (why do you think we call certain alcoholic beverages "spirits?") Alcohol has the ability to make people black out, which is when they forget everything that happened. This often happens because their good soul leaves due to how polluted and traumatic life conditions are here on Earth; it will stay connected by a tether but leave its body behind for dark entities who take advantage of free roaming with no logical restraints or thoughts about anyone else's wellbeing. The law of attraction is not just about the universe and you, it's also a battle within your soul.

Alcohol makes this problem worse because they break down how alcohol can completely stop that connection between them both from happening at all. It becomes difficult to remember what exactly caused us so much pain in our lives but when we do remember those painful memories are accentuated by negative thoughts stemming from addiction or alcoholism - which means if someone has an addictive personality type then their life will be filled with trauma as opposed to people who have a more stable lifestyle where everything seems better than before even though one may think there isn't any progress being made whatsoever. What does the phrase, "separation is an illusion" really mean? The idea that we are all separate beings with a singular identity or self-sufficiency in this world is only one perspective of reality. When you consider how everything on at least atomic level shares qualities such as electrons and protons (which make up atoms) then there's no difference between any two people because they share these essential building blocks. In conclusion, when considering what it means to be "self-sufficient," remember not to fall under illusions like belief systems which tell us otherwise!

We are all made up of the same form on earth. We are particles of energy vibrating at different frequencies, like in a radio frequency spectrum that changes along with our moods and emotions. When we drink alcohol, it causes us to move down onto lower frequencies while also pushing the more spiritual vibrations higher and further away from us - think about how people call beer "courage juice," because when they're drinking their ego comes out completely without any thought for consequences or what is best for them as individuals by shutting off their spirit mind. People are drinking near-alcoholic levels just to conform and be accepted.

Think of how normalized it's become in mom get togethers, play dates, park outings with the kids or date nights for a drink after work. The belief system has led us to believe that alcohol is not a registered poison and one of the leading causes for cancer. To be free from blockage caused by illusion, try detaching yourself just for a while. The law of attraction works because it alters your own energetic vibration ranges in order to match up with universal fields energy flow surrounding us all throughout time. It's always now. Not tomorrow, not yesterday - but right here and now in the present moment. We lose track of time when we put toxins into our body because they have a way of messing with neurotransmitters which regulate how you think about yourself and your life experience as well as what is happening around you on an everyday basis. When we drink, a moment appears and then is destroyed. The only thing it takes for that to happen are the few seconds of time between when you lift your glass up from its resting place on the table or bar top until you put it back down again in anticipation of taking another sip. The Christian theory is very clear as well. Proverbs 23:20 "Do not join those who drink too much wine or gorge themselves on meat, for drunkards and gluttons become poor, and drowsiness clothes them in rags." Ephesians 5:18 "Do not get drunk on wine, which leads to debauchery. Instead, be filled with spirit." All religions and cultures are running on the same fuel of universal truths. I wanted to explore this idea, so during my research for this book, I studied several different religious beliefs from many parts of the world. They all had one thing in common: they believe that everyone has a purpose and had a strong belief when it came to alcohol. It's called different things in different cultures, but the bottom line all came down to the exact same story.

> "BY THE TIME YOU WAKE UP TOMORROW MORNING, A PERCENTAGE OF WHO YOU WERE TODAY WILL HAVE DISAPPEARED FOREVER, AND A SIMILAR PERCENTAGE OF YOU WILL BE TAKING ITS FIRST EVER STEP ON PLANET EARTH IN THE ROLE OF YOU. FAST FORWARD A FEW MONTHS AND VIRTUALLY EVERY PART OF THE YOU THAT EXISTS TODAYS WILL BE GONE, REPLACED BY ENTIRELY NEW CELLS. LET GO OF THE PAST. YOU WERE NOT THERE ANYWAY. FORGET ABOUT THE FUTURE. YOU WILL NEVER GET THERE EITHER."
>
> -Craig Beck

COURTNEY HANSON

Dear Alcohol,

It's been a long road between you and me. Even between the times of absence and breaks you somehow find a way to steal my happiness. It's time I break up with you once and for all - not a break but a divorce. I am fucking done. You have ruined my relationships over and over. I have no friends, my family is always waiting for me to fail, and you have taken so many opportunities from me. It wasn't always bad. You allowed me to have glimpses of confidence or took away extreme pain on nights I couldn't make it through. You helped me pass time on my loneliest nights and allowed me to come out of my shell. Then the next day hits and I feel guilty, ashamed and worthless. I've tried so hard to just have fun with you but somehow you grip me down to a point I have no control. You cloud my head and take over my body turning myself into someone who's a stranger. I'm done with letting you destroy me and everything around me. Whenever your around for a few days nothing comes but chaos and destruction. You've had me put in jail, almost lose my children, my husband, pushed me into an affair, the list goes back for over 15 years. I'm hurt, I'm mad at myself - I thought I was stronger than you, but the bottom line is you almost took my life. My values and reasoning went out the door - you talked me into almost every "I never" that I said would not happen to me. I remember two years ago going out with mom friends for karaoke and getting so drunk I went home early. The next morning, I was embarrassed and mortified at my actions - I cried for a week feeling like a horrible mother. Somehow you consoled me and told me it was okay. I saw everyone around me having wine nights or a bottle at dinner and I tried so hard to just fit in, to just be normal. I knew every time how I felt, I knew the guilt was real, but you told me was okay to keep pushing through. You would help…There was always a reason for you to show back up - a celebration, a sadness, a gathering, a stressful day, you just kept showing up no matter how much I tried to avoid you. The guilt over time became less and less as you took my soul little by little. I began to rationalize making the abusive relationship "normal." I even switched at a time from white to red because that was healthy for my heart. You slyly began to eliminate my capacity to put my guard down, to trust, to be honest with anyone including myself.

It got to this point I would have one or two of you and then thought fuck it we'll just finish the bottle. You caused my pain from my family to turn into anger. You caused me to call them and say horrible things I can never take back. (However much deserved.) You have made me miss important moments and milestones that I can never get back and for this I loathe you. Our last encounter you took over my body, so I had no control of stopping - I felt so horribly the only glimmer of hope too feeling alive was more of you. I wish we could have worked; I really do, and I think at this point I can say I've tried so hard. I think of all the camping trips that I can't boat and drink, all the mom nights I'll awkwardly be the one woman show with a water bottle, the New Year's Eve or date nights of a little tipsiness and crazy fun sex. But then that all goes away when I think of the morning of July 4th. To puking blood, shaking on my bathroom floor, to having to be spoon fed ice chips, to no longer being able to work because I no longer had the ability to speak without crying. I am sure there will be times I'll miss you, but I want to thank you for taking my damn near killing me because now all of my "maybe" questions you answered crystal clear. You no longer have power over me. We are through...For good.

You lose. I win.

-Courtney

The Inner Child

The Divine Feminine is an energy, which means she can't be seen or heard, but she can be felt. She is the feminine that exists in all living beings on earth, including the ocean, moon, and trees. She is sometimes known as Yin energy, Shakti, Kali, or Gaia.

The divine balance of masculine and feminine energy creates a sense of perfect peace. Our inner child is full of pure love, light, joy, and freedom. To create such purity in ourselves requires the duality that comes from our true self's connection with both halves. The feminine is harmony, beauty, peace and love. She shines with light in all her many forms: joyous laughter of children at play; the luminosity from a newborn's smile; the radiance that glows between lovers who have found their soulmates after searching for so long.

The masculine needs to be nurtured by this goddess just as much as she does because both need each other equally if they are going to make it through life successfully. Despite the challenges of life, we are all searching for ways to be ourselves. We suppress our true selves and resist our desires. When we do this, we are denying ourselves of enlightenment.

The divine power is within each one of us, but sometimes this feeling gets lost. A calming, spiritual energy lies within each of us and can be embraced to find empowerment. The Divine Feminine is a type of energy that everyone can access and tap into – not something tangible or some gate kept secret club.

It's connected with the body, nature, cycles of creation and transformation - The divine feminine refers to the part in our consciousness responsible for qualities such as intuition or feelings; nurturing receptivity and interconnectedness.

The divine feminine is a powerful force. It can be accessed by anyone, and it cannot be encapsulated in one definition or form of expression because its true potential transcends the physical world. For example, fertility may come to mind when you hear about this energy but know that it extends far beyond biological boundaries into realms of creativity and love - both accessible for all regardless of gender. There are two energies inherent to our humanity: the masculine and feminine.

These forces give us a direct connection with divinity, showing up as strength in one's inner warrior or intuition in their Goddess within. When we're out of balance, there is an imbalance between these energies where they act against each other instead of together for growth and healing. We live in a society that is constantly telling us to be tough, strong and unemotional. We are taught to embody our inner Warrior while not realizing the suppression of our inner goddess. We must create balance.

The Divine Masculine and Feminine are two opposing forces that work in harmony to create balance. In Vedic philosophy, the duality of existence is born from these opposing energies. The goal for both archetypes isn't to overpower or cancel each other out but rather find peace with one another by balancing life's aspects which happen through interaction. This idea is seen throughout many ancient Eastern philosophies with concepts like Yin & Yang, Sun and Moon or Shiva (the creator) and Shakti (his consort).

The left side of our brain is tied to logic and reasoning, while the right side has been linked with creativity and connection.

This becomes even more apparent when we consider that people are thought to use one hemisphere or another for different tasks at any given time; your unconscious mind might be responsible for analytical functions in decision-making, whereas you may switch over into a creative mindset as soon as it's time for intuition or creation. This is Western Societies spin on the masculine and feminine within hemispheres of your brain.

Our energy bodies are made up of innumerable strands that weave together to form an intricate network. These threads, also called nadis in Sanskrit or meridians in acupuncture and Chinese medicine, transmit our life-force or prana from the physical body through each level until it reaches the crown chakra at top which is often associated with spirituality. The 72000 karmic knots on these spiritual currents correspond to nerves in the human anatomy - just like a plateful of spaghetti.

One such point where many of these energies converge is known as a chakra; one's lower back for example would be located at second lumbar vertebrae (L2). Just below this location you can feel flowing rivers meeting over your backbone creating what we know as the root chakra.

Ida nadi governs the feminine, left side of the body. The Pingala nadi governs masculine, right side of the body and activates opposite sides in our brain since they are so different from one another- This is where things get mind blowing: although we know that each gender has a certain dominant "side" it seems to be reversed when considering which half dominates what part of ourselves. For example, if you are "left brained" you are probably more dominant within the right side of your body "the masculine" and vice versa for right brained and left side "the feminine." An old proverb that says "the eye sees only what the mind is prepared to comprehend" takes on new and more inclusive meaning in light of these findings. Science has found that holistic right hemisphere directs our attention to larger collective thoughts, we see the need to jump from project to project in order to complete a bigger picture. The left side is focused on the linear straight line of logic.

The hemispheres are divided in two so they can work together more effectively: one hemisphere will control speech while another processes visual stimuli; both halves have a hand each when you pick something up with your fingers or sip from a glass.

For us to heal from feeling chronically out-of-balance or unbalanced in a certain area, one word: acknowledgment that our bodies are a vast and intricate energy system.

Before we can truly tap into the magic of the feminine energy, we must first allow that little you inside to feel safe, secure and protected. Most of us are relying on the "hustle" masculine energy today and through this I hope you find some balance within the yin and the yang. Tapping into this energy allows manifestation to make sense and flow effortlessly, your life begins to unfold in ways you once dreamt of, and you are stepping into your purpose further and further with each exercise you complete. Inner child work is about adult self-doing the healing of wounds that were denied to us as children. We are beginning to realize how capable, competent and nurturing we really can be; this process primarily involves acknowledging painful events from our childhood, so they don't continue influencing our life in adulthood. The inner child is the most powerful part of ourselves that we are not aware. It can be a source of mental disorder or destructive behavior patterns, but it also has an extraordinary power to heal and help us grow. The inner child is an important part of who we are. It doesn't matter if you're eighteen or eighty, this child lives inside everyone and it's integral to understanding what makes us tick.

We were all once children; the only difference between a three-year old today and one fifty years ago is that they now have more things in their life: responsibilities, jobs, spouses etc. However, most adults don't know about these feelings deep down within themselves because people grow up so quickly that often there isn't enough time for them to really explore those childhood memories before being pulled into adulthood situations or circumstances. When we are children, our inner voice is often the only one that speaks to us. As adults, this child-like side of ourselves can be hard to find and communicate with. For those who have been through trauma or other significant life events at a young age, it may seem like they were put on mute for an extended period while their personality developed in ways that made sense based on what was happening externally around them but not inside themselves where it mattered most. We must learn how to take our inner child seriously and communicate with little us. The needs of this perennial inner child remain unchanged from what they were back in childhood-she needs love, acceptance, protection and nurturance—which is why it's crucial that we listen.

The signs of a wounded inner child

- You feel there is something wrong with you.
- Always seeking approval or the need to be liked.
- You experience social anxiety or stress when going outside of your daily routine or comfort zone.
- You have a hard time saying no and are a people pleaser. You do not have a strong sense of identity.
- Your self-sabotage or have the need to have chaos and conflict in your life. You hoard people, things, emotions.
- Letting go is very difficult for you. This can be memoirs from thirty years ago or an ex that was toxic.
- You feel inadequate. Your negative self-talk is constantly criticizing you.
- You have a problem forgiving yourself for mistakes or your past. This can show through rigidity or perfectionism.
- You have a hard time with commitment and trust. You have deep abandonment issues and are clingy or run away in relationships. Co-dependency is often a problem here.

Identifying the inner child –

We all have specific patterns of childhood that are related to how we were raised. See which pattern resonates the most with you and notice the similarities in what is coming up in your life today as an adult. Circle the one that you relate to the most.

The playful child: This child is healthy and often neglected in adulthood. Is there a time when you were feeling playful and spontaneous having fun without guilt or anxiety?

_____
_____
_____
_____
_____

The fearful child: This child received a lot of criticism and regularly experiences panic or anxiety when not receiving confirmation they are doing well.

_____
_____
_____
_____
_____

The abandoned child: This child often comes from not getting enough attention from parents. It can be as simple as parents worked and were busy to the more extreme side of abuse or neglect. As adults they don't believe they are worthy of being loved.

_____
_____
_____
_____
_____

The disconnected child: This child never had the opportunity to learn what it means to bond or be close to someone. This often happens when only one parent is present or if someone passed at a young age.

In adulthood they have a hard time trusting and stay isolated. Intimacy is very fearful.

___

The spoiled child: This child tends to throw tantrums when instant gratification is not met. This carries on into adult hood as well.

___

The discounted child: This child was treated as if they didn't exist. Maybe after a sibling was born or an event happened within the family. In adulthood self-belief and positive validation is virtually absent.

___

The first exercise we are going to write a letter to our younger selves. To begin this process, I want you to close your eyes and visualize your childhood. How old are you when the first thing comes to mind? Got it? This is the age you are writing to little you. A few questions to keep the dialogue flowing when you begin... Start out with your name –

Dear _____,

How do you feel?

_____
_____
_____
_____
_____
_____
_____
_____
_____

How can I support you?

_____
_____
_____
_____
_____
_____
_____
_____
_____

What do you need from me?

_____
_____
_____
_____
_____
_____
_____
_____
_____

This should open the dialogue and create safety and security. Begin free flow writing after these prompts. It doesn't have to make sense just let the pen flow.

Beautiful work. Time to reverse the letter. This exercise is the exact same but reversed. After reviewing the letter, you wrote to little you, I want the inner child in you to respond back to adult you and answer the questions you asked. What does she/he need from you to feel safe, secure and loved? A few questions to keep the dialogue flowing when you begin... Start out with your name –

Dear _____,

I feel _____ this event hurt/scared/made me feel unloved.
_____
_____
_____
_____
_____
_____
_____
_____
_____

You can support me by...

In order to begin my healing journey, I need you to promise...
_____
_____

This should open the dialogue and create safety and security. Grab your journal and begin free flow write after these prompts. It doesn't have to make sense just let the pen flow. Often we will have detachment to little us – if you do run into a little writers block just start putting bullet points of what comes up intuitively for you. (Have Kleenex available this can be very emotional.)
_____
_____
_____
_____

WITHIN

Inner Child Meditation

Get in a comfortable position either sitting down with your hands on your lap or laying down with your hands in receiving position. Children often have a hard time labeling emotion especially if they have been told to "be quiet" or "shut up" these emotions become repressed and to avoid the feeling of punishment we maintain this "must be good" don't be seen – don't be heard behavior. Emotions are meant to be heard and experienced. As you close your eyes imagine adult you looking at your child self. Notice what emotions are popping up and just observe them, feel them through and walk through the experience with yourself. Assure the little you they are safe and it's ok. Sit and talk for about ten minutes and just see what comes up for you. Every experience is valid and ok. At the end of your meditation walk up to the little you and see if they will allow you to give them a hug. If they pull away at first, this is ok. It may take a few times to get a hug. Immediately after the meditation journal about all that came up for you. Events, memories, emotions let it all out.

Dissociation to your inner child.

Your inner child is an incredibly important part of who you are. It's like a little person inside your head that knows all the things about yourself, and it has been there since day one with only its experiences to guide it – without any input from society or other people. But sometimes for this innocent being to cope with daily life our subconscious will store memories away, so we don't have such heavy thoughts weighing on us at once. Sometimes when trauma happens these memories can come out into conscious awareness as well!

Be gentle and kind towards yourself during this process. Dissociation with your inner child is very common when healing trauma. "Dissociating from oneself can be seen as an escape mechanism, which also helps people cope mentally and emotionally." I wanted to share with you my personal inner child letters and show an example of dissociation. When I was young, it felt as though there were two parts of me: one that always needs help but felt unsafe in my environment which was constantly changing; the other who wanted to fix everything yet only felt normal within chaotic situations. As a result, I struggled for years to figure out how to connect to little me because for so long I had to be the "grown up."

Dear Courtney,

My dear girl – I wish I could have rescued you from all the pain and neglect. You deserved to be loved, you deserved cuddles, you deserved to be tucked in with a kiss, you deserved to feel worth something and wanted. I promise you from the bottom of my heart it had nothing to do with you – you did not deserve the hand you were dealt but what I do know is you are strong; you have compassion and are an empath capable of feeling so truly and deeply. You will make a mark on this world sweet girl. I know now it hurts so bad, it's hard to see light when we are swimming for air, but you must trust and know now everyone will hurt you. It's ok to be vulnerable, it's ok to feel and let people in. Not everyone will leave you. When I see tears in your eyes it breaks my heart, I want to protect you as you should have been protected. I want you to know you are wanted. Don't stop being kind because the world has been cruel. Don't stop loving because you haven't felt loved and don't stop feeling because the easy way is too numb. You don't have to wear mask - not everyone's going to like you and that's okay. God will bring in your life who is supposed to be there. I want you not to have to grow up so fast, I want you to do you and not care what others think of you – just follow your heart. I love you so deeply and want you to see yourself the way I see you now. An innocent, pure, kind and loving child meant to move mountains. You were carefully crafted and hand-picked. You have a destiny. There are no mistakes – you are special are worth all the nurturing and love in this world. Don't let your head tell you anything different. The ego can be such a scary space at times. Please connect- please don't shut off what you were destined for. You went through the dark so you could shine the brightest light. I love you very much. Promise me you'll just keep going no matter what.

– Your future self.

Now this may seem like a great inner child letter, but it is as detached as they come and here's why... When I wrote my inner child letters, I could barely even remember certain aspects of my childhood. I had compartmentalized so many memories for my success in adult hood that opening that can of worms seemed dangerous and daunting. They were locked away in this box within my subconscious and I wasn't sure if they would be accessible to me again. I had created this reality which was not the truth in order to cope. When I wrote this first letter I visualized as if I was writing a letter to my daughter. It was the only way I could begin to tap into this part of me. If you are currently detached and struggling with connection of little you, begin by writing to a son, daughter, nephew, niece, someone you love unconditionally. This allows you to at least get the pen to paper moving. Let me share now with you my letter once I had done inner child work and was connected to the little me.

WITHIN

Dear Courtney,

I know what you see when you wake up. You see a girl with empty eyes hidden behind coke bottle glasses, you see loneliness and you think no one will ever want you, so anyone who shows you the slightest attention you bend over backwards for - even if it hurts you. You see frizzy hair (you always wanted straight), you see ugly clothes you can never seem to put together, no matter how hard you try, you see psoriasis and that you're "different", you see the popular girls and wonder what they have that you don't, you wonder why everyone has boyfriends but you, you wonder why grandma left so soon and feel it's so unfair, you wonder why your parents hate each other and why your sisters are so loved, you wonder why you move so much and dream of one day having a home, you love pets and take in all the strays because you can relate to them and they make you feel safe, you wonder why your bullied and don't stand up for yourself, you cry more than you smile sweet girl.

You have dreams and enjoy them because it's a brief break from the harsh world. You crave desperately acceptance from someone - anyone. Being kind and smart you feel isn't good enough. You love art and imaginative play because then you can create your own world where you can be who you want to be. Your soul is beautiful I wish you could see this, you're different because you feel so deeply, you relate so easily, and you hurt so quickly because you're vulnerable. I wish I could go back and give you the love which you so desperately needed. You're beautiful just the way you are, and you do not need to change for anybody - ever. Kids are so mean they made fun of you because of their own insecurities. You were the target because you were so passive - people knew you would take it and not fight back. Being popular is overrated most "popular" girls end up pregnant in high school or working at Mc Donald's. The universe knew you were destined for more. You're going to grow up and use this pain to help a lot of women in this world. I don't want you to hurt anymore I want you to know all the pain was for a purpose. I wish you could see what I see now and know it's going to be okay. I know the darkness you feel. The depression, the hopelessness, the wanting to be someone else even if it's just for a day. The exterior will change over time - learn to love you for you. Dissociation to your inner child. You're funny, you care, you want to see others smile no matter what they've done to you. Grandma is your spirit guide I promise she is always with you and watching down to make sure you're okay. Your dad loves you so deeply but has no idea how to parent a lost little girl - that is not your fault. Your mom couldn't parent you; it has nothing to do with being worthless it's her own issues. You can't bond because you're always prepared to move, you just can't see this yet and blame yourself. I love you so much and you serve to be nurtured and snuggled and told how beautiful and loved you are. I know it was a survival mode to be a chameleon, but you were truly born to stand out. We are all born with imperfections, but you know what? This is what makes us special. If we were all made the same life would be so boring. I wish you would cherish your innocence instead of craving the need to grow up so quickly. Your prayers are heard, and your tears are seen no matter how much you try to pretend it is all okay. What happened to you was not okay.

I know you acted out towards your dad because you so badly wanted him to be a mom, but he couldn't - he tried to be there for you, but you were angry. You should have been angry. It is valid you were angry. You are the generational curse breaker. It stops with you - this is powerful. You are powerful. History of abuse and abandonment stops with you. You're too young to know the truth right now but when you're older I promise it will all come out - it will all make sense. I wish I could bring the twinkle back to your eyes that every child deserves to have within its magic. I want you to know how brave and resilient you are even if that's not what you see in the reflection. Some day you be a mom and remember these feelings you will cherish the spark and make sure. Your children know how special and loved they are. You'll give the extra snuggles, the tuck ins, the bedtime kisses, the constant stream of love because you know what it's like to not have that. You will cherish making people feel valued and validated. Your soul is radiant, and you have a mission with your life. No child deserves the childhood you were dealt - it was horrible with glimpses of fun and memories. Hold on to that fun - Dissociation to your inner child. Clench it so close to your heart. Fun is what will make you smile. You will heal and you will learn your worth. You will know this journey ends with a happy ending like all the fairytales you read. You dear are the princess not the frog you see in the mirror. You will not sit on the sidelines forever - I promise you will have a time to shine and know your worth every beam of light which comes your way. Please keep your head up, keep shining, keep being unapologetically you because you're beautiful from the inside out.

Things will get better sweet girl - this is a promise I won't break.

- Your future self

They say that when you're in a tunnel, and it's dark as night on one side of the entrance but light shining brightly from the other end. You'll be satisfied with where you are until someone shines their flashlight right into your eyes, blinding them to everything else around. In this way, people who have dissociative disorders experience life similarly-identity is only defined by its proximity to others rather than what an individual chooses for themselves so much like how physicists teach us about quantum entanglement: two entangled particles even if they can't interact physically due to distance will always share physical properties no matter which direction time goes or space expands because there is some sort of invisible connection between them despite never coming close enough together before being separated again.

When a person survives trauma during their childhood, the brain and personality may form in an abnormal way. This can lead to dissociative disorders later if they continue using dissociation as a coping mechanism for complex traumas.

What are symptoms of Dissociation?

- Have an out-of-body experience.
- Feel like you are a different person sometimes.
- Feel like your heart is pounding or you're light-headed.
- Feel emotionally numb or detached.
- Feel little or no pain.
- Memory loss of certain time periods, events, people and personal information.
- A sense of being detached from yourself and your emotions.
- A perception of the people and things around you as distorted and unreal.
- A blurred sense of identity

Before you begin these letters to little you try some of these grounding techniques to center and prepare yourself.

1. Breathing slowly.
2. Listening to the sounds around you.

3. Walking barefoot.
4. Wrapping yourself in a blanket and feeling it around you.
5. Touching something or sniffing something with a strong smell.

Take time to play.

A wise Buddhist once said that inside each of us dwells a young, suffering child. And to protect ourselves from future pain, we all try our hardest not to remember the misery and anguish this innocent soul has felt for them not feel those pains again. But often when we come across feelings so deep, they make their way up through cracks only known by someone who's been hurt before; it's because our inner wounded child is calling out for help. If you don't take care of your wounds, how can you stop others from entering? Think back to what you used to enjoy as a child. Did it spark joy in your soul? Was there anything that made time seem like no big deal and all the world was at peace with itself for just those moments when you were doing them? If so, try taking up two of these activities again, but this time put away your phone or any other distractions; become fully immersed in each one. Feel the memories come flooding back to you – is that me growing taller on my tippy toes while painting little trees green or am I finally getting good enough at dancing without looking down? Tap into little you. Spend time with her.

Journal Prompts – Self Forgiveness

What is something I am judging/blaming or shaming myself over?
_____
_____
_____
_____
_____
_____
_____

I want to forgive myself and start feeling...

When I made choices in the past, I was coming from a place of...

I now know that I was doing the best I could with the tools I was given at the time. I see that my inner child was desperate for the need of...

As an adult I am going to nurture and help you feel safe by...

___

If I were a loving parent speaking to an innocent child who felt guilty, alone, scared, invalidated what would I tell them?

___

I am proud of myself and deserve equal forgiveness. I acknowledge myself today for these things...

___

COURTNEY HANSON

Dear future self,

I hear and understand every word you said and I love you for taking the time to acknowledge me and know I am hurting. I miss you. We haven't had a connection in such a long time. I need a few things for you to allow me healing, to allow to just feel whole again. I need you to stay sober so you can feel me when I reach out to you. I need you to feel your feelings all the way through so I can too. I need you to keep your distance from parents, so I won't feel scared or triggered, at least until we have a more solid foundation. I need you to create magic in the holidays again. I love celebrations and traditions. You are healing me a little bit every day, I feel your love and presence feel connected and loved. I haven't felt loved in so long. During my childhood I missed out on a lot of things. It has caused me sadness, jealousy, and pain. Will you make this up to me by always being present with my future children, telling them how loved they are, show them how capable they are, build them up and show them they can do anything, and you will support them? Will you never settle for anything but our dreams? I want to inspire and help people know their worth love and acceptance. I want you to never be complacent and follow our heart its usually always right. My entire existence was crippled by bullying cruelty and trying to be someone I wasn't to impress others. Will you help me heal by being unapologetically genuine and you without a care in the world of what others think of you. One last thing I need for you is to allow people in. We deserve a happily ever after. Let your husband love you so we can feel free. Everything I've been through was for a reason to leave us right where we are at now. Please keep pushing forward no matter how uncomfortable it is.

Please don't abandon me again.

I've missed you so much.

-Courtney

I understand

I see

I speak

I love

I do

I feel

I am

The Chakra for the inner child – Sacral and Root Chakra

The sacral chakra, also known as the Swadhisthana chakra, is our inner child center. It relates to our internal urges and instincts- not just those we feel sexually but all of them! This chakra houses a part of us that has been denied or neglected; this place in which we often try to hide. The Sacral Chakra is our emotional center. It's influenced by early relationships and environments, which often hold trauma. The Root chakra also helps govern disassociation, feelings of unbalance, security and stability in the sacral area or anywhere else.

Signs of a blocked sacral chakra

- Constipation
- Urinary and Kidney Infections
- Back Pain
- Gynecological Cysts
- Abnormal Menstruation
- Infertility
- Impotence
- Depression
- Low Self Esteem
- Jealousy
- Insecurity
- Detachment
- Fear

Signs of a blocked root chakra

- Sluggishness
- Colon Problems
- Bladder Issues
- Lower Back Pain
- Left arm, leg or foot issues

- Cramping
- Inflammation
- Restlessness
- Insecurity
- Excessive anger or aggression
- Impatience
- Greediness
- Obsession with materialistic items

Healing your sacral chakra

The first step to any healing is to acknowledge we need healing in this area.

Water – With the Earth element's grounding and refining properties, you can cleanse your body from toxins by drinking plenty of water. A good idea is to drink half of your body weight in ounces each day. You will be flushing out heavy metals or chemicals with this process as well, so it pays off in more ways than one. In addition to consuming your daily dose of H2O, try taking warm baths infused with orange essential oils (or other colors depending on what chakra are most damaged). These work wonders because they nourish both our physical bodies and emotional selves simultaneously- soothing any pain we may feel at home while increasing mental clarity during challenging times. The refreshing cool water that comes with a cold shower can be such an enriching experience.

Try it and see for yourself! Cold showers have been shown to stimulate the vagus nerve, which is often connected to anxiety, so in other words they're perfect for those of us who suffer from this condition. Start out small – maybe just 3 minutes at first before working your way up- but make sure you don't get too used to them because over time cold showers may not produce as profound effects anymore on your body or mind. For centuries, people have been going to natural bodies of water such as lakes and oceans for their spiritual cleansing. It is believed that bathing in the waters will cleanse one's aura from negativity caused by stress or other factors; however, this act does not require a person to be submerged entirely- simply being around these sacred places can work wonders! We all know how great it feels after taking an ice-cold shower on a hot summer day – but did you also know that your body benefits greatly when you take time out every week to enjoy yourself at scenic locations?

Studies show that spending even just ten minutes away from our busy lives has noticeable effects: lower levels of cortisol (stress hormone), improved heart rate variability & blood pressure, and decreased feelings of anxiety.

Nutrition for unblocking – Nuts, Seeds, Pumpkin, Orange, Melons, Mangos, Citrus Fruits, Butternut Squash, Fermented Foods (Kombucha), Carrots and Sweet Potatoes. Get creative and find ways to incorporate this into your everyday meal plan.

Get Crafty – The sacral chakra is all about creativity, so tap into coloring, painting, baking or gardening. Whatever feels good for you.

Hip Openers – Doctors and researchers have been trying to figure out how trauma affects our bodies for decades. From the head down, it's easy enough to see where it takes a toll on us: headaches make their way through your skull; teeth ache in pain from grinding or clenching; but what about those joint pains? A new study by doctors at Stanford University has revealed that when we are under duress of any kind – be it mental or physical trauma – there is an increased pressure placed upon joints like your shoulders, knees, hips as well as within muscle tissues such as the psoas muscle which connects upper-body with lower-body muscles together. This muscle passes anteriorly to our hips in which we can release through simple daily stretches. When we go into fight, flight or fuck (sympathetic nervous system) our body also has a fourth dynamic response which is freeze. When we freeze our body holds on to this extra energy to keep us safe so that we can respond "fight or flight" to safety. As children when we are in a traumatic experience, angry, or in pain we shake. We have giant temper tantrums and throw ourselves on the floor. Why? This is how we allow this energy out of our bodies. As we get older, we are told to control our emotions. Temper tantrums are frowned upon or punished for "acting out" – so what do we do? We push our emotions deep down into this muscle from a very tiny age.

Practice Chanting – Vam is the mantra that supports healing for sacral chakra. It's powerful when combined with hip opener exercises, such as child's pose and table stretches in yoga class or professional massage therapy sessions–making it one of the most important mantras to learn.

Crystals are always a good idea – Incorporate in crystals like amber, coral, orange calcite, citrine, orange aventurine, carnelian and hematite.

SHAKE

Make it a part of your morning routine to shake. Whether you jump up and down and shake silly or dance around your kitchen – physically shaking your body every morning is a way to release this stagnant energy.

Hip openers for the psoas muscle –

- 3-legged dog (Downward dog splits) While in downward dog and pulling your navel into the spine left one leg straight up and rotate sides. You can also begin to bend your knee with the leg lifted and draw circles with you knee to continue opening deeper.
- Lizard Lunge Twist
- Shin to Shin or Butterfly
- Runners Lunge – Bend the front knee to 90 degrees and stack your knee on top of your ankle. Lengthen and engage the extended leg. Release tension in the neck by extending your spine.
- Lizard or Blaster Pose – From your lunge position inch your front foot out to the side corner end of your mat. Take the back knee off the floor and slowly lower down onto your forearms – if this is too intense always know you have the option to drop your knee and untuck your toes in the back leg.
- Pigeon Pose

- Downward Dog
- Yogi Squat
- Plank hip rollers are also a great way to open up this area. From plank position simply rotate your hips from side to side.

Burn earthy element oils – sandalwood, cypress, cedar wood, rosewood, patchouli, cloves, black pepper and ginger.

Nourishing foods to incorporate – strawberries, beets, radishes, tomatoes, potatoes, things which grow from the earth allow us to ground through our root chakra. Also, foods which are red in color.

Set intention and allow permission – Claim healing for your root chakra and write your intentions for healing this area.

Rub a metal spoon on your foot – Take a metal spoon and rub it on the sole of your feet to your heel. This is activating new energy to come into your root chakra.

Grounding crystals – onyx, hematite, black tourmaline, re jasper and red agate.

Root Chakra Mantras
"I am grounded and centered."
"I am here right now."
"I am at home in my body."
"I am safe and secure."
"I have everything I need to create the life I desire."
"I don't chase I attract. What's meant to me will come to me." "With every breath I release anxiety and fear."

Sit in a comfortable position on the floor in easy pose. Wrap your arms around you as if to give yourself a hug. Slowly rock in a spiral rotation for a few moments with your eyes closed.

- My strength is greater than any struggle.
- I am fearless.
- I am getting stronger every day.
- I am in awe of what my body is capable of.
- I am who I want to be.
- No one can make me feel inferior.
- I inspire others.
- I know my worth.
- I choose what I become.
- I am brave.
- I am fierce.
- I have the power to change my story.
- I have courage to say no.
- I am proud of the progress I make daily.

The Maiden

The maiden archetype is a representation of the young and powerless female character in need of being rescued. This usually happens by men who are heroes, such as when they save her from demons or monsters created to create conflict within the story that moves it along while also representing what drives their desires for success and motivation. She displays an innocent quality with youthful features.

The maiden is very sensitive and emotional often very in touch with her feelings. This is usually a phase every woman goes through when they are younger, but some never grow out of. She represents innocent playfulness and fun, possessing a sense of curiosity and energetic exploration. Maidens enjoy developing new strengths, adopting new knowledge but struggle deeply with being alone. Their innocent nature creates this sense of compliancy and passiveness. She may be waiting for life to happen for her instead of taking the bull by the horns. The maiden is usually presented as very feminine – think Sleeping Beauty or Princess Aurora.

When in balance: The maiden is enchanting, charming, and full of vitality. She has an open mind that's curious and pure in a world where these qualities are rare.

When out of balance: The maiden projects, pretends, denies, fantasy land, emotional codependency, attracts abusive relationships, diffidence.

The main wound: She doesn't trust her intuition, steps too far into the masculine, becomes to logical and does not feel safe expressing herself fully.

Circle all that relate to you.

Overdeveloped Maiden Energy:

- Sexual Promiscuity
- Free experience as a "wild child"
- Forcing or abrasive
- Distracted
- Thrill seeking
- Inability to commit

Lack of Maiden Energy:

- Fear of our wild nature as women
- Shame of the body and it's sensuality
- Rigid, prude, cutting off or shaming deep pleasure or desire
- Keeping your life force shut off, never coloring outside of the lines
- Insecure
- Holding on to things longer then they serve, fear of letting go
- Allowing ourselves to be objectified

When to call the Maiden in – The maiden is sure to be your best friend when you are feeling not only overwhelmed by responsibility, but also need for a break from the routine. As she helps us honor our wilder selves and free our inner child, we may find ourselves much more stuck in life than before. If it feels like there's too many commitments or that indecision has gotten the better of you lately, do yourself a favor and reach out to this ancient goddess who can surely help release you back into an authentic state once again.

Accepting all aspects of yourself.

Make a list of twenty things you love about yourself. This can be something you're proud of or kicked ass at, or simply just amazing qualities you have. Don't be bashful.

1. _____
2. _____
3. _____
4. _____
5. _____
6. _____
7. _____
8. _____
9. _____
10. _____
11. _____
12. _____
13. _____
14. _____
15. _____
16. _____
17. _____
18. _____
19. _____
20. _____

Bring your sexy back.
Close your eyes and imagine yourself in the most authentic form.
What is she wearing? How does her hair look? Is she barefoot or in heels?
Dress up yourself in the vision which comes to mind.

Celebrate.

- Turn on the tunes and freely dance around your living room. (Alone or with friends).
- Give yourself a foot bath or foot rub.
- Make an alter or do a ritual of self-love.
- Manifestation Bath: Place some of your favorite herbs into the bathtub. Lavender, mug wort, chamomile, passion fruit, essential oils, fresh fruits, flowers and psom salt. Surround the area with candles and crystals. Amethyst and Rose Quartz work amazing.
- Honor your sisters and celebrate with them the growth and success you all have accomplished.
- Go somewhere new and feel the sense of adventure. Go alone and notice what comes up for you. Pick up a new hobby. Maybe you've always wanted to play the guitar or start photography? This is your time for connection and play.
- Lay on the floor with a book and take a nap.

"SHE REPRESENTS LIFE'S BEGINNINGS AND POSSIBILITIES."

The waxing moon is her symbol.

Diffuse flowery essential oils – Rose, Jasmine & Ylang Ylang.

There are many ways that you can enjoy your sexy time. Whether it is self-pleasure or with a partner, releasing the passion and desire within will help connect to this aspect of yourself as well as come into alignment more easily on all levels. Let go of rigidness and embarrassment in order to truly feel free during these moments so make sure both partners are having fun.

Rituals & Connections.
How to connect to the waxing moon.

As some of you might know, the moon affects the ocean with its tidal pull. What is less commonly known among humans though is that our bodies consist of up to nearly 70% water as well! As many of you are aware, there's a direct correlation between how strong and close to Earth we can see a full moon in relation to lunar phases at any given time; it entirely changes which kind of tides occur on earthbound oceans when they're affected by gravity from all those moons hanging out far away in space. It turns out then, not much is different within our bodies during different moon phases.

The phase of the Moon is called Waxing because it's a time when our night sky starts to get brighter, and that light shines on us from the moon. The Crescent means less than half of the moon can be seen in this scenario, but we should try not to focus too much on what could or might happen as there are always other possibilities for things if they don't go according to plan. Instead, let's shine a little bit more light onto why you're doing something – do your thoughts come back with some intentions?

The phase of the Moon is called Waxing because it's at its brightest point during this period; hence shining like wax against darkening skies lit by tiny crescent moons. The moon is calling you to action, but are you going to answer? Most of us have some sort of goal we've always wanted. You're not alone in this struggle; there's no shame in admitting that things haven't gone as planned and it might be time for a change.

The waxing moon is your time to ask what you are really doing to complete your goals? The moon is our guide, reminding us to take inspiration and create a new reality.

Waxing Gibbous Rituals

A ritual is always something which feels sacred to you. In order to have a clear space, you need to energetically cleanse it. Light some incense and visualize the room being filled with white light that is made from your life force energy; this will help guide any new energies into place as well.

Next, set up an altar in front of yourself where you can center all these different types of energy together while also writing down how you're feeling about what's been going on lately- anything that pops into mind (whether good or bad!) At last, take time for reflection by lighting one candle representing each type of energy present at the ritual before finally journaling everything out. If you're stuck in journaling begin with these prompts. What opportunities are coming up for me? How can I raise my energy level – what is no longer serving me? What inspires me lately? Where has my focus been? What signs are continually popping up from the Universe for me? Start to notice the driftwood (signs) all around you. Ask for a clear sign like an epiphany or picture of Elvis to represent certain questions in your life and pay attention when they pop up – take time over the week after asking to journal any insights that come from it.

During the phase of this moon, signs of what's to come are often seen. This is a great time to tap into gratitude and re-align with an abundance mindset instead of one rooted in scarcity. Write down some things that went your way recently and make you happy; take moments each day during the next few days when nothing but positivity will be allowed–ask yourself: "What am I grateful for?" And remember as if everything has already been done." The most important part is to let go of the "how" and remain open with faith to all possibilities. Sometimes doors are closing that you don't want to because the Universe has something better in store for you. It can feel unnatural as humans sometimes because we so deeply want things to get better that even if they're good in their current state, there will always exist an underlying desire or discontentment towards them–which could lead us into thinking about how much better life would be were this thing not happening right now.

Sometimes we worry too much about what will happen or how people might react instead of focusing our energy inwardly for those moments where life feels eternal because we can shut the outside noise out – we can release control and trust.

From Maiden to Queen – Persephone

One of the most known maiden archetypes is Persephone, she was said to be daughter to Mother Goddess Demeter. While her mother is busy calling plants forth from earth with a thunderous roar, her playful daughter spends much of her time in flower fields and playing amongst the tall stalks that rise up into an azure sky. Hades had been watching this for weeks; he finally decides on snatching his niece away as revenge against Zeus who has given him dominion over all souls below Earth's surface but forbids any intercourse between gods and mortals so long as they are still mortal – Demeter wanders heartbroken over her daughter's loss and refuses to let the crops grow.

The Gods decide to intervene, and Hades is forced to give up his bride, but Hades was two steps ahead. He promises her that if she eats the pomegranate seeds in hell then he will grant her released to roam on Earth with Persephone or go back home and live as though nothing has changed there either way for half of the year. Demeter's daughter Persephone was originally referred to as a kore aka a maiden. With Persephone spending half of the year in the underworld her mother grieves through the falling leaves of fall and the cold death of winter. Hecate (aka the crone) acts during this time and accompanies Persephone as her guide.

Let's backtrack a little and discuss the spot sacred to God Dionysus. Nysos, also where the maiden roamed and played. Usual for his wild, ecstatic female followers-the Maenads–Dionysus was famed with his maenad women roaming through forests in an intoxicated trance that sometimes culminated in violence against animals or even men who came across their path. Now let us look at the maidens' playmates: Artemis (the huntress) and Athena (the war goddess) – you must realize they saw something interesting enough to hang out with the maiden. Underneath the innocence possesses a dangerous ferocity just waiting to escape.

Now let's chat about her family dynamic. Zeus was a notorious womanizer, but not with Demeter. She wasn't his wife, and yet she still became one of the most powerful goddesses in Mount Olympus-the mother everyone knows as Mother Earth to this day who reigns supreme over her own territory. She took her job of motherhood just as seriously- It makes sense that Persephone would be Zeus's heir considering he is her father! Now here is where it gets spicy. Persephone is the queen and goddess of fertility. (Yes, we read that right she transformed from the innocent maiden to a queen.) For ancient people, there was no more important woman to their existence than her–she represented life in its most primal form. It was believed that when Persephone descended into the Underworld for a season each year she wasn't doing so willingly; it was part of women's sacred initiation rites where they descend through darkness, enter Hell with their evil twin (personification), be guided by spirits from above as well as below who helped them rise again having gained power sourced from both birth and creation.

We all have a dark side to us that is always seeking redemption from its own darkness. Hades personifies the fallen aspect of our consciousness trying in vain to redeem itself by trapping light it sees outside, but unable to see the hidden light within ourselves which we can only remember when we are at peace with who we really are and letting go of what no longer serves us so as not be consumed by those old limiting beliefs anymore. Hades is almost the representation of the wounded inner child within all of us. Persephone is doomed to live in the underworld for half the year, yes, she is forced – but on the Earth she was disempowered.

Her mother was overbearing in her personal archetype, which can be seen within every family. There is a possession of children that diminishes wild souls at an early age through limited access to freedom as they grow up with sheltered lives full of parental expectations and rules for them to follow. Think about how many stories we hear about young women running off with older men (the bad boys.) We are all seeking empowerment.

We are all seeking the feeling to be free. The soul so deeply longs to remember its true nature that at times it will bring us to the brink of suffering to awaken us: as though this were not enough, all through tragic Persephone achieves liberation from her mother's grip. The attachment she had with Hades is what gave him power over her and threatened both their existences; but then there came a time when they could feel something like love for each other–when he helped free his queen. Persephone's battle is one we can all relate to. The freedom of independence gives way to the grief and loss of youth, innocence, relationships with friends and family–a time that may have been our happiest before adulthood took over.

When Persephone is tricked into eating a pomegranate, she symbolizes how we must go through our own hell before she can be reborn. The pain and terror that comes with her journey are the same trials everyone must face on their way back up from Hades. However, when you taste all of those hidden gifts in your dark depths like fruit does for its seeds, it becomes easier to birth these gifts to the collective after experiencing so much first-hand knowledge about life's demons. We must consider the law of polarity. Like anything there is a ying to the yang. Darkness to light. In the underworld, danger and addiction are never too far. Without our inner Hecate (the wise woman) we can easily get lost in all that unfold in this dark psyche. The descent of the crone and the grief of Persephone's mother ensure our rebirth. Enlightenment is not an end state, but a mastery in being both human and divine-when we are initiated through our own darkness, when we know how to protect ourselves from its grips.

Persephone is a powerful goddess who becomes queen of the underworld when she can fully embrace her darkness and meet it with light. She then rises to become an empowered woman, but only if she embraces both power and femininity. The maiden must first find themselves before they can be found by another person or society's opinions about them take on more weight than their own journey does for them; this may seem difficult because not everyone has encouragement handed out freely in life – especially women.

The Solar Plexus

The solar plexus is the location of some of your most important organs. Located in front of your aorta, it works with other parts to regulate these vital systems – including digestion and metabolism. It's also connected to emotional wellness through its connection as part of the sympathetic nervous system; so, when we experience stress or trauma this area can be deeply affected by those experiences too!

The solar plexus (sometimes known as celiac) is an essential organ found deep inside you that distributes nutrients throughout our body while regulating many bodily functions such as digesting food and metabolizing hormones for things like sleep cycles and moods- all without us ever knowing about them always happening within us. Connecting to the solar plexus chakra is an important way for a woman to connect with her inner maiden.

This connection can be achieved through affirmations, visualization exercises, and meditation techniques which help you reconnect your relationship with yourself as well as other people in your life who are close to you. As women we have learned over time that it's not acceptable or safe for us show our feelings outwardly (especially anger). We often feel like if we speak up then there will be consequences – sometimes even physical threats of violence against ourselves and others; but connecting back into this power center allows one freedom from these fears by opening oneself up again towards accountability — especially when necessary. The Solar Plexus Chakra represents a person's sense of self, whether they feel confident in themselves or not – this is also known as our ego center. For individuals who are feeling less than polished on the inside and out can get their power back by connecting with their true selves.

This will help you reclaim what has been lost-self-esteem, confidence, strength and femininity. One way to feel more at ease in connecting with this chakra is to associate with yellow. Eat yellow foods, engage in activities that you are most comfortable with. This can be done through meditation, placing your hands over the diaphragm and feeling yellow light flowing into this area, or even just recalling positive memories from past experiences. Breath of fire is a powerful breath work exercise that can awaken the chakra area. Breath work, such as deep breathing exercises and hyperventilation techniques, are often used to help people clear their minds and relax. Breath of Fire is one type of practice which helps us develop our lungs by encouraging maximum inhalation in order to build up oxygen intake inside the body through this ancient Japanese technique.

- I accept myself exactly as I am now.
- I accept myself unconditionally.
- I accept love from myself and others. I am at peace with where I am now.
- I am perfect, just as I am.
- I am free.
- I am spontaneous.
- I am enough.
- I am creating my own love.
- I embrace who I am.
- I am open to seeing myself in a new life.
- I am more than my body.
- My imperfections are what make me beautiful.
- I am exactly who I need to be

The Mother

The mother archetype is a natural caregiver – she represents our maternal instinct, the desire to create life and provide sustenance. The desires of mothers are driven by their actual idea of motherhood. Even if childless the mother archetype is responsible, protective and finds great satisfaction in caring for others. Mothers often put their needs on the back burners to ensure everyone around them is taken care of first. They become neglectful of their own needs and often find it very difficult to set personal boundaries which leaves them feeling depleted in energy. There are two types of mother archetypes. One is the caring mother and the other is the neglectful mother. They both carry these characteristics as a whole.

- Stubbornness
- Persistence
- Strength
- Patience
- Obsession
- Single-Mindedness

The mother archetype is seen in every woman. It can be found from the moment you nurture your baby doll, to when you stand up for and take care of your younger siblings. Two good examples are Cinderella's fairy godmother who represents a nurturing mother figure while her stepmom embodies an abusive one with much neglectful qualities.

If you feel you weren't adequately mothered, this inner mother is here to support your inner child with love & nurtured support.

THE GREAT MOTHER

The great mother is full of compassion, love and forgiveness. She is the embodiment of strength; determined to see past your wrongdoings for a chance at redemption. When we embrace this archetype within ourselves, we give out love as medicine to our children and those around us in need - every action made from the heart center with kindness in her eyes.

When in balance: The Mother symbolizes all the gifts and love that mother earth has to offer. She is a nurturing figure who teaches us how to trust our instincts, follow natural rhythms, find balance in life—and she can connect with your inner child and heal you. With her as part of your spiritual journey, it's easy for anyone from any background or belief system to feel safe while on their own personal path back towards wholeness.

When out of balance: In her shadow side, the mother archetype can over-give to the point where she neglects herself. She is unable to show up as her best self and therefore struggles with losing identity because of this. This might lead in some cases for codependence or controlling tendencies that make it hard for a mother figure to let go when they should. The Great Mother, who represents both death and life. She holds opposing forces of destruction and creation in her hands - it's up to us to embrace this paradox by accepting that everything has an opposite side.

The core limiting belief of The Mother "I am not enough."

When to call the mother in – We all call in different archetypes at different phases within our lives. You do not have to be a mother in order to embody the mother archetype. The three facets of every goddess are birthed from,

Maiden (daughter), Mother (mother) and Crone (grandmother). The mother is not just about procreating. She has the power of creativity and creation, which are her birthright as a woman. Creation can be anything from innovation to art to design--anything that nurtures abundance in some way. The archetypal goddess of all things created is none other than Mother Earth herself; she symbolizes what it means for women today: being creative while also nurturing oneself.

>"I am enough, just as I am."

Divine Mother,
Help me to rest in my heart and offer unconditional love and compassion to all of my relations and to my own inner child.

THE SHADOW MOTHER

The shadow is not inherently bad or good. It has it place in all aspects of our lives, including the mother archetype and how she influences. When the dark side of Mother becomes too large over one's psyche, they may lose touch with what it means to be nurturing. Not only to themselves but others as well, but when we embrace this aspect within ourselves instead of fear, it becomes liberation for both self and those around us.

We will not take care of our own personal needs such as our body, our own hobbies, self-love, or our own children. We are checked out essentially. This is the feeling of not a good enough mom or inadequate in our everyday lives. Narcissistic behaviors show denying our children and those we care about any form of love or attention. We deny basic needs.

A mother who lacks a sense of self-love can be seen in their shadow side as manipulative and controlling. This type of parent is often gossipy with the intention to shame others for what they see as flaws, so that people will not focus on theirs instead. They are also very controlling because this way if they don't get any attention than those around them won't have it either. A child raised by such parents learns how painful love really is - never experiencing true affection themselves from an early age which leads to low entitlement levels later down the road since no one ever believes that anything good could happen without something bad happening beforehand. The Mother Wound is a complex trauma that all of us have experienced to some degree. It lives as strong limiting beliefs and can be ignited by other experiences in life, such as the father wound or even just an experience with your mother. The research conducted has found it within many women's unconscious minds-

> "The world goes on through its twist and turns, I go on in its meandering ways, but I am still Who wants to watch the waves of life's ocean…floundering."
> - Gururaj Ananda Yogi

The Mother Wound

There is no other way to put this - The Mother Wound affects us deeply when we ourselves become mothers without that example growing up of what that was supposed to look like in a healthy way. Abandonment creeps into many relationships, and self-love can be difficult with the scar inflicted by one's own mother not wanting them the idea of being abandoned or unwanted has always been something I found heartbreaking. But becoming a mother myself, it really hit me how much abandonment will creep into my life (it's a sneaky emotion) because my mother was absent when I needed her most in life. It is hard to role model a behavior in which you were never taught.

The mother wound can be defined as your mother not being emotionally attuned and available to you as a child. She may have been present physically but emotionally absent from her children's lives in many cases. Or she may have been absent all together. When she wasn't around or paying attention, kids felt hurt and rejected because they were left feeling like their needs didn't matter at all to anyone else other than themselves for so long of their life.

The Mother Wound is the pain rooted in our relationship with our mothers that we have inherited and passed down from generation to generation.

The wound has a profound effect on all of us, but it's especially deep for those who are born female in patriarchal cultures because they will never be able to find true peace without healing this part of their story.

The mother wound is what women carry around through generations by passing them onto subsequent daughters or granddaughters; whether she was victimized herself or simply inherits beliefs about womanhood handed down over time, her daughter's psyche could end up wounded as well when these wounds go unhealed. This is where you hear the word "generational curse" come into play. The Mother Wound is a phenomenon that has been identified in many ways: on an individual basis, women who have experienced trauma from their mothers often struggle with patterns of self-sabotage.

On a cultural level, it's the pain of being female and not feeling empowered; this wound can be passed down through generations as we cope individually to try healing our wounds. Finally, on an eternal sense there are spiritual implications for one who feels disconnected from her body or other people - she must realize that those feelings come from something much deeper than just physical separation and isolationism because they stem back to "the mother" herself. Some people place the blame for their Mother Wound with someone other than themselves to avoid taking responsibility. Healing your mother wound is a way of accepting personal responsibility and moving on from it. When we have mother wounds often, we feel like victims and see emotions as the enemy. Unhealthy coping techniques, from overeating, numbing out, or to just cut off emotions all together can be a way that we deal with the feelings associated with having had an unhealthy relationship in childhood. Learning ways to express your emotional self without being aggressive or harming yourself is important for keeping healthy mental boundaries; this also helps you develop healthier relationships throughout adulthood if you are able to take control of what's happening inside your headfirst.

Writing letters without sending was a powerful way for me personally to tap into this consciously. It was a way to gather my thoughts and come to a space of forgiveness from anger.

COURTNEY HANSON

Mom,

This letter is to explain why I'm so mad at you, why I can't forgive you for the life of me and my thoughts which so many only know the surface of because you play such a manipulative game. At Christmas you did an excellent job of letting your true colors show with all you text the family about me when I needed you the most. Let's start at the beginning. You never wanted me, I know that I was a whoops but as you told me you had an abortion before me with my dad and couldn't handle going through that again. Then we fast forward - A mom's job is to protect her children no matter how inconvenient I was for you. You let Dickon beat my sister with belts, you let him do inappropriate things to me. You stayed… You exposed me to a very dark world at a very young age. You didn't keep me safe. Then you lied my entire life saying it was my grandmother's money that got me taken away. I saw every document and recording as an adult, and it was all bullshit. My dad was told not to let you see me until I was eighteen. I begged and cried for you nightly, I wanted my mom, and I forgave you because I didn't understand. I just needed you. When I got old enough to communicate properly my dad let you come over to my grandmas to see me. Sometimes you showed, sometimes you didn't. I remember sitting on my playground set writing you a "wake up and smell the coffee" letter begging you to pull your shit together and love me despite my dad. Something so fucked up is every time I saw you; you would tell me how much like my dad I was. (I knew your hate for each other.) What you didn't know was that at home my dad was telling me how much like you I was. Everything is kind of a blur, you never came to my talent shows, choir performances, band concerts - nothing. I would always look for you in the crowds. In eighth grade I got to spend the first month of summer with you. It was clear you didn't care if I was there or not. You had your new family and that was your only concern. I did make friends in the neighborhood though and had fun riding bikes with them. I remember that summer I so desperately wanted your attention I was pounding my knees on the gravel in the driveway till they bled, I ran inside saying I fell on my bike so you would nurture me and you told me I was so dramatic and not to wake up my little sister and go back outside. I remember that summer you vacuumed every morning to make lines on the carpet, so when I flew back to Illinois, I tried so hard to be just like you.

WITHIN

Before you put me on the plane you put my hair in two French braids, and I refused to take them out for a week because that was our last bonding moment. Every morning in Illinois I would wake up extra early to vacuum my room just like you did, in a weird way it made me feel like I was with you again. Everything I did though was made fun of. It's why I am so defensive. Remember that time I was going to The Christian Academy - I had to wear a uniform with a cardigan and the first time you ever saw me in the uniform you began laughing at me calling me conservative. When I moved in with you freshmen year, I felt all my dreams had come true. I finally had my mom - but it wasn't at all like what I saw my friends and their moms like. I was always the black sheep on the back burner - You would call me low nipples, make fun of my nerdiness when that is all I knew because you weren't around to teach me, and youtube didn't exist. I was raised by a man who knew very little of hair and makeup trends. I was super into singing, piano and clarinet it was always a connection I had playing piano and singing with my grandma. I was always told how talented I was till I moved in with you. Freshmen year I got the lead soprano solo at honor choir and was singing Tale as old as time - It was my first and last school event you ever went to. I had practiced for months and afterwards your only response was "singing is not your thing, maybe try out for volleyball next year because your tall." I quit the choir the next year and never sang again. I know I joke about it in my first book, and we've brushed it under the rug, but you humiliated me in front of everyone that day. I took a blow to my self-esteem which I didn't think could get any lower. You took me on four trips my entire life - all because they were convenient, and the entire family was going. I started to lie about everything - I wanted your love so bad; I would make up stories just to have conversations with you or act like I needed your advice. I made you scrapbooks telling you how much I loved you and would be the best daughter ever. I lived with you for all of a year and you never let my friends come in the house. I remember Jessica peeing in the yard. We were all "troublemakers" to you. Remember the weed you found of my sister and blamed me for it? My dad sent me a computer eventually and I just sat in my room instant messaging friends at school because at least I had someone to talk too. You never noticed I was depressed or isolating. I think you were just happy you didn't have to deal with me. Then Christmas my sophomore year I lit a candle and forgot to blow it out, we came home, and you kicked me out. You knew my dad was living in a hotel and didn't care. I spent the remainder of that month living out of the Comfort Inn. No check in, no apology, nothing from you. I spent Christmas eating lunch meat ham in a hotel watching law and order. Fuck you for that. Something changed in me that night. I started sneaking cigarettes, skipping school, partying. I don't think we spoke for six months. We finally got a rental in the ghetto, and it was such a bad neighborhood a lot of kids from school weren't allowed to come over because of the drugs and shootings in the area. You came to see there and said what a dump it was, and you knew my dad had gotten cps called and you did nothing. You let me come for visits when it was convenient for you. I had to walk four miles just catch public transit to get to school there and back. Eventually I just stopped showing up. You weren't there for any of my school dances, you were supposed to do my hair and makeup for tolo and flaked the morning of because of "work." My junior prom is when life started to spin out of control. I decided to smoke pot for the first time before and accidently left a cigarette in my purse. My dad found it and said no to prom. I had already gotten ready and was about to leave. I decided to steal his car for the night and go any ways. He showed up to my prom with police and when I saw them, I was terrified and ran. I was scared to go home so I spent the night at a party with the car. Police found me and arrested me on felony charges at 17 for taking motor vehicle without permission. I stayed in juvenile hall for sixty days and at this point I was good at adapting. It had become a survival skill for me. I could talk or fit in with anyone, anywhere. You came to visit once in juvi and all you could talk about was my corn rolls I had in my hair. The court agreed to drop the felony if I went to Visions which you and dad advocated for because then you wouldn't have to see me or deal with me for nine months. You both put me in a lockdown facility, no makeup, no razors, no electronics, no outside communication, no visitors, no mirrors. You took my senior year or high school away from me. I was in there with fourteen-year-old prostitutes. I shut down and did whatever I had to just to get through. In there I basically learned how to get away with things. I was never exposed to anyone or anything like that until then. My friends were all just pot heads that liked to go to parties and dance. While in the facility my dad had moved to Indiana with some girl, so you were my only option once released. It's weird that year living with you I remember very little I was in such a fog, I know it didn't

WITHIN

last long and I moved in with Jessica until moving to Indiana a year later with my dad after I had a bad run in with cocaine. That was short lived, I started drinking and partying a lot with college friends. I was now an adult, so I came and went as I pleased. At that point I didn't want to feel anything I felt I had been robbed of being a kid and now had to grow up but had no clue how to adult. I didn't know how to cook, do laundry, dishes - absolutely no life skills which was your job to teach me. Because of you I never could hold a relationship longer than three months. The first boyfriend I ever had I was forced to live with after a month of dating. We went to a bar and I had a fake wrist band, he brought me home drunk I think I had just turned 18 and he was 22 my dad at the time lived above a salon in a studio. No kitchen just a microwave so I lived on potatoes, sandwiches, and frozen burritos. My dad told me he was done with me and had my boyfriend at the time take me he could no longer deal with me. Even after I broke up with him a month later, I lived there till I could move back to Washington. I called you and you didn't care. I asked for help flying home and you couldn't help. When I finally made it back you saw me all of three times. All I wanted was for you to love me or at least want to be in the same room with me. You and dad tossed me around like a pawn. No regard for me just how you could hurt each other. Like an idiot though any chance you opened to me I jumped at the bait. I never brought a thing up or stood my ground because I wanted that relationship so fucking bad. I ended up moving to California and I tried so hard to build a relationship with you. I started going to AA, had 18 months sober, I begged you to come down for my sober 21 and you wouldn't. I begged you to come to my engagement party - you didn't. I wanted your approval so bad and was told he looks like a weasel and your ring is too small. A month after my engagement party I cheated with my boss and got pregnant. I was terrified and couldn't even take care of myself let alone a baby. I begged you to come help me set up the nursery and stay with me the first couple weeks because I would be alone, but you told you couldn't get off work. You work at Nordstrom's. Let's keep it real, you didn't want to. My sister and dad came down to help learn to nurse, how to change a diaper, took care of my c section wounds and fed me because I was incapable of walking the stairs. If it wasn't for them, I would have had no one. All you ever did was bash anything I did for the next two years. I made him organic food and you mocked me, I didn't know about sunscreen, and you called me a bad mom because he got sunburned, you made fun of his ears and for him being a ginger. We finally came up that year for Christmas so you could meet him, but you belittled more than anything. You worked the whole week we were up there and never once attempted to bond or help so I could have a break. When I flew back, I felt so sad everything I imagined about that trip failed again. I tried hard to make it work with Liam's dad and took so much emotional abuse from his PTSD I just couldn't do it anymore. I called to get advice over that few months and you just told me to be stronger and that I was a mom now. We talked off and on over the next four years mostly you are telling me how something was wrong with Liam and he has behavioral issues. I would catch myself talking shit about my own child just to make conversation with you and for you to praise me and tell me good job. Shame on me – I still feel guilt for agreeing with you on anything. I then got pregnant with Audrey I was so excited to tell you and your response was "Oh booh not again are you sure about this?" During my pregnancy when I found out I was having a girl you were excited and spoke to me a little more. After Audrey was born you never came down no matter how much I begged. Any fight I had with my husband I would call you and it would be my fault. Finally, when Audrey was 18 months, we came up to visit. I had horrible pneumonia and I laid on my sister's couch dying, and you said your fine do a Dr. video call – I did, and they told me to go to a walk-in clinic immediately. You sat in the car with Audrey while I went in with my oxygen at 84% I text you from the drs office I had pneumonia and when I got in the car you were on the phone with your plastic surgeon asking if I was contagious and if it was safe to be around me. You didn't offer to pick up anything or ask how I was feeling, nothing. I didn't want to ruin the trip and for the first time in my life we had family pictures the next day which I didn't want to ruin. Audrey had a 103 temp and couldn't breathe, and we still did pictures because that's how much they meant to me. Towards the end of our week trip, we had a special time playing tourist in Seattle. It was the most maternal I have ever seen you act, and I will cherish that day the rest of my life. It was just you, me and the kids. We laughed, we took selfies, you loved on both the kids, and I felt for the first time there was hope for us to grow our relationship. I flew back and called you nearly every day after that. I felt like I could tell you anything looking back I see why though – My stepdad had just had his stroke and you were scared, then my little sister got in a bad relationship, and then things got hard with me, and you left again. My custody battle with Liam's father got ugly and you made comments about all his cps calls on me to gain custody and made remarks to put me down whenever you could. During my custody battle I thought best to not talk to any of you which what I did for the next year. I can't remember how or why we even started talking again. But we became close - My sister came out as polyamorous and you called me crying for the first time ever. During that time, I was pregnant with Tristan. We had been trying for over a year to get pregnant and your response was still "can you handle one more?" After the traumatic birth and me having to be at the hospital alone I felt you really loved me. You posted about Tristan on your gram asking for prayers (now I know it was for the attention factor.) None the less, I felt you loved me and were there - truly present. We talked so much that for the first time in over twelve years you decided to come visit me in California. We were closer than ever, and it was your first-time meeting, Cameron. By this point I had been with him for six years. You fell in love with my husband and said how much my stepdad would love him and how alike they were. The trip was so normal - we adventured every day, you got to see Audrey for the second time in her life and you fell in love with her as well. You told me Liam you just didn't know how to connect too. When you left, I cried so hard I just wanted you to stay, to be Mimi, to be my mom. I felt so close to you - you said several times when you were down here and I would clean something a certain way or say a certain phrase "Oh, you're so much like me I can't believe I've never seen it before." To me I knew that was a way of you saying you loved me. When I wrote my first book you posted it all over and wrote me a card saying how much you loved me, what a good wife and mom I was and how proud of me you were - You sent me two more cards like this to for the following Mother's Day and for my birthday. I still have them saved. Just reading I'm proud of you made me want to move more mountains, to be a bigger wonder woman, I wanted to impress you, I truly thought at this point in my life you were here to stay. When Tristan was three months old you came down for a second time and we went to Tahoe together and it was amazing. The whole trip again was smooth and beautiful. The visit just couldn't have been any more perfect. Cameron had just started the fire academy for his promotion, so you wanted to help me get in a groove, I felt so much love and so much support from you. Audrey was so excited to see her Mimi and for you to sleep in her princess bed with her. Everything was as close to perfect as it's ever been. I knew something was wrong with my hormones at this point, I knew I had postpartum Depression, but everything was so perfect I couldn't dare risk ruining it or tell you how I was feeling inside. You kept telling me what a wonderful mom I was and how strong I was, and I wanted to push and prove to you how much better I could get. When you left, I talked to you daily. When my older sister told my younger sister she was poly I was the first one called. When anyone needed advice, I was the go-to. When you left after that trip I couldn't stop crying again. I had lost my husband and now felt I had lost you. I was unsure our next visit and I slowly fell into a habit of drinking wine every night to calm down from being solo all day. It never caused a problem at this point it was just a part of my routine. You began a relationship with my older sister again and slowly started slipping away again. In our dynamic of four only three can be in the triangle at one time. There is always an odd man out. During the summer we made the drive up to Seattle and stayed for two weeks. I think this is the trip you saw something was off with me. You lectured me a few times on my parenting and drinking. "Why are you always tired." "What's wrong with you?" We had one huge blow out that week when I caught my little sister and you talking shit about me in the bathroom. I called you out and you said I was defensive and had my little sister begin screaming at me. I went downstairs and just sobbed. I felt alienated and out of the circle again. I drove home and we continued to talk about once a week but slowly began to distance ourselves. The emotional part of the affair began shortly after this - I slowly started to distance and pull away from everyone and everything I loved. The day after Tristan's first birthday, the affair went from emotional to physical. I left and called my big sister crying and confused almost on this emotional rush and high. She saw a way to get back in the trio and everything I begged her not to share, she ran and told you. I called to tell you and you basically told me what a piece of shit I was and how you never thought I would be capable of doing something like this and how ashamed of the woman I had become you were. We all had several volatile conversations and it hit the peak of explosion when I flew to Seattle and didn't see you. I stayed at my aunt and uncles, and you sent attacking text, threatened to call CPS, you didn't even hear my side of the story or why I left because you were listening to everyone but me. When I needed family, you were yet again, absent. You didn't even once ask if I was okay. When I was in Seattle it hit me like a ton of bricks to the head - you don't love me, you only want me when I make you look good, when it's easy and convenient for you. Fuck you for not being a parent or even just having an ounce of empathy when all I wanted was a hug and told it was going to be okay. You didn't give a shit; you never have, and you never will. For this, you can't be in my life moving forward. I will find a way to forgive you. I will find a way to love you from a distance. But physically, emotionally, spiritually you have taught me what a god damn warrior I am. How resilient I can be. How to mother myself. I release the hold to you. I release the toxic behavior on all sides. I am going to heal. I am going to help thousands of others heal. But before I do that.

Fuck you for never being there...
Fuck you for being the first to turn everyone against me...
Fuck you for your lies and games...
Fuck you for making my son feel less than loved...
Fuck you for your decisions and missing out on my amazing family's lives...

I share these letters to not bash my mom, but with the intention to show the true nature of the *victim mentality*. This was a letter I wrote while in trauma therapy - looking back on it so many memories and truths are missing. I created a certain scenario within my head to justify my acting out and behavior. She made a lot of mistakes and I spent years living in fear, thinking the world had it out for me because she left me when I was younger. It wasn't until - after working through issues with abandonment myself as an adult- did I realize that this is just how things are sometimes; nobody's perfect and everyone has a story. We made our soul contracts to work through lessons, to heal, to grow, to nurture. Again, this is not the sexy part of growth. Forgiving my mother has helped put everything into perspective.

Abandonment issues are a sneaky emotion, and we start developing subconscious safety mechanisms as children. It is possible that these patterns, formulated in our childhoods, gravely affect us in adulthood without even consciously knowing why we are self-sabotaging or having destructive behavior. The feeling of not being able to relax because you feel unsafe can be damaging for your mental and physical well-being.

The anxiety level is very high, which makes it difficult to concentrate on anything else but the potential threat in front of you. It also interferes with childhood development as kids cannot fully explore their environment when they are constantly scanning for danger or worrying about what could happen next.

Children are not born with the ability to identify and deal with danger in their environment. In order to feel safe – even in an unsafe environment - very young children use a subconscious defense called idealization, which is where they put their parents up on pedestals and see them as perfect, all-knowing, godlike creatures that can protect them from anything threatening or dangerous around them.

This makes creates a safety net for us within the subconscious mind. Keep in mind on a conscious level we have no idea we are doing this. One of the most difficult things in life for children is when their parents abandon them. Children often find themselves at fault and believe that they are inadequate because it could be no other way according to this passage by Dr. John Gottman, a leading researcher on marital stability and divorce prediction who say's "parents have all of the power". This sense of defectiveness is where the Mother Wound begins to take formation. As we get older the secondary emotion comes into play. Shame. Shame is an emotional infection that sets in on top of the wound. It's a little closer to awareness, but it still resides beneath consciousness.

The Internal Critic is a mean and controlling voice. It constantly points out your flaws, makes you feel like an imposter, or tells you outright that others will eventually leave because of the way things are going. What's more? The IC always harps on abandonment issues: fears of rejection when it comes to anything from limiting beliefs about oneself to coping skills past memories which bring up feelings related to shame but can't be pinned down for certain reasons. This is where we become triggered subconsciously and have no idea why we are reacting the way we are as adults.

We usually direct this within two ways, internally or externally. The energy goes inwards constantly beating ourselves up, ruining every opportunity, sabotaging relationships so we don't get hurt or we feel the need to take our anger and pain out on others. Externalizing this hate is no better than internalizing it because both actions can lead us down a dark path of resentment.

In order to be able to love ourselves, we first need find our inner mother. We can't move forward if we don't take care of the parts that got left behind when growing up and this is something only an internal mother could do for us.

A healthy mother archetype allows us to experience a sense of love, security, nourishment and containment. When we can embrace ourselves and our suffering more fully, it becomes easier for us to do the same with others. We need to have a compassionate heart in order for there be compassion on an even larger scale—we cannot hold the global heart if we don't have one that's holding up under pressure.

> Go back and take care of yourself.
> Your body needs you,
> your feelings need you,

your perceptions need you.
Your suffering needs you to acknowledge it.
Go home and be there for all these things.

Healing the Mother Wound

In our culture it is difficult for women not to grow up with trauma caused by their mothers or fathers and/or the society in which they live. For many people there are various ways that can help heal these wounds, but one was very vital for me - forgiveness! It takes courage because we need to forgive those who have hurt us deeply without any hope of reciprocity from them ever again as well as forgiving ourselves so that we may move on instead of being weighed down by bitterness and anger forever.

There is a cycle of pain that has been passed down from generation to generation. We can break this pattern, but we must be aware and understand the root cause before it will heal.

Epigenetics: Epigenetics is the study of how your behaviors and environment can cause changes that affect the way your genes work. Unlike genetic changes, epigenetic changes are reversible and do not change your DNA sequence, but they can change how your body reads a DNA sequence.

Trauma IS passed down at a cellular level, but the fabulous news is that it can be reversed.

The field of epigenetics gained momentum about a decade ago, when scientists reported that children who were exposed in the womb to the Dutch Hunger Winter famine toward the end of World War II carried an identifiable chemical mark on one gene. The researchers later linked this finding with differences between their health outcomes later in life including higher-than average body mass.

We also need to consider the responsibility through limiting beliefs, religions, and traditions that have been put on mothers to be the "perfect woman".

When a woman feels she is not good enough, because of societal norms and expectations, it can create an unhealthy Mother Wound. When women refuse to abandon their desires in favor for the cultural ideal of motherhood, they are left feeling suffocated by excessive pressure that breeds rage, depression, and anxiety which then gets passed on to her children through subtle or even aggressive forms of emotional abandonment or manipulation such as shame, guilt, or obligation and this creates the maternal wound. If we embrace the divine feminine and all the healing in which it offers without confronting and healing the Mother Wound, this is nothing but another sugar coating and form of spiritual bypassing.

You are entitled to having your own experience of the wound, you're not your mother and therefore the bravest decision is to step out of the cycle. Pause, and get awareness. Often times when we do this, we take ownership or feel like we are betraying - it is crucial to allow yourself space through this journey.

As a woman who carries deep wounds from her mother's absence in my life, I know how much pain can be felt when you feel like your mother isn't there with you at every turn.

I find it really empowering to think about how my mother was doing at the age I am at now with children. It allows me to come from a space of empathy and step out of resentment. For example - when my mother was my age, she had already been through four marriages with three children from three different men. I triggered an abusive relationship she had with my father and a life of trauma and abandonment she created for me within her previous marriages. She was finally happy with who she is still married to now and had a newborn baby - her life was perfect but when I was around it was inconvenient and brought up her own personal wounds, she was not ready to heal from. At the same time, I can't help but wonder what our relationship would be like now if her life had been different and there were no traumatic events in her own past.

Often our mothers do not have the tools or strength to protect us and show up as they should have.

The Mother Wound is a sacred passage that you are blessed to have the opportunity of healing. It will give birth to your best self through its own transformation, as it heals both personal and human wounds alike by bringing back unity with life and others in this world. We often have trouble realizing what we've taken on and how much grief it has caused. Start asking yourself, "What messages do I internalize?" Or when someone says something unpleasant about you in front of others: What is my first reaction? Why am I triggered in this way? Rewiring our brain is an important part of healing from the mother wound. Rewiring means that we are developing new connections between neurons in our brains, and it can be difficult at first, but with repetition these neural pathways will fire off automatically making them like you've been doing this your whole life. Brains want to heal themselves.

But how do we do this? It starts with mindfulness - No one knows for certain how the human brain works and changes over time; however, there are many theories that suggest what might be happening inside of it based on new research findings. One theory is called neuroplasticity (or "neuro-rewiring"), which says that by practicing various skills or habits repeatedly enough to strengthen them in a particular region of the brain—we can change its physical structure with repeated practice. This can be as simple as deciding who you want to be and what you want your life to look like and showing up for that person every day - taking on the persona if you will. Reparenting is also a powerful method - Reparenting yourself is providing your little you what your mother should have given you. It's a lot of grieving to get over the idea that our mother wasn't there for us in any way, shape or form.

Reparenting may sound off-putting at first, but it doesn't need to be complicated - One day I realized that if I don't give myself what my mom never did then nobody will and after working fiercely here are the top ways, I found to reparent myself: validate all experiences; talk lovingly about oneself out loud; use affirmations when possible; do activities little you loved; practice breathing techniques and movement. Wrap your arms around you while seated in easy pose and rock in a spiral motion allowing your whole body to sync together in comfort, love and ease.

I am so glad you were born. You are a good person with the capacity to do great things and I love who you are and want to be there for every step of your development. When life gets hard, come talk it out with me; together we will get through this difficult time knowing that my support is always available when needed most! It's okay if sometimes being perfect can't happen because all feelings deserve respect. Nobody deserves more understanding than someone they care about deeply - not even themselves! Remember: mistakes aren't failures on your part but just lessons in disguise which help teach us what we need or don't need as humans living in an imperfect world where everything changes constantly, and nobody has any control over anything outside of themselves. You are the most amazing, beautiful person I have ever met. You can do anything you want and be whoever you need to be in order to find that which makes your world brighter. Sometimes we get lost along our journey but with a little help from those who love us it's so much easier for us to see what was all around us this whole time! I'm very proud of everything about you; how strong-willed, talented and kindhearted you are - You are an inspiration by being yourself no matter what anyone says or thinks

Demeter

Demeter also known as Mother Earth is the daughter of the deities Cronus and Rhea. Demeter is most known for her story with Hades and Persephone, but a lot is left unsaid about what she went through upon Persephone's taking. As a mother she was distressed - so distressed she caused a famine. Demeter is also associated with Gaea (Earth) - Demeter and Persephone were the central figures of Eleusinian Mysteries, the most famous secret religious festival in Ancient Greece. Demeter's name consists of two parts.

Meter - mother and De - Gaea. Together they create Mother - Earth. Demeter is usually portrayed as a fully clothed and matronly looking woman either enthroned and regally seated or proudly standing with an extended hand.

Demeter is the goddess of agriculture. She presides over grain, fertility and growth while also being a protector from natural disasters such as floods or drought. Demeter is usually represented in art wearing either traditional Roman clothing with her matronly look on display for all to see or confidently standing proud extending one hand outwards towards someone else who may be sitting down looking at her admiringly.

The scandal is to be said that Zeus (Persephone's father) who was also Demeter's brother knew all about Hades and aided him throughout the taking of Persephone's. Demeter went from roaming the Earth for nine days heartbroken to fiery and anger.

She was so pissed she left Mt. Olympus and went to grieve her daughter among mortals disguised as an older woman. While being disguised as a mortal she ended up with King Celeus of Eleusis, where his wife Metanira gave Demeter a job as a nurse to her baby, Demphon. In gratitude for the kindness Demeter devised a plan to make Demophon immortal. She did this by give him baths in fire each night slowly burning his mortality away. Metanira walked in on this ritual with no clue Demeter was really a Goddess and began to freak out.

Demeter revealed herself to Metanira and told her the only way Eleusinians would ever gain her kindness back is by building a temple establishing a festival in her glory. The King agreed and built her temple. Demeter spent the next year in grief refusing to do her duties, being neglectful, and the people started dying out of hunger and lack of crops. Zeus finally realized that if he didn't bring Persephones back to Demeter the people would be wiped out from hunger.

Demeter had seven children in total - Persephone, Ploutos, Philomelus, Despoena, Arion, Eubuleus and Chrysothemis.

Embodiment of The Mother

When we think of the Mother Goddess, it is important to realize that she will always be a figure with great power. Mothers have more than enough creativity and feminine ability in them to create life or anything they want for themselves. Women possess creative powers which can be used not only when giving birth but also in art, music, innovation, and invention. Feminine power is an indicator of our nurturing ability; this provides us abundance all around ourselves as women are given many opportunities by society today.

Create

You can make your life more beautiful by incorporating handmade items into it. One way is to make art, another would be to cook something delicious or tap in that creative center inside of you and do what makes you happy! You don't have time for every hobby? That doesn't mean there aren't some simple ways for making the things around you a little prettier: sewing up curtains from old sheets, painting an abstract masterpiece on empty wall space--whatever brings out the artist in yourself

Wear Moveable Clothing

As a woman, our energy is designed to flow and move. Yoga pants are great for working out in but if you want the most feminine look try throwing on some harem pants or something with more of an airy feel like a dress that flows nicely around your body.

Connect to Plants

Plants are known for their healing properties and the ability to ground ourselves. Connecting with mother earth while feeling her love is simpler than ever! Plants help heal our bodies, minds, emotions, and more- it's no wonder why they're the universal symbol for "life." The Earth provides an endless number of resources that we can tap into in order to reconnect after what feels like an eternity without much connection. Humans adapt over time from their natural surroundings as well as adapting mentally by living life on social media instead of experiencing things firsthand.

Every full moon the spirit of the mother emerges.

It is important to harness her energy in the right ways. It is easy to slip into the need for "control" during this time. The moon has been a symbol of feminine power for all time. It is understanding, intuition, birth and death; it's also about reincarnation and spiritual connection. The Moon represents our deepest needs as individuals - this means we can use its cycle to make us better listeners to ourselves. The appearance of a full moon symbolizes many things that we can't see. Cosmically speaking, it's the time of month where energy peaks and then releases - "a cosmic sigh." The full moon has the power to show us what we need to release from our lives and let go of, preparing ourselves for a new chapter. It is easy when you think about it: just as the moon gives way at nightfall so too can your anger give way with kindness on yourself during this time in order to prepare for another phase in life.

Perform these steps to harvest the powerful energy of a full moon.

1. Meditate - Take as long as you need in a silent meditation, allow your breath to guide you and be your medicine in release. Inhale through the nose and long exhales through your mouth.

2. Fire - The act of lighting a candle has been associated with intuition for centuries. The spiritual meaning behind the practice is that fire represents transformation, and when we light candles it helps us to release negativity in our lives.

3. Let it go - If you want to make things better, there are some steps that will put you in a much more positive place. First and foremost is identifying the weight on your shoulders by writing down what has been weighing you down for long enough. You'll then be able to see clearer than before with these written thoughts out of your head. Identifying this burden can help change it so that not only do they no longer weigh as heavily but also don't affect us anymore at all! To truly let go, start by recognizing the things dragging you back into old habits or bad situations which could have taken hold if left unchecked too long expressing them through writing may give clarity where thinking about them would not suffice because we've become used to ignoring.

4. Visualize - Imagine the fulfillment you would feel at your fulfilled potential. Let it fill you with a joy so intense that tears well up in your eyes as if someone had given life to an empty shell of who you might have been and brought color back into its world again for the first time in decades.

5. Speak your intention to the moon - Forgiving someone or yourself can be difficult, but it is necessary. When you speak the words "I forgive" to a person and feel negative energy drain away; when you know that any negativity will not linger in your life because of what has been released into the universe for handling—it's worth investing some time to do so. Forgiveness frees us up from all those worries about being judged by others, removes feelings of resentment, brings peace within ourselves and with other people close to our hearts. All this while also allowing room for self-growth as we continue learning on mistakes made along our journey through life! Forgive somebody else? Speak aloud: I forgive _____ (person) feeling negativity draining away may release them into the moon's energy.

Connect to your menstrual cycle

When we menstruate, our body releases a hormone called estrogen. This shifts the chemical balance of our bodies and can cause symptoms like irritability or fatigue. The power behind these periods goes beyond just those 5–7-day cycles in which women experience menses each month! Try tracking your monthly cycle by monitoring not only how you're feeling physically but also whether you felt especially creative during that time; this information could provide insight into what areas need reinforcing through the menstrual process for better overall wellbeing. Women across different cultures often have synchronized period dates when they spend time together because everything is connected--this was first observed centuries ago in Africa where it's documented as "moon months" among tribes who lived near water sources. This is our time for wisdom and creative flow; we receive information differently at different times of the month which explains how some days feel more productive than others! From menstruation to ovulation (and back again), we're preparing to give birth - sometimes literally but also figuratively. And this process doesn't just happen in a linear way, it's cyclical: from one life phase into another and then back around again like clockwork.

Acts of service

If you want to be more connected with others, try being kind. This could mean buying a cup of coffee for someone or volunteering at community service events. The energy flows where attention goes and when it comes from unconditional love, the results are boundless.

Practicality

The idea of manly tasks such as fixing a leaky sink or changing the tire on your car might seem to be an insurmountable task for the inexperienced. With some quick tutorials and practice you can learn how to fix these things yourself in no time. Take your power back.

Use what you have and have what you use

The sun rises in the east and sets out west. The sky is blue one moment, then colorful with shades of purple the next; a perfect example of how creativity can be found all around us. Learning to tap into the power of your archetype is a chance for novel creativity. You can learn about where you get your best ideas by taking this opportunity to explore other realms and flex that creative muscle.

Gather

Join other women in ceremony, moon circles or dinner to feel part of the community and collective consciousness.

Make Space

Clearing out the excess creates a space for abundance. The mother is often associated with the provider-the safe space, so clear as much clutter from your life and take time to slow down. Spend some time appreciating what it feels like to receive instead of chasing after every shiny object that comes into view because you'll discover how rewarding being in an abundant mindset can be.

You must be careful when you fill up your cup because what goes in, must come out. You might spend so much time with other people that the only way to recharge is by spending some quality "me-time"; otherwise, it will continue being drained and neglected as well. There's nothing wrong about keeping a balance between giving yourself attention and taking care of others around us who depend on our support and motivation for them not feeling alone or forgotten. Think back over this week: What worked? Where did I let myself down? How can I do better next time?" The human brain is uniquely wired to respond not only to what we want but also what we don't. It does not react linearly, so when the emotional part of your brain receives input that's contrary to how you feel about something then it becomes twice as strong and difficult for logic or reason to get through - this can be very destructive if dealing with thoughts about self-esteem because they are already vulnerable emotions in need of support and protection from outside forces such as criticism.

What we resist will persist.

Chakra Connection of The Root Chakra

The root chakra is the first center in an individual's astral body where energy from other parts of oneself can be drawn. It is located at the base of your spine. It also governs our sense of security, stability and safety; as well as to what degree we are grounded or focused on reality. This controls how connected you feel with your physical self and surroundings when encountering them via touch, sight etc., while it also has a lot to do with how safe people typically make themselves feel which reflects their level of spiritual growth at a given time period. The Mother archetype is not attained until one becomes self-sufficient in all areas of life, both financially and emotionally. The financial security that comes with being a good manager for oneself allows the individual to love themselves unconditionally because they know what it feels like to be loved by someone else instead of relying on others for this affection--such as during divorce or illness. When we have this foundation securely within ourselves, our cup will run over with emotions so much more powerfully when feeling unconditional love from those around us; after all, these people are just getting an overflow from your overflowing feelings too. The mother archetype embodies these traits - she's nurturing but also has deep roots that push through any obstacle in her way. It may be hard to get there sometimes, especially when you're first getting started with embodiment of The Mother; but once you tap into this place within yourself, I can guarantee anything will seem possible!

How to tell if your root chakra is blocked.

In what areas do you not feel safe?

_____
_____
_____
_____
_____
_____

In what areas of your life do you feel there is scarcity or not enough?

_____
_____
_____
_____
_____
_____

Where do you feel you have no control or choice?

_____
_____
_____
_____
_____
_____

Where do you lack boundaries?

_____
_____
_____
_____
_____
_____

> Do you trust life supports you and you make
> healthy decisions to support yourself?

_____
_____
_____
_____
_____

Exercises to open the Root Chakra

- The mantra is LAM - this opens prosperity. belongings, and feeling of security.
- Being out with mother nature. Grounding and walking barefoot on the ground itself.
- Yoga poses like mountain, warrior one, squat, goddess and child's pose.
- Imagine a reddish brownish cord attaching from your tail bone to mother earth and feel the love she sends flowing through this cord. Continue to envision this color embracing the lower area of your back. You may feel heat or tingling during this exercise.
- I fear nothing while I am in my body. There is no danger. I enjoy being calm and quiet here. Being in my body is comfortable, because my power is here, my wisdom is here, right where I need them.
- I am important in the lives of my children.
- By allowing myself to be happy, I inspire my family to be happy as well.
- I am the best mother for my children; I was born to be their mother.
- I am doing my best as a mom and that is enough.
- I am grateful for my ability to create life. I will remember to put oxygen on my mask first. I choose to take care of myself.
- I will be kind to myself.
- I will not worry about small details today.
- The foundation of my being is my body. The foundation of my peace and centeredness, is my calm, peaceful and loving body, I agree that this human body is a lovely place to be.
- My body is quiet and lovingly supportive. I am in a relaxed state and my heart supports me.
- I do not need permission to feel glorious.

The Huntress
– Warrioress

The Huntress is the independent female spirit. She represents a woman's autonomy and ability to pursue a life of her own choosing. The fierceness with which she pursues goals, along with an unyielding independence that allows for self-sufficiency in all aspects of living makes up this strong yet free spirited persona whom one would be hard pressed not to admire should they find themselves fortunate enough to earn her trust as well as gain access into her dangerous domain where it becomes apparent just how passionate about what she believes in the Huntressed really is; through being exposed more so than any other personality type before now we see why she has always been considered such a fierce activist who stands up or fights against injustices.

The Goddess Artemis is the epitome of a powerful huntress archetype. She's wild and unruly, but also nurturing in her own way; she teaches archery to young girls who are expected to protect their homes as they grow up while still taking care of themselves out there in the wilderness. In some cultures, the mythical figure even hunts down her male partner in order to tame him for marriage. Now let's explore the huntress and her archetype.

The goddess Diana, also known as Artemis in Greek mythology, is often associated with being a hunter of animals- especially deer. This association probably stems from the fact that she was originally worshipped by women who were out hunting game for food or other domestic purposes including clothing ornamentations like furs and pelts to keep themselves warm during winter months. Often depicted wearing short tunics over their bare skin while they hunted through forests on foot or horseback depending on where you lived at time (Greek vs Roman), carrying bow & arrow, spear gun etc.

The huntress archetype is a powerful one. The woman who hunts and fights with all of her might, without hesitation or fear. She does not shy away from the unknown dangers that lie ahead because she knows what it will take to get where she wants to be in life. The mythological character often depicted as a warrior goddess of natural childbirth was indicative for women living during hard times: they needed their own inner strength and resourcefulness so there would always be enough food on the table no matter how difficult things got outside. It's this same instinctual drive which drives today's modern-day hunter—the need to outsmart prey rather than waiting patiently like an animal caged by nature's limitations.

Greatest Strengths
Self – reliant
Courageous
Goal-oriented
Sympathizes with women's causes

Huntresses are powerful and intelligent beings, which is a clear strength of the archetype. Their quick-thinking allows them to anticipate their enemies' moves before they happen, making it difficult for people to take advantage of them in battle. They also have superior vision that includes night vision - an ability that can be quite advantageous when fighting during nighttime battles or other dark situations where visibility may not necessarily favor those on the hunt.

The Shadow Side
Avoids being vulnerable.
Resents other women.
Can push people away.
Can be aloof.

While in the huntress state, a woman will avoid all signs of *vulnerability*. But as soon as she is confronted with intimacy and must show her true self, she flees from it like prey before a predator's creeping footsteps. The passion of the huntress turns to rage. In her mind, there is no need for mercy or forgiveness as she seeks out justice in a world that demands it from all around her.

The woman who experiences this archetype in shadow may be subject to bouts of cruelty, uncontrollable anger and vengefulness- but only when something has been done wrong against them first; they are not coldly cruel without reason, nor do they harm others with any sense of self-righteousness like those who experience these qualities within their light side would have before being confronted by an antagonist's darkness.

The Huntresses experience in the shadow of competitive spirit is one that often results into an obsession to be better than everyone else and will stop at nothing less. In this stage there can exist a destructive aggression as they try to create their own legacy on top of all others. Potentially cruel.

Artemis

Artemis was a goddess of ancient Greece. She protected the countryside, greenery and animals as well as being in charge of childbirth. Artemis is one of the Greek goddesses that prefers to stay in forests instead of Mount Olympus. Artemis was the daughter of Zeus and Leto, a Titaness. (Back to Zeus being a total drama starter and ho.) She had one brother - Apollo - who is best known for being king of Olympus, music, prophecy and more importantly the sun god. Artemis' birth could not have been easy as she faced many obstacles from her very beginning including that at some point during labor or delivery - Hera (the queen goddess) sent two giant scorpions to kill baby Artemis on route in order stop them both because they were considered rivals by other gods fearing their power if paired together but luckily Mother Gaia intervened shielding little Arty with soil and turned into an island called Ortygia where people still pray today. Artemis has always possessed great strength even as a child. Artemis' major responsibility was to cater for wild animals and the wilderness. Artemis was the patron goddess of childbirth and midwifery. She picked up this role because she helped her mother Leto give birth to her younger twin brother Apollo, one of the most prolific gods in all mythology. It seems a bit odd for Artemis to have this role considering that Artemis herself was an eternal virgin. Like many Greek gods and deities, Artemis did have quite a hot temper. She was known for having the ability to give diseases to young women who disobeyed her instructions. Conversely, she had the ability to heal young girls that were ill. According to one account of Artemis' story, the river god Alpheous falls madly in love with her and goes ahead to capture her. Because she had sworn to be chaste all his life, he evades Alpheous advances by rubbing mud on her face. A similar account states that it was Arethusa rather who fell victim first after Artemis found out about his intentions of rape when they were both at a temple attendant position where he placed a spell turning her into a water fountain at the Temple of Artemis. The Constellation of Orion is not just a group of stars in the sky. The constellation symbolizes two important figures from Greek Mythology: Artemis and her close friend, hunting partner, companion for artistry - Orion! Imbued with powers by Zeus himself to represent these divine beings, this celestial form has been admired through the ages as one that was born out of tragedy but still manages to shine brightly even today. Long before the start of Troy, a king named Agamemnon incurred the wrath of Artemis after he killed an animal sacred to her. The goddess punished him by sending plagues and winds that prevented his army from sailing toward Troy for many days. Agamemnon sacrificed his daughter Iphigenia to Artemis in order appease the goddess and lift her curse. Once Agamemnon made this sacrifice, he was able to lead an army of Greeks back home with a clear conscience for their victory over Troy. In a small deviation from the story we know, Mycenaen king Agamemnon was spared by Artemis when she took pity and whisked Iphigenia away before his blade could land on her head. Soon after, he would go to live in one of her temples, where he spent the remainder of his days with his daughter beside him.

Artemis was a goddess of the hunt and had many appearances. Her favorite portrayals show her as an elegant, winged goddess with silver bow in hand for slaying beasts or other enemies that stray too close to home territory. A deer may be seen next to Artemis; this is because she would often send those who hunted prey all over land into hunting grounds where they were guaranteed success if they could only resist being eaten themselves first. The virgin huntress, Atalanta was known for her beauty. However, she did not take well to anyone who dared compare a mortal's appearance with hers and so Artemis quickly dispatched a wild bear to scare the daylights out of innocent youths in order that they would cease their endless comparisons. Artemis punished the daughter of Lelantos and Peribola for doubting her maidenhood, so she allowed Dionysus to defile Aura. The goddess descended into madness as a result, going about killing people until finally one day Aura killed and ate one of her own children in addition to others. Greek mythology is dark huh? As I went on hours of endless study within each Goddess my mouth just dropped with the stories which were passed down. It's like a train wreck you can't look away from and for good reason, they are truly fascinating! An Artemis woman is not the motherly type, having a boyish and athletic figure that would be more likely to give birth to children than raise them. But if she chooses to become a parent, she will be very protective of her children without being domineering like many other mothers might tend towards. She'll enjoy raising independent kids who can relate with their parents better as they age themselves while not losing sight of how important unconditional love from early on in life is for bonding purposes. When embodiment of the Huntress enters our midlife years, she has a difficult time of it if she has not cultivated some other goddesses in herself. She is so used to being an independent and goal driven person, that by the end of her twenties or early thirties, she's reached many goals set for herself years ago. Many times, this will lead them into complacency as they can feel satisfied with all their accomplishments without seeking new challenges at later stages in life. This may be a time where she becomes more introspective and takes the opportunity to explore her spirituality, psychological and psychic abilities. Her youthful attitude will remain unchanged as long as it is possible for her to continue exploring these things. She will still travel if she can because of how much joy that brings into life so keep an eye on this adventurous spirit. Artemis is usually younger, in her 20's or 30's. She isn't one of the "mature" Goddesses as they are called. This isn't really about maturity; it shows how age can affect a goddess' appearance and personality traits which often changes with each decade that passes by for example Artemis was portrayed to be an independent maiden who enjoys spending time outdoors but when she got older from being young to middle aged she became more concerned with building relationships so finally at old age you would see this same woman care less about independence due to not wanting isolation anymore. In Greek mythology, many gods have different personalities depending on their stage of life whether its infancy through adulthood all the way until death happens typically after someone has lived well into their 80s.

Setting Boundaries

A boundary is a line that keeps two things apart. When you stand in your truth unapologetically, it becomes easier to know where the boundaries are and what's right for you because there isn't anything else getting mixed up with these truths. You have the right to not think twice in setting your' personal boundaries. A great way of understanding personal limits is through taking care of one's own body - starting at standing in our truth without apology or regret which allows us to identify those lines (or boundaries!) between ourselves and others' desires, so they don't get crossed over unintentionally while hunting down life goals.

- Express your thoughts and emotions without fear of judgement.
- Ask for your needs to be met.
- Say no without feeling guilty.
- Prioritize your self-care.
- Be treated with respect.
- Decide what to do for your body.
- Feel safe.

Establishing boundaries is one of the most important things to do in order to be happy and healthy. It teaches others how we want them to treat us, teaching respect and consideration for our needs. Setting these boundaries also protects your time and energy, which you deserve. Here are some signs you may have weak boundaries or none.

- Anxiety.
- Overwhelm and burnout.

- Resentment.
- Compulsive behavior such as eating, drinking or overworking.
- Feeling unable to express your emotions.
- Weak sense of self.
- Lack of purpose or direction.

It is impossible to set clear boundaries if you have no idea what they are yourself. **Take some time to consider your rights and write them down.** For example, you may feel with your family you have the right to put your needs first before them. With work it maybe you do not work outside business hours. With a relationship it may mean no one raises their voice to you. Really take some time here to notice what triggers you or makes you feel unsafe.

Your Rights – Non-Negotiables

Core Beliefs – Your personal value system

What is the first thing you believe? What else do you believe about yourself and your life that can't be changed or modified by others yet are still a part of who we are as an individual. Whether it's our belief in something specific like religion, politics or even fears; this list should help guide us to start figuring out what beliefs actually matter most when making decisions for ourselves. Ask the question why do I believe this? Where did this belief come from? What is my core belief system?

1. _____
2. _____
3. _____
4. _____
5. _____
6. _____
7. _____
8. _____
9. _____
10. _____

With the information from above, begin to put into place what your boundaries are and how you can communicate this in relationships within your own life. Instead of a fight approach, try delivering your boundaries from a place of cool, calm and collected. Think of it as simply informing people of how their actions cross your boundaries and how you will remove yourself from the relationship/situation if the behavior continues.

Tie it together.

The Huntress is the Solar Plexus Chakra – Our Power.
Repeat out loud.

May I know my true power, worth and potential. May I feel safe and secure in my power, worth and potential.
May I feel love and loved in my power, worth and potential.
May I find freedom from any fears holding me back from my power, worth and potential. May you know your true power.
May you know your true worth and potential.
May you feel safe and secure in your power, worth and potential. May you feel love and loved in your power, wroth and potential.
May you find freedom from any fears holding you back from your power, worth and potential. May we know our true power, worth and potential.
May we feel safe and secure in our power, worth and potential.
May we feel love and loved in our power, worth and potential.
May we find freedom from any fears holding us back from our power, worth and potential.

Place your hands at your solar plexus. (Three inches above your belly button.)

"I break any contract I have ever made with another consciously or unconsciously, that has given them power over my sense of self, the authority to approve or reject anything about me, including my voice, creativity, spirituality and way of living of my own free will I now choose to directly perceive my own inner power and turn within with kindness and compassion to see myself through the eyes of unconditional love." Place your hands on your heart and repeat "I love and approve of my power."

The Warrioress is ignored by society. We neglect the importance of her inspiring strength to those around us when we don't honor her with our attention or respect.

The "Warrior Woman" archetype has been generally neglected in this patriarchal culture because she doesn't fit into traditional roles for women which are typically domestic. The huntress archetype is to be called in when you feel like a victim, your masculine side is weak and stuck unable to take action, or if there's been loss of focus from self-doubt and confusion. You may be feeling these things because it feels as though the boundaries that keep us safe are being breached. The wild outside world gets closer than ever before. The huntress archetype is all about service. She fights in the name of love, as the embodiment of fierce love; a force that brings with it, kindness and compassion for her enemies. The spirit inside this woman has been known to be warm but also giving when she needs to defend herself against those who would do harm unto others.

When we embody the Warrioress, she helps us break free from societal norms that try to confine her. She is not like the Wild Woman who seeks freedom by rejecting society; rather, a Warrioress embraces and accepts herself as confident, strong and powerful in order to bring about their purpose. You must stand and speak your truth. You must ditch the victim mentality. You must become the doctor and start nurturing the patient.

You can face the evil in this world once you have faced what is inside of you first because they are all just reflections of who we really are deep down on our soul level.

Victim Mentality: People who have a victim mentality have usually suffered through trauma or hard times but haven't developed a proper way to cope. As a result, they develop a negative view of life. Because they don't think anything is their fault, they have little or no sense of responsibility in their lives.

Warrioress Mentality: This mindset is more than aggressiveness and determination; it is about overcoming challenge and adversity. It's about possessing, understanding, and being able to utilize a set of

psychological and physical skills that allow someone to be effective, adaptive and persistent.

She is life and being, starry-bright, sparkling, blinding, mobile, whose sweet strangeness draws man on the more irresistibly the more disdainfully it dismisses him; an essence crystal-clear, which is nevertheless intertwined with the dark roots in all animate nature; a being childishly simple and yet incalculable, sweetly amiable and diamond hard; girlishly demure, fleeting, elusive, and suddenly brusque and contrary; playing frolicking, dancing, and in a flash most inexorably serious; lovingly anxious and tenderly solicitous, with the enchantment of a smile that outweighs perdition, and yet wild to the point of gruesomeness and cruel to the point of repulsiveness. All of these are traits of the free, withdrawn nature to which Artemis belongs, and in her the piously intuitive spirit has learned to perceive this eternal image of sublime femininity as a thing divine.

THE HOMERIC GODS – GREEK RELIGION

"I can stand up for what I believe in without shunning someone else's truth."

"I can stand strong in my own presence without making others feel less-than."

"I can speak up for myself and listen to what others have to say. I can be seen and heard without raising my voice."

"I don't need to fight to feel better about who I am and what I know - I just need to know myself enough to let others be who they are too."

"I don't need to explain every decision I make. I don't need to accept every invitation to an argument. I don't need the opinions of others to understand who I am. I do what I need to do to keep my light, so that I can be light for those around me."

"How people treat me is their karma; how I react is mine.

It's not my responsibility to change other people; other's responsibilities do not belong to me. I can hold a space for others to work through their problems without taking them on as my own. It's not for me to decide the lessons someone else needs to learn."

"I can respect the feelings of others and still honor my own.

What other people do and say may affect me, but at the end of the day, what goes on inside of me is my own responsibility."

"It's okay to spend time alone without explaining myself. It's okay to say no and feel good about saying it."

"It's okay to let go of my own expectations now and then. This is my life, and it's my job to figure out what is best for me."

"It's okay to let my scars and imperfections show because I'm beautifully human and I'm proud to be here."

"I don't need permission to follow my own heart. I am allowed to ask for what I need. I am a giver, and I am not above receiving. I honor the balance of give and take in my life."

The Wise Woman – Crone

Carl Jung, the Swiss psychologist and founder of analytical psychology tells us that you can find a wise woman in all walks of life. She is like an archetype but isn't limited to one personality trait or characteristic; instead, she's whatever kind of support that we need at that point in our lives.

The Wise Woman is an archetype that has been present since time immemorial, with a strong presence in fairy tales and myths. The concept of the wise woman (or witch) stems from early shamanistic practices as well as ancient goddess worshiping cultures who believed female knowledge was sacred. They embodied this idea by invoking the deities or divine feminine to communicate messages through divination sessions involving tarot cards, tea leaves, bones/scapulae and other natural items found in nature such as plants. These women were not only spiritual leaders but often also doctors for their communities - utilizing remedies ranging from herbalism to astrology when healing those around them; they held immense power within these roles due solely to being born into them.

Witches are often seen as benevolent or even heroic in Western cultures because of the deep roots they have with literature, but folklore can paint a more sinister picture. The masculine counterpart to witches is "wizards", and this contrast leaves little doubt that it takes specific characteristics for someone who wants to become one: mastery over occult knowledge (or at least know how not fuck up), while embodying humility and emotional intelligence-both traits necessary when learning anything worthwhile on their own accord.

The energy of the Mana personality is often not very well understood. This can be attributed to a general lack of connection with one's own energies, and their abilities within our society--and in turn this has led us into an over-dependence on other people for answers instead. The Greek Goddess Hecate embodies three different aspects: as a goddess linked to childbirth; as an oracular deity able to see into past events, present happenings and future outcomes; and associated with sorcery--a wise woman whose powers extend beyond human knowledge.

Women of today must possess the qualities of both masculine and feminine energies. She understands how important it is to live a balanced life, understanding that each side has an equally valuable contribution to make in her spiritual journey.

The individual gets this balance by mastering her body-- physically, emotionally, spiritually; as well as cultivating emotional intelligence through empathy for others' feelings with open-mindedness so she can be receptive rather than reactive. She is a survivor who has walked through pain and hardship but overcoming this only strengthens her resolve to help others.

She uses the lessons she's learned from past trauma in order to teach others how they can cope with their own problems.

Where others might resent the circumstances that led to their situation, she has chosen forgiveness. She is like a mother figure who protects those around her and always gives them support in any way. People are drawn to her for guidance because of knowledge about tradition and history; people value what she can give as it comes from our ancestors' experience which we have been able to preserve through time thanks to this woman's dedication. She pushes and challenges people to their highest potential while walking by their side.

"My temple is my body. My world around me my altar. My words are spells. My every thought an intention. My actions rituals. To manifest all that will be. I am sacred. I am divine."

The Sass of the Wise Woman

She is a healer and shaman, but also enjoys life's absurdity. She sees laughter as medicine for the soul because it reminds us of our own humanity. She is an enchanting woman who laughs often. Her wit and sense of humor are amusing, but she's also mysterious in her own way.

She knows that laughter really does heal the soul, so she tries to share this with those around her by being a source for happiness and joy. The Crone is the embodiment of enlightenment. She can see through illusions and bring order to chaos, but her shadow often makes people uncomfortable when they are unable or unwilling to face their own truths about themselves in that moment.

The crone is the 3rd and final phase of a woman's life. She has learned her lessons, mastered them to an extent, and now she cuts away what no longer serves you so it can be released into nothingness for new growth opportunities with ease; this process may feel like death at first but there awaits a rebirth of sorts which brings light back into your conscious awareness.

The Shadow of the Wise Woman

Your Crone Shadow can be your best friend or worst foe. The Hag is the shadow of over-identification with this archetype, and it is characterized by active opposition to giving up power while in denial about her age. This leads women into the passive shadow state: Denier--constant self-doubt which breeds confusion and a feeling that they are powerless against anything going on around them. The person with this profile may feel incapable of trusting anyone in the world, and they are hypersensitive to their environment.

They fear psycho spiritual energy because it feels like a threat, so when someone is being irrational or emotional around them, they can't help but overvalue rationality. Christianity has systematically removed any connections with the Crone archetype in its ideology. This happened most notably during witch burning times of the 15th to 17th centuries and through the Inquisition which occurred across Europe, as well as Puritanism coming from New World settlers. In the patriarchal culture, women's embodied ways of knowing and their ability to speak truth to power are a clear threat. Therefore people in positions of power push out female public service workers with university credentials because they fear an overthrow from this intellectual collective that has been silenced for generations.

In the past, women were often killed for being a woman. They would be drowned, hung or burned at stake and sometimes they had no other reason but just to have been born with uniquely powerful feminine presence that threatened social order. Even living long could lead one branded as a witch by society's standards of what was normal in terms of slave behavior; this is how strong their influence on others has always been throughout time periods such as these. The wise woman is an ancient part of our collective consciousness.

It's time for her to be embraced and respected in a way that she never has before, because this will take us into the future! We are all familiar with some painful memories from history -- things we don't want to remember but can't seem to forget either. These events live on inside each cell as they change who we become, what direction life takes us down; it also shapes how open-minded or closed off we feel towards learning new things about ourselves.

Unfortunately, many people still operate under patriarchal notions which view women only able participate in two roles: maiden/mother - one where they must remain pure forever and one where their main responsibility is fulfilling any need children might have.

Hecate

Hecate, the goddess of magic and witchcraft is also known for her fierce appearance. She was born from an egg that fell under a blackthorn tree on earth which had been thrown there by Zeus as he became angry with his father Kronos who swallowed all but one of their children (Zeus being saved). She appears as a gigantic woman with torch in hand. Her hair snakes down all around her face while she walks on ten feet formed from serpents--her passage accompanied by thunderous roars that shake the sky above. She will stop to give you one last warning before sending you into your worst nightmare: "I am Hecate! Look upon my works ye mighty and despair!" Hecate appears as an ancient female deity carrying a flame-lit sword; her appearance would be enough to strike fear onto anyone who might cross paths with this dark entity at night. The loud noise associated with these entities are said to consist of deep baying howls like dogs and strange shrieks. Hecate grew up in exile, not knowing where she came from until Demeter found her wandering through the wilderness alone when searching for Persephone whom Hades abducted to be queen in the underworld. Hecate has long been associated with witchcraft and the occult, even necromancy. Her name has been connected to dark magic and disturbing rituals in the works of Shakespeare and well into modern times, including Harry Potter's nemesis Severus Snape who is portrayed as a follower of Hecate's teaching about Dark Arts. Hecate was a goddess of magic and the underworld, but she also played an important role at home. She protected borders as well as being associated with some revered deities from Olympus. Yet, Hecate's origins are still unknown and changeable to this day - much like her powers. Hecate is a goddess from Greek mythology, but she predates the written record of Hesiod and Homer. There are some indications that her story was already evolving at this time as oral tradition changed stories over generations. Hecate may have been changing even before we had any texts to study about her in ancient Greece. Scholars of ancient Greek religion have noted that Apollo was occasionally given the name Hecatos, which they interpret to mean "one who reaches far." These academics believe that Hecate may once been another name for his twin sister Artemis's identity. Who needs a GPS when you have Hecate? She was the goddess of boundaries, or anything that falls between two places. Her statues were often placed at crossroads and borders to create light for both sides. Though her torches could only illuminate one side of each boundary, it still helped guide travelers as they crossed over into new territory. The Greeks believed that the boundary between life and death was not only a moment in time, but also an actual place. This physical location is where souls cross to pass into one of those two worlds forever. The goddess of the underworld, Hecate was pictured as a woman with two faces. She watched over both life and death. Her keys gave her power to open and close the doors to the underworld of Hades. Hecate is the goddess of Earth, Heaven and Hell. And for that reason, she has three female bodies to represent her involvement in all aspects of our mortal world.

How have these qualities identified the most with you?
_____
_____
_____
_____
_____

Which of these do not resonate with you?
_____
_____
_____
_____
_____

The Embodiment of the Wise Woman

When we are fully embodied with the wise woman, our lives come from strength and compassion. She is a master of the four elements; earth, water, air and fire—she can even move them! We know she's awakened when her ability to align herself in body-mind-spirit comes through as wisdom. Sometimes referred to as "high priestess," this alignment allows for knowing what your true self looks like so that you may live more authentically every day. When I'm embodying my inner Wise Woman - one who embodies power (strength), resilience (compassion) and visionarieship (vision) among other qualities - life has an ease about it because there's no need for me act against myself or suppress any part within.

> Wisdom is divine knowledge. Wisdom is everywhere in the Universe. It surrounds us. it is present in every one of us. It does not belong to anyone of us, but we all can access it.

Receive wisdom from your Spirit Guides

You are not here to experience this walk solo. You are here with your sisters, mother earth and your spirit guides. To awaken the wise woman means becoming a vessel of divine knowledge in service for others - waiting patiently as we call on them or invite them into our lives when needed most. While they can't support us if we don't even know that they exist, spirit guides carry ancient wisdom which helps along the journey so long as you're willing to make room for it within yourself.

Morning Prayer

I thank you for being present in my life and guiding me through the many paths I walk. Thank you so much for blessing all these areas, as well as keeping them safe from harm's way. I'm asking that blessings may be bestowed on myself, those around me who are near or far away with love to help us grow together spiritually stronger than ever before. I invite divine creator angels, teachers and spirit guides to share their wisdom with me today and every day of my life. Blessings upon my home, blessings upon jobs, bless health, treasures, love, and my sacred soul purpose. And so it is.

Self Confidence and Growth

- Make a list of all your past achievements.
- List your strengths.

- Write down the names of three women who inspire you and embody self-confidence and wisdom.
- Write down words of the qualities these women carry that inspire you.

The Wise Woman Tradition

What if you had the power to heal yourself with food, medicine and plants? It's not just a fairytale. A growing number of people are turning to botanical healing for their anxiety, depression or simply as an alternative method in general. "Western doctors prescribe drugs that can have negative side effects," says Dr Erica Reed from the University of Kansas Medical Center. "People need other options than pharmaceuticals alone".

You might be asking "why would I want something natural when it comes with risks?" But there is no such thing as risk-free living; we all take chances every day by choosing what clothes to wear out into public, which route home from work takes us on at night…the list goes on.

This asks us to surrender to our intuition about what is needed and truly listen for the answer. Plants are amazingly intuitive and have their own ways of guiding us on a spiritual path. Take time to reflect during your next walk outside by noticing which plants seem the most inviting or important when you feel an urge to pick them up for some reason- usually because they're at different stages in life that resonate with something inside of you!

After picking one plant from the ground (or finding it high in a tree), stop and ask yourself what stage is this plant at? What qualities does it hold? And finally, how do I think these specific properties will benefit me if used right now as part of my spirituality practice? Developing one's connection with nature can help cultivate intuitive skills that are innate within all beings but often go unused due to our fast-paced lifestyles filled with constant distractions such as social media and technology. After making your choice verify the plant is edible and medicinal (Plant-O-Manic is a great site for this.)

Make a tincture

There are two ways to do this. The edible and the energy. If you can't verify what a plant is, then don't eat it! However, if you've verified that it's medicinal purposes work for your needs, start with just one drop of oil at first before increasing dosage appropriately.

> *For Energy Repeat all steps but place by your bed - do not intake.*

- Find a tincture that has an airtight lid. Fill the container with your plant - use the flowers and leaves rather than the stems or roots. Pack it as much as you can.
- Fill the container with mixture that's 45% alcohol and 55% distilled water. To avoid mold, make sure the leaves, flowers or stems are entirely in the mixture that container is filled to the top.
- Secure the tincture and wait for about two weeks. Strain out the plant material and you now have your tincture. Drop a small amount under your tongue and just observe. how do you feel?
- Begin to journal what comes up for you both physically and emotionally while interacting with what you are drawn too.

If you are ready to take the leap of faith and dive into your own spiritual journey, then this is for you. Challenge yourself by sitting in silence with an open mind as we delve deep within ourselves through guided meditation strategies that will help us get back on track when life throws curve balls at us!

Do not question what comes up or allow your thoughts to interrupt - simply flow with the state of healing traditions and opening the doorway to wisdom from ancient times past.

The Moon
AND YOUR CYCLE

The three stages of feminine life- the maiden, mother and crone all represent a season. The maiden is springtime; she represents new beginnings: rebirth, fertility in crops or animals as well as relationships with others. In contrast to this youthful optimism stands summer's potent power embodied by the maternal goddesses Isis and Demeter who care for their respective communities deeply but sternly-- creating abundance while also maintaining order so that it might endure into future seasons when they are reborn again from fall/winter back to childhood at dawn once more. Lastly there is winter which marks our passage through death towards renewal; these cold months often offers nature its most beautiful landscape (the snow) where one can find solitude amidst vastness. Due to her deep connection with the earth, many people have misconceived that she is a scary entity. In reality, this energy comes across as supportive and nurturing instead of frightening or negative-minded. She brings an abundance of richness in life and rebirth every winter when spring arrives. Aside from the season cycles, we as women are guided by our own cycles and pulled from the moon. If you are currently cycling with a monthly bleed the crone embodies the time when we have our period. In cycle wisdom, when we bleed it is our opportunity to rest, rejuvenate and go inward. This invites us to slow down and explore just as winter does.

How can you trust your inner wisdom more?

___

How does aging make you feel?

___

How can you honor your inner wise woman more authentically?

___

> Grounding is the one thing you need to master
> before we dive into third eye work.

The third eye is a powerful tool which allows us to explore our spiritual world. However, in order for the spirit of this realm to be experienced fully it must first be grounded with physical sensations. When we ground ourselves by connecting these two worlds more often-we are able to experience them on an even deeper level than before. Grounding is pretty magical and provides us with energy to work with our chakras in a healthy and balanced way. There is duality and the law of polarity is in everything.

Grounding Exercises

- Place your hands in cold water. (Also, a great way to cleanse energy.)
- Pick up or touch items near you.
- Breathe deeply. In for 4 through your nose and out for 4 through your nose with making an "ocean" sound in the back of your throat. This is called balance breathing and brings us up when we are down

and down when we are up. Imagine you are fogging up a mirror on the exhale but make the exhale from your nose.
- Walk barefoot outside. Feel the earth beneath your toes.
- Hold a piece of ice.
- Move your body - this could be as simple as taking a brisk walk.
- Do a body scan - start at the crown and work your way to your toes acknowledging everybody part. Where you can let go or feel tension, where you can relax, what feels good. You can also run your fingers over your skin during this exercise.
- The 5,4,3,2,1 method. This is especially powerful when experiencing anxiety. Working back from 5 use your senses to notice what is around you. 5 things you hear, 4 things you see, 3 things you touch, two things you smell and one thing you taste.
- Recite mantras and pay attention to the vibration of your voice as you say each one.

Anja

Almost every Kriya you read uses the sixth chakra to focus and activate the pituitary gland and bring ANJA awakening to the third eye. A simple practice of bringing your eyes to focus in the space between your brow is stimulating to the Anja chakra. Anja means "to command". Yogi Bhajan explained going through life without intuition is like driving a car which as no side mirror and no rearview mirror. All you can see is straight ahead. Yoga Mudra: Sit on your heels and interlace your hands behind you back in Venus lock. Straighten the arms and fold forward bringing your forehead to the ground while lifting the hands high away from the back. Close your eyes and focus on the third eye by gently rolling the yes up and inward. Breath long and deep. Venus lock for women is an interlacing of all the fingers starting with the right little finger on bottom. The thumbs are parallel to each other with the tip of the right thumb on the web between the left thumb and index finger. The tip of the left thumb rests on the mound below the right thumb.

"Go inside and listen to your inner voice. Every question has an answer. Your soul is full of wisdom and knows the way."
- Yogi Bhajan

Exploring the Third Eye Chakra

You are in touch with the universe when you tap into your third eye. The seat of wisdom, intuition and higher consciousness resides here as well. It is also where we come to find answers from within ourselves. The chakra associated with wise women is the Third Eye! Not only does it provide us insights but allows one-on-one contact between our inner selves.

To practice opening this area - Pay attention to your dreams. Begin a dream journal so you can see what's going on in the hidden corners of our minds. We often don't remember dreaming and that is because we're not meant to, but when it does happen the lesson being taught from within becomes clear as day.

_____
_____
_____
_____
_____
_____
_____
_____
_____
_____
_____
_____
_____
_____
_____
_____
_____
_____

Imagine the third eye as a diamond with many facets. Sit comfortably, close your eyes and imagine yourself in front of that precious jeweled object. With each breath you take, it becomes clearer to see inside this gemstone until all is revealed in its brilliant light - just like when our mind starts to become clear during meditation! This may be hard at first but if you keep trying every day for 10 minutes or so before bedtime then soon enough your powers will start coming into focus more clearly each time you meditate.

- Take a long and deep breath. As you exhale, move attention to the center of your forehead, in-between the brows and just above the brow line, and imagine an indigo-blue chakra. The dark indigo glow of the chakra illuminates your mind and then spreads to the rest of your body.
- Imagine an entrance to your mind through the third eye. You open the door and walk into the empty room. Feel free to decorate the room any way you like - choose color, decor, look and feel. Create your' aesthetic.
- Make it suit your tastes exactly, so that it becomes your personal sanctuary.
- Find the most comfortable spot in the room and sit down.
- You look out onto the world from there. Bring into focus the same thoughts, issues, situations and ideas that occupy your day-to-day life. You silently contemplate upon them.
- See your sixth chakra spinning and gaining strength. As it spins faster, the chakra's indigo light washes over you and pervades every cell, every pore in your body.
- Breathe deeply and feel the energy bursting forth from your third eye as rays of dazzling deep blue light.
- Rest in awareness.
- Gently stand up and walk to the door through which you entered the room. Walk out and look back at your inner sanctuary and feel at one with it.
- When you are ready, open your eyes and arise.

Are you seeing colors, shapes, or images? To expand this meditation, incorporate in the crystal's amethyst, ametrine, laborite, lepidolite, lapis lazuli, tourmaline quartz, sodalite, blue tigers' eye, hag stone, blue quartz, kyanite, blue apatite, blue obsidian, and black obsidian. Lemon oil is also able to bathe the pineal gland with light and help awaken the gifts of the third eye.

On the next page journal about what came up for you during the meditation. Describe in as much detail as you can.

COURTNEY HANSON

Signs you may be blocked.

- Inability to set goals and stick to them.
- A disconnection to your intuition or instincts.
- Not knowing what feels right or wrong. Feeling of disconnect from other people. Narrow mindedness.
- Disconnect or lack of interest in nature and mother earth.
- Denial.
- Unconsciously judging others constantly.
- Poor vision/ Memory problems.
- Unexplained depression, anxiety or just feeling blah. Intense sensitivity with light.
- A diet of high processed foods.
- Difficulty visioning your future.
- Never remembering your dreams.
- Lack of imagination.
- Very realist mindset.

Things to remember before these exercises.

Do not force anything. This is a process, let it come naturally and be gentle with yourself. A risk is often disrupted sleep, anxiety within your relationships which feel empty, increasingly sensitive and anxious. Remember to walk through this one step at a time. Find something you love and that works for you, once you feel ready for more than try something new.

Extra Resources

1. Silent meditation is a way to exercise your third eye, which can be done very easily. By doing this you will connect the mind and spirit as one in modern society where social media rings are constantly going off with notifications, negative self-talk about ourselves, or marketing that fills our heads. With the use of silent mediation, we get to listen for what's hidden instead - listening closely to messages from our guides and angels who want us to hear them during these hard times in life. When meditating rub circles around your third eye area gently but continuously.
2. Lucid Dreaming is like being in a movie. In traditional dreams, we watch the events unfold as if they were on television screens but with lucid dreaming there's more control and it feels very real because you are present for all of these interactions happening within your dream world. There can be many benefits to this technique such as breaking bad habits from waking life or trying out new things that may have been too scary before just by entering them into our mind through a different perspective without any risk involved! One way to begin this practice is to wake yourself up during REM sleep then go back after ten minutes awake. This allows connections between both worlds where memories stored in one place will start spilling over into another giving us yet another chance at reality-testing.
3. Practice using your intuition. Trusting yourself is half the battle. Following and listening to your first instinct. Be aware of your gut and what it is telling you, so often we are trained by society to quiet this or push forward. We have this instinct for a reason. It is

important to learn to identify your fight, flight or fuck response vs. the actual intuitional instinct. Tarot is a great way to play with intuition also the act of realizing when you just "know" something.
4. Express yourself creatively. See a pattern? Creativity is in almost every archetype and the reason why is because it allows our energy to flow naturally in a joyous state from the soul out into creativity, allowing us to loosen up rigid thoughts and think outside of the box.
5. From the moment we take that first breath, our connection to Mother Earth is there. We feel it when we're lost in a great book or find ourselves so deeply engrossed in nature's beauty and wonderment. And while these are all amazing ways of connecting with this earth goddess, why not dive into some plants? Get grounded by rooting your toes deep into soil-drenched ground and bask under green leaves as they provide shade from the suns blazing rays! Inhale fresh air filled only with her scents - pine needles mixed delicately among long grasses swaying gently back and forth on warm summer days.

COURTNEY HANSON

"I trust my intuition."

"I deserve to be happy and successful."

"Everything that happens to me is an opportunity to learn and grow."

"I stand up for myself and I stand by my decisions."

"I have the power to change my life at any point in time."

"I believe that my unshakeable faith and determination has led me where I need to be."

The Wild Woman
– Mystic

"Be wild; that is how to clear the river. The river does not flow in polluted; we manage that. The river does not dry up, we block it. If we want to allow it it's freedom, we have to allow our ideational lives to let loose, to stream, letting anything come, initially censoring nothing. That is creative life. it is made up of divine paradox. To create one must be willing to be stone stupid, to sit upon a throne on top of a jackass and spill rubies from one's mouth. Then the river will flow, then we can stand in the stream of it raining down."

-Clarissa Pinkola Estes
Women who run with the wolves.

The wild woman is a force to be reckoned with she's instinctive, born of nature. And while many people think that the archetype resonates closely with other archetypes like maiden, mother and wise woman--the truth is it encompasses all three at once. She doesn't want to play by society's rules-she just doesn't want to be tamed or pinned down.

She is in full control of her life, and she won't let anyone tell her how to live it. She's a rebel with an attitude that will never bend for society; instead, she'll push back against anything telling her what to do because there are so many ways, we can be ourselves.

The wild woman is an instinctual animal nature of a woman. This energy within the psyche remains latent until entering midlife, when we become more aware and crave freedom to be ourselves. It can be hard for women in our society that have been "civilized" as they struggle with connecting this innate expression of who they are because it does not come from one singular place but instead multiple energies like love, creativity or sex appeal. She is not a singular energy.

She has been a muse; she's had her head in the clouds- from here on earth to the heavens. She is vaster than any one person could know and more powerful with every single idea that comes into being. Her creativity knows no bounds; it flows through each of us as we try to make sense of our lives' journeys. The wild woman is a sensual, creative being that dwells in the crevices of your mind. She doesn't care about relationships or societal norms if she feels safe and loved. The traditional misconceptions are easier to digest than reality for many people because this side of human nature can be dangerous at times when it's denied like some other parts we don't want to see. The wild woman represents that unshaken and integral part of us. It's for this reason that it is so much more powerful when a woman discovers her true being than if someone else were to do so, because she has overcome the constraints on society imposed by gender roles as well as living up to expectations from others in order not only to be herself but also become who she really is deep down inside. The wild woman archetype can be a powerful guide in your spiritual journey, helping you to regain alignment with the divine.

Strengths of the Mystic - She is a woman who values peace in an increasingly distracting world. She does not seek external goals, rather she strives for personal fulfillment that would make other people's skin tingle with goosebumps. Her self-respect and patience are her qualities to admire the most, because it shows how whole of a person, she already is without any reassurance from anyone else. Sometimes when faced with distraction or chaos one might crumble at their core; but this girl will stay strong no matter what adversity comes knocking on her door.

The Shadow of the Mystic - Preferring to be alone, she becomes detached and disconnected from her emotions. When love does come around for this introverted woman it is difficult for her to express herself fully because of the distance that comes with being by oneself so often. She can appear cold and bitchy as a result of not wanting others close or even letting them get too emotionally invested in their relationship without fear they will leave like everyone else has done before. This lack of assertiveness can create this prison within her own body.

Empowering the Healer within

"The wolf licks her own wounds and carries on. She makes sure no one is left behind in her pack and creates justice. There is no need for revenge just the creation of justice."

Embracing Your Cycles

Your' cycles actually an integral part of the female body and is guided by hormones like estrogen and progesterone. This monthly purging process can serve as a time for self-examination in order to improve your mental health or work through any emotional challenges you may have faced over the course of one month before it comes back up again!

When women are taught from such a young age about their cycles, they reject what very thing gives them life - our natural biological mechanism being menstruation (a rise). The denial occurs when we're younger and leads us into adulthood where many people still feel ashamed or embarrassed at times due to having periods. We deny the natural biological mechanism that is our inner wisdom. Your period is a time and place where you can tap into your infinite power.

The way to get the most out of this sacred part of womanhood is by harnessing it's magic; when mastered, there are few things more powerful than tapping into your feminine energy. Mother Earth is an incredible spiritual being who connects with us in a way that helps to better understand our own abilities. She has her own cycles and when we intertwine them, it can help you see patterns of your strengths, productivity levels or creativity among other things on the list.

Winter Menstruation - Day 1 - 5 This is the time of your cycle when you might feel sluggish or tired. It's also a great opportunity to catch up on some sleep and relaxation before things get busy again. The days of menstruation are a time when our bodies are trying to release the blood in the lining of our uterus. It's like we're getting all these signals from our body telling us "hey, I need you to take some time off and just chill." This is especially true if you compare this process with winter where leaves fall from trees as animals hibernate preparing themselves for colder months ahead. This is exactly what you should be doing during this time. Take a break and find ways to rejuvenate yourself - go on walks, eat warm cozy foods, journal your thoughts (gently!), light yin yoga for some balance in the body, take deep breaths of fresh air outside or beneath an open window at home with soothing sounds running through them like nature videos or white noise machine apps. This is the time to let go of all that's weighing you down. You have some releasing superpowers right now. Winter, with its full moon-like qualities, is a time for forgiveness, letting go and reconciliation. Write out anything from your past or present-- resentments you still carry and people who have wronged you--and burn it. Release it all into the Universe.

Spring Menstruation - Spring is 6 - 11 Spring is in the air, and after your cycle you might be feeling a surge of energy. Ever notice how springtime just feels energized? That's because it does! Estrogen gives you the motivation, inspiration and productivity to get creative. You feel more energetic and vibrant as libido increases by the day. During this time, get curious and begin creating! Maybe it's a scribble or vision board. Tap into what you truly want in life during this phase think BIG

-do not limit yourself to any one idea or dream because anything is possible at any time. Eat lighter foods as your appetite will be a bit more suppressed during this time.

Summer Menstruation - There's this little thing that happens in your biological clock every month. This time you feel like a goddess, sexy and vivacious with more energy than ever before.

This is the shortest phase and only a few days long. This is your ovulation. Your peak. You're feeling invincible right now, so get your sweat on and feel the blood pumping through you. You might do something a little different from what's expected of you at this time or even try to take up that hobby again because it never seemed like too much work before!

Right now, is an ideal time for intense workouts; new poses are no longer intimidating and just seem natural to explore. Your intuition has been heightened, which means all those ideas in your head are worth exploring while they last - give yourself permission to be who you want during this time. This is your time to shine - You are looking hot, damn confident and ready to wow any audience whether that's public speaking or a girl's night out.

Fall Menstruation - During this phase were hanging for a while (day 12 - 16) and this is when our estrogen takes a tank and progesterone begins the rise. Progesterone is the hormone that gives you a feeling of relaxation and helps you sleep better. It has been also found to reduce stress levels as well, so it's important for those who are often anxious or stressed out to utilize this time in your cycle. You know the time is coming when you are about to get your period. It's that funny mood swing where sometimes, everything just starts irritating you and suddenly nothing seems fun or interesting anymore. This is when we often fall into imposter syndrome. We scroll through our feed, wondering if anyone will notice that, we are not good enough and constantly criticizing ourselves - which could be really hard to explain to an observer looking in. There are times when we can't quite pinpoint what is going on, and this time seems to be one of those moments. There's no telling how long it will last or why everyone around us feels the same way as if they're all suffering from some sort of delirium. During these fleeting spells where there doesn't seem to be any rhyme nor reason behind our behavior let yourself have a little grace. Nourish yourself with brown rice bowls, proteins, fish and healthy fats during this phase. Our superpower of this phase is decision making. This is your "I can set any boundary and own that shit" phase. Make tough decisions during this time.

Maybe you like to take a deep breath and count backwards from ten. Maybe your go-to style is an angry dance party in the middle of your room, or maybe it's writing about what makes you happy on some paper that gets burned into ashes after. You know yourself best - so explore what letting go means to you.

Letting Go - The first letting go ritual is writing down all that you are ready to release. Meditation before always allows some clarity in this ritual. Think about what's taking up space but not serving you so well- maybe it could be someone or something, a habit or an emotional response? Maybe there's just too much clutter and your life needs more simplicity right now? The next step would then be the act of releasing these things/people into nature as if giving them back to mother earth herself from which they were created. The letting go process is meditating on everything we want to let out; anything that isn't benefitting us anymore can feel like baggage weighing us down. Take time during meditation for quiet reflection, listing those people, places and things which do not get space in your life moving forward. What are you clenching on to? It's easy to feel overwhelmed and stressed out in life. When you're feeling that way, it can help if you identify the cause by going inward or writing down what is bothering you on paper. Sometimes just recognizing how we are responding to a situation will ensure that this doesn't become a pattern within our lives. Sit back, relax and watch the smoke rise as you burn your list. As it does, practice 4 - 8 breathing- taking in a deep breath for four counts before releasing an "ahhh" sound out of your mouth at eight counts while you release everything to the universe. This is your sacred self so add or subtract as needed!

Sisterhood - If you are not already a part of a moon circle or women's group - it should be a priority. This is the perfect time to gather in gratitude and when we are around other women we are supported, embraced and nurtured. We can tap deeper into these traits within our self when we have felt them from other women. We have the safety to feel, cry, scream and howl under the stars but we do it together. It allows you to feel a part of a tribe and as one in the collective; honor this sacredness however feels good for you.

Life isn't about finding yourself. It's about creating the woman you always wanted to be, even if she doesn't exist yet.

Herb Connection - In modern society and in many ancient cultures, we are taught that the world is a place of balance. Yin to Yang, light to dark, pain to pleasure; these dualities exist everywhere from our everyday lives on Earth all the way up into space where opposites attract each other with magnetic forces.

In every aspect of life there exists this natural balancing act between opposite polarities or "laws" - one cannot thrive without its counterpart coming along for the ride. The feminine energy is a yin energy which means it is receptive. Feminine energy likes to receive. It connects to the roots of us which are creative, flow, sensual, empathy, guiding and nourishing. During our winter phase or actual bleed, we can nourish our bodies cramps and pains with natural herbs and remedies to allow peace and tranquil moments. To promote that "go within" nourishment our body needs. You can mix these in teas, use in oils, take herb baths, find your personal favs and go with that.

Lavender and Chamomile - Allows a sense of calm and relaxation and can provide grounding.

Turmeric - My personal favorite here is the turmeric latte - such a cozy drink to relax with at night before bed. This is anti-inflammatory and can reduce pain.

Red raspberry - This allows toning of the uterus and acts as an aid to other herbs flowing them to all the right spaces your body needs.

Cramp bark - Eases the pain of cramping and back pain. This soothes the muscle tissue and can bring warmth to a painful area.

Ginger - Ginger is also very helpful to stagnated and painful pelvic areas. Provides relief.

Mug wort - Allows us to tap into our intuition and really opens the subconscious and conscious connection in the dream world.

The Vessel

We have this sneaky inner voice that tells us we're not good enough, but the truth is you are. You deserve to love yourself as much as anyone does and would if given the chance. For many of us it's hard to just take care of ourselves because we hold so much stress in our bellies-aka the second brain. But when we do something for ourselves like get deep into meditation or find ways to release tension, then all those negative thoughts fade and peace enters instead.

Doing things for self can be difficult at times due to life's constant demands on your attention; To start a relationship with your body you first need to be thankful for this amazing vessel which carries and nourishes you daily. A simple breath is sending oxygen to your entire body - take time in gratitude for how it's always there when worries are weighing on your shoulders, picking you up after you've fallen, or soothing away the aches. We are walking miracles.

Embodying the Wild Woman

- <u>Meet your shadow self</u> and engage in regular shadow work
- Bring awareness to your deepest emotions and feelings
- Get to know yourself intimately
- Unleash your raw, authentic nature
- Journey all the way to your edge, and keep going
- <u>Track your menstrual cycle</u> and meet your Wild Woman each cycle

"The Wild Woman carries the bundles for healing—she carries everything a woman needs to be and know. She carries the medicine for all things. She carries stories and dreams and words and songs and signs and symbols, she is both vehicle and destination."
- Dr. Clarissa Pinkola Estes

Intuition

Intuition is a strange concept, and some people will tell you that it's just an excuse for not thinking. However, this couldn't be further from the truth.

Our intuition exists inside us; or more specifically in our brain - which has two different operating systems to handle stressors: Fight-or-Flight mode (technically we have a third one where trauma stores itself away but let's save that for another chapter).

Intuitive thoughts happen when these fight or flight modes are triggered by your environment and/or stimuli. These triggers can come as either physical sensations or emotional responses. The first reaction is an instinctual, effortless response. A bike approaches quickly on a sidewalk and you put your hands out instinctively to avoid getting hit head-on with the front tire of the bicycle. This intuition exists in all humans because it's part of our natural survival instincts when faced with danger or uncertainty during times like this one where there are very few other options available for us but to react immediately without much thought at all. Intuitive power is the ability to make quick decisions about if something is real, fake or feels good. It all happens outside of our conscious awareness and science backs intuition up! Intuition can be strengthened by tapping into your brilliance which lies inside you - but how? I gotchya covered with a few tips on 'how to feed it'.

Paying close attention to our intuition can be difficult. We are all guilty of ignoring it, but when we do make the effort and listen closely, great things happen! Take a moment and slowdown in life so you notice what your body is telling you. When something feels off or hesitant about an idea that comes up - give yourself permission to explore this voice inside immediately because they're usually right on target with how we feel for good reason

Trust your gut. Your gut is also known as your second brain, and for good reason. Society is constantly telling us what to look like, how to act and feel for us to fit in with their idea of "perfect." What if we tapped into trusting our intuition? The enteric nervous system has about 100 million neurons which can be more than the number found in most people's spinal cord. It is a little-known fact that we are more than just our skin, bones and organs. We have an entire ecosystem of microbes living inside us which help to keep everything running smoothly. They play such important roles in regulating digestion, immunity and even moods so it's not surprising when you start feeling off after the breakup or death of someone close; your gut instinct has been telling you something was wrong for weeks now but because these things have never happened before all you could do was trust what felt right. Therefore, we get sick; we feel shivers up the spine, goosebumps on your arms, our body is reacting to alert us of certain situations and people.

Let it go. When Elsa sang her famous anthem, "Let It Go," she was singing about more than just the cold and snow. In fact, this song is a great reminder that we put up barriers to our own happiness by not letting ourselves have negative thoughts or emotions. I know it's hard when you're in an emotional state but try your best not to let those feelings control you - they'll only get worse if left unchecked! You can use tools like affirmations for yourself as well as visualizations of peace around others who are hurting instead of being angry with them; these exercises will help reduce stress levels which would otherwise be blocking good energy from meeting us on all fronts: physically (our health), mentally (feelings) and spiritually.

Watch out for the vampires. We all have at least one in our lives. That person that you walk away from feeling the need to take a nap. They suck the energy right out of you with no regrets or even knowledge that they have done such a thing. Be very deliberate about who you have around you on a regular basis. Surround yourself with people who empower and inspire you. The "I want to be you when I grow up" people. There are two types of people you choose in your life. The first allows the power to stay with you and the vampire demands the power over to themselves. Choose wisely my friend.

The surroundings. Some people get lost in their thoughts and never really experience what is happening around them. If you are one of these people, start paying attention to the nuances instead of just your own desires or distractions. Pick up on every nuance that shines with pure joy as well as those moments when there appears to be a disconnect from life itself; pay close attention so you can begin understanding how they affect each other in your day-to-day life because not everything will have an obvious explanation right away. Write down observations whenever possible so that over time patterns might emerge for more productive living while also exposing some things about yourself along the way.

Meditation - Try this meditation technique next time you're feeling restless. Pick up a candle, light it and stare into the flame. If thoughts come to mind, then watch them float by but do not attach yourself to them just yet- bring your attention back to the flickering of the burning wick! Keep watching as long as possible before choosing an amount of time that suits you best (maybe 10 or 15 minutes). Use these moments in silence and focus wisely because they will leave positive effects on your energy levels when finished with practice over periods of consecutive days.

> "Surrender and accept that whatever is happening in the moment, is the Universe is working on your behalf."
> - Mastin Kipp

Surrender

Surrendering is being truly present. Being in the moment, and noticing what you can touch, feel taste or see. Do this from a place of love instead of fear- notice your surroundings without judgement to release anxiety about tomorrow's choices and shame for yesterday's decisions

"Surrendering comes down to one thing: mindfulness." You hear it all over social media these days but how do we practice it? It all starts with awareness; paying attention here (right now) so that you're fully aware of not only yourself but also whatever else is around us at any given time. "We make our choices from two places--love or fear," says author Pema Chodron. Where are you making these choices from?

Your past does not define you. You went through those situations and made those choices to learn a lesson, even if the path was tough at times. Your experiences have led you here today so instead of feeling shame or guilt about something that can't be changed, shift your mindset around it to gratitude for walking through hard shit and learning lessons which make us wiser and freer in life.

What you are ashamed of is your freaking superpower. It's the thing that will help you reach so many others in your path and get them to change their lives too! But it also means we need to let go sometimes, because there are some things out of our control- like where life takes us next? So, write down thoughts regularly whether they're journal entries or affirmations about what YOU want for yourself... just see what comes up when writing at least 10 minutes a day.

A journal is your weapon. It can be a sword that battles all the demons in your mind, or it could be an ice-cream cone on sticky summer days. You may not know what you are going to write about when you open its pages and start writing; but anything goes.

Identify your limiting beliefs and fears.

Take a moment and write down the top five things that you fear the most.

1. _____
_____
_____
_____
_____

2. _____
_____
_____
_____
_____

3. _____
_____
_____
_____
_____

4. _____
_____
_____
_____
_____

5. _____
_____
_____
_____
_____

What would happen if these fears came true?

1. _____
_____
_____
_____
_____

2. _____
_____
_____
_____
_____

3. _____
_____
_____
_____
_____

4. _____
_____
_____
_____
_____

5. _____
_____
_____

You just empowered your inner strength. You're on the verge of a new chapter - you released the power out of your fears. It's that simple.

Shadow Work

We must do some shadow work in order to understand our limiting beliefs. But what can we immediately do? We can start asking ourselves questions like "does this belief belong to me or was it told to me?" This way of questioning will help us clarify if the certain moral, decision or choice is something that is truly ours. If the answer does not align with your non-negotiables, then know for sure that those thoughts and feelings were imposed on you without your consent. Tap into what YOU want; use discernment when faced with decisions or choices in order not accept anything that does not align with the highest good of all. There are many different types of shadows, but one type is that which we create in our own minds. Shadow work can be a difficult process for some to face head on because it means confronting aspects of ourselves that may have been buried and forgotten about by both the unconscious mind as well as society's expectations or standards. A shadow is a person's hidden self that they refuse to accept or acknowledge as part of who they are. This work allows you to take a piece of yourself that has been banished and bring it back to light. This can be anything from exploring your feelings in the aftermath of an abusive relationship or family members death to finally facing deep seated self-destructive behaviors like alcoholism or drug abuse. Shadow work will help heal our emotional wounds by giving us permission to feel all parts of ourselves - good and bad alike; It is often easier to get in touch with feelings that are otherwise ignored or suppressed. The shadow self may also help you meet your' life purpose and play an important role in personal growth as well as spiritual development by cultivating empathy for others' struggles and pain points. Our shadow is often expressed through denial or anger because it conflicts with the idea of how we want to be seen by others - that whole ego scenario; but we all have these dark spots inside us which can turn into powerful allies if illuminated properly during this process. Shadow work allows us to get closer to understanding what makes us tick both lightheartedly and deeply so there isn't anything left unseen. Shadow work is the process of identifying and exploring your own suppressed emotions, thoughts, or impulses. It can be helpful to think about shadow work as peeling back layers from an onion so that you find a more complete understanding of yourself. As we delve into this important self-knowledge exploration there are some simple guidelines you may wish to follow:

Be gentle with yourself during any emotional upheaval while going through these inner processes; give yourself permission to take time for it all make sense at your' own pace.

What emotion do you try to avoid? Why are you afraid of this type of feeling? What would happen if it was felt all the way through and not just a fleeting moment in time?

_____
_____
_____
_____
_____
_____
_____
_____
_____
_____
_____
_____
_____
_____
_____
_____
_____
_____
_____
_____
_____
_____

COURTNEY HANSON

WITHIN

Can you believe how many things we take for granted? There are so many things that I usually don't think about until they're right in front of me, like a chair. Chairs let us sit down and have some relaxation time but when was the last time you thought to yourself "wow this is amazing! A chair!" Probably never because it's something everyone takes for granted. Think about things you take for granted daily.

_____
_____
_____
_____
_____
_____
_____
_____
_____
_____
_____
_____
_____
_____
_____
_____
_____
_____
_____
_____
_____
_____
_____
_____
_____
_____
_____
_____
_____
_____
_____
_____
_____
_____

COURTNEY HANSON

Which of these adjectives trigger you? Think about why it triggers you. Is this the word someone has used to describe you before or a word that you identify with and find truth in its meaning, even if others don't agree with your definition for the term?

Arrogant, liar, jealous, mean, cruel, possessive, bitchy, bossy, loser, greedy, mysterious, sneaky, codependent, sick, fat, disgusting, stalker, stupid, idiot, fearful, sexist, masochistic, narcissist, insignificant, frigid, racist, victim, egotistic, ugly, arrogant, careless, passive, aggressive, lame, boring, tactless, irresponsible, incompetent, lazy, unfair, childish, know it all, gloomy, depressed, pushy, stubborn, inferior, weak, impatient, unreliable, self-destructive, over sensitive, heartless, resentful, dominant, bad, ignorant, uneducated, tasteless, insecure.

_____
_____
_____
_____
_____
_____
_____
_____
_____
_____
_____
_____
_____
_____
_____
_____
_____
_____
_____
_____
_____
_____
_____
_____

COURTNEY HANSON

What is it that you resent? Why do you have those resentments? How has holding on to this resentment helped your life in any way at all?

The way I spend my daily life is how I will spend the rest of my life. How do you feel about this statement?

What does it mean to be worthy? What is the difference between being good and bad, right or wrong? Why do we have this question of worthiness at all in our society so heavily entrenched in capitalist values that define success as money, fame, power and social status alone.

Why am I afraid to trust others? Why have people been hurtful towards me in the past, and how could that make me seem untrustworthy today? Have I hurt people?

Which of my weaknesses is my superpower?

COURTNEY HANSON

What's one thing that stresses you out the most?

How do other people see you? Do they judge your appearance and personality the same way as yourself or do their perceptions differ completely from what you think about yourself? How does this make you feel?

Much of who we are, what we feel and do is shaped by the people around us. Who has the most influence over you? Is it healthy for them to have this kind of control?

Do you ever envy people who seem to be more successful than yourself? Who do you envy? If so, why do you think that is the case and what can we learn from their success?

Think of a relationship you turned your back on. How has it been positive now looking back?

Do you ever find yourself judging how others see you? Do they really know who you are, or does a mask of your own design hide the real person from view? It can be difficult to distinguish between what is reality and what we project onto it. How do you feel judged on any given day?

COURTNEY HANSON

Write about the last time you tried to manipulate a situation and how you felt about it?

When was the last time you ran from your responsibilities? What were they, and why did you choose to run away at that moment in time instead of following through with what needed to be done?

If you could say one thing to the person who has hurt you the most right now, what would you say?

Many people might think of spanking when they hear about punishment. Others picture themselves in court, standing before a judge as the sentence is read: "For your crime we hereby punish you to life imprisonment without parole." It can be minor or extreme - each person will have created their own story around this word. When you hear the word punishment what is the first situation which comes to mind?

Speaking your truth

It's so hard to say what we really want, because deep down in our heart there is fear. We make decisions from two places in our life - love or fear. It can be difficult and sometimes feel like you have a lump in your throat that won't let anything out. Sometimes it feels easier just to stay quiet or scream as loud as possible when everything boils over - does any of this sound familiar? You are the only person who can understand and relate to your own feelings. I've told my children, "Your words are powerful" since they were old enough to comprehend the meaning behind this statement. The deepest pain is denying your true self for others' comfort because you feel like it would make them happy if you just put on an act. You have an immense amount of creative control over what you say and how you feel about yourself--you're in charge. When people hear negative things said about themselves from someone else, there is so much potential harm that could be done by those harmful statements simply being left unchecked or unchallenged. We make decisions from two spaces within ourselves. Fear and love. Speaking your truth means being true to who you are, no matter what. Do not try cover up or hide anything for approval of someone liking you better; be the truest version of yourself that exists and say whatever is on your mind! Hear these words from a wise woman - "Speak when thy tongue can make thee understood." Below I have compiled some tips about how to start speaking out more often: before long, it will become second nature.

- It can be hard to identify our own feelings sometimes, but with some effort we will start recognizing them more and more often. Take a moment to make small note of your moods throughout each day so that you have an idea at the end how you were feeling or what made you happy or sad. Analyzing one's emotions is not always easy which leads many people ignore their true feels in order avoid any discomfort from being vulnerable. If you have nothing to say - don't force it. Embrace the silence.
- It's always important to be honest. In your day-to-day life, you may find yourself in conversations where the other person is talking about something that you have no idea about. As hard as it can sometimes seem, honesty is the best policy so tell them. You'll learn

more than just how far their knowledge stretches when it comes to this subject but also gain some insight into things outside of your everyday world which might help broaden or change perspectives altogether. Get curious and be bold.
- If you disagree with something - say it. A therapist once told me "The minute you start yelling - is the minute the other person stops listening". You can disagree kindly but still get your point across clearly.
- When someone ask you, a question answer it truthfully. Where do you want to eat? Instead of "I don't know" state what you're feeling like eating.
- Tell someone you love them. A friend, someone who inspires you, someone who motivates you, let them know verbally how much they impact your life.
- "A lot of people are afraid to say what they want. That's why they don't get what they want". - Madonna
- Mean what you say and say what you mean. If you want something - SAY IT.

Universal Energy withing the Wild Woman

1. Rub your hands together FAST
2. Create friction for 30 seconds
3. Pull your hands apart slowly. Do you feel the magnetic pull between your palms? THIS is Universal energy.

Imagine a violet light emanating from your palms and radiating out over the area you wish to heal. Whether it's an injury, chakra or body ache - this healing technique can be used anywhere! Hold until you feel warmth in that place (or tingly sensations). After practicing on yourself for a while, take some time each day to use this technique while visualizing someone else who needs help with their health and well-being.

With your eyes closed - Place your hands on each chakra and imagine the chakras color. As you are in each area with every inhale visualize the light growing, swirling and becoming stronger. You will feel drawn to certain areas longer than others - this is totally normal and a sign that certain chakra is blocked.

Chakra Color Guide
Root - Reddish Orangish Brown
Sacral - Orange
Solar Plexus - Golden
Heart - Green
Throat - Blue
Third Eye - Indigo
Crown - Violet

"I am tapped into my divine fem energy."

"I listen to my intuition and trust her."

"I am water: a perfect balance between structure and flow."

"When my body tells me to rest, I rest."

"I hear the calling and I go."

"I embrace my sealskin and return to my home."

"I naturally know what I need to do."

"I go out in the woods and have no fear."

"I build my own life, bone by bone."

"I wear bravery like a crown."

"I howl to the moon."

"I know where my soul resides."

"I am wise. I am wild."

"I am woman hear me ROAR."

The Lover

The Lover is about immersing oneself in the sensations and emotions of life. She revels in sensuality with a playful, yet celebratory attitude that spreads joy to all she encounters when we embody her energy within ourselves. When living from the perspective of our Lover we are resting deeply into bodily sensation without abandoning any part or parts; feeling what is present completely at this moment, not allowing anything else to occupy us even for a second. Our playfulness reveals an uninhibited side as childlike innocence emerges through spontaneity and creativity, so everything becomes new again each time it's played out before us like a child on Christmas morning opening their presents.

She is the definition of "I don't chase I receive - what is meant to be will come to me."

She is a woman who wants to live life fully and without fear. She embraces the significance of her senses, as she knows they are integral in how we experience this world - whether it be through sight or smell, hearing or touch. The love of connection and experience is a very important part to the person that she strives to be. She has an all-encompassing passion for life itself, which manifests in spontaneity as well as wanderlust. The healthy Lover accepts and loves herself as she is - she also understands that no one is responsible for our happiness but ourselves, she is fully embodied that the answers come from within. When she opens to surrender and self-fulfillment, she becomes unstoppable. Her promise is to make the world filled with love, her desire is to attain intimacy, her goal is being in relationships with things she loves - maybe it's traveling, money, sex or an actual person. The fear is being alone or abandoned. Her strategy is becoming more attractive to others and has a gift of gratitude and passion.

The Lovers motivation is in belonging and feeling that sense of connection. If the lover were a movie think - Romeo & Juliette, Titanic, The Notebook, and Moulin Rouge.

> Divine Lover, teach me rest be in my body, to feel what
> is there completely, without the stories, and to come to
> love myself and my body, exactly the way I am.
> - INITIATORY PRAYER

The Shadow of the Lover

Don't you know that she's toxiccccc. Who doesn't love a little Brittney am I right? More of a country fan? I've got you... "I dug my keys into the side of his pretty little souped up four-wheel drive." The Shadow Lover is the victim, but she's not a passive one. She'll always be checking up on you and wondering if you're going to leave her for someone else. If your other relationships are also of importance in your life, then this can cause some tension between all involved. The Lover will unconsciously spiral to a space that is destructive to all around her in fear of abandonment. We are talking slash the tires, go through your phone while your sleeping - all the cray behavior. The shadow lover is often misunderstood because people don't seem like that type when they first meet them, being manipulative or scary tends to come out after time has passed by (sometimes years) before it becomes apparent how serious these signs were from day one- making people feel isolated and alone without knowing why. In times of trauma, our Lover falls into shadow. This is because she cannot stand to be seen in the light when that person who was meant to protect her has left and abandoned their duties. As an adult this can happen easily through a breakup or divorce, loss of someone we love dearly or sexual assault - if they had mothers and fathers who couldn't contact them properly or didn't hold us or truly see us, our Lover may not feel safe enough to come forth. If the shadow of the lover, you can expect to experience these emotions -

- Clinginess
- Feeling the need to gossip about other women
- Lack of self-love
- Vain
- Unexplained anger
- Guilt and shame
- Withdrawing from normal situations
- The need for attention
- Making ultimatums "if you don't do this then I will..."
- She begins to take on the world's problems and neglect herself. She has forgotten that she is Love embodied, which means if there are any issues out in the world then they are just reflections of her own inner self-worth.

(One of the key points of embodiment is mirroring the love you put out into the world back to yourself or the Lover becomes drained, and a huge void begins to form.) If in a relationship the lover becomes the ball and chain with the need for every ounce of control within the situation. The partners usually feed off each other and it comes to the point of breaking in a very dramatic explosion.

Embodiment of The Lover

The Lover archetype helps us to loosen up and build more connections with others. When we are feeling rejected or desire a romantic partner, this is the archetypal support system for getting what you want out of relationships. This archetype is about connection, desire and healing past feelings of rejection or being unloved. Self-love is not just about how you look on the outside; it must come from within. One way of incorporating self-love into your daily routine is by nourishing and loving your body with simple, less expensive activities such as reading a book or journaling in an uplifting environment that makes you happy. By doing these things regularly we create a sacred feeling that stays alive for when we are going through tough times. To support the body in its natural healing process, it can be helpful to implement simple changes and rituals into your life.

- One of these is drinking lemon water every morning which provides hydration for our cells as well manages inflammation with vitamin C absorption.
- Hikes or walks provide fresh air while also giving us a chance to connect with Mother Earth by feeling her beauty around you; something that may not come naturally when we're stuck inside all day.
- Yoga gives us strength both physically and mentally through poses designed specifically for flexibility (especially important after having kids).
- Taking extra time putting lotion on can help hydrate tired and dry skin while also providing a protective barrier against environmental aggressors like pollution from city life.
- Bringing plants into your space is an inexpensive way to cleanse the air which may be polluted by household cleaners of other dried out items around us all day long. Additionally it's good practice to nurture them because they will provide plenty of oxygen during this process so now, we have purified our environment & increased feelings of calmness too.
- Blast music and dance around, take a bubble bath with candles, indulge in self pleasure and creating your own satisfaction. Later in the book we will discuss climax manifestation which is a beautiful practice to try while embodying the Lover.
- It is important to find a therapist or healing modality that feels right for you. There are many different forms of therapy, and it can be difficult if not impossible to know which one will suit your needs best without trying them out firsthand. Some people enjoy working with their minds through journaling while others may prefer meditating on the breath itself in order to clear distractions from their thoughts during sessions. Shadow work has been known

as an effective form of psychotherapy where clients explore limiting beliefs and how they have shaped our lives over time - often we carry these things into adulthood even though some were prevalent only when younger ages (such as being bullied by classmates). Beginners should start slow so they can see what method works best for their needs.
- Dress like a goddess. Think of clothing that will make you feel sexy and feminine, with nothing too tight or constricting. Wear clothes which flow against your body so the female energy can move freely without any obstructions.
- Write yourself or someone else you love a spicy love letter.

A love letter to you.

COURTNEY HANSON

WITHIN

I love you deeply,

Aphrodite

Aphrodite, the goddess of love and beauty who is identified with Venus by Roman mythology. Her name means "foam" in Greek which highlights her birth from Uranus' severed genitals after his son Cronus threw them into the ocean foam. Although worshipped as a goddess of love and fertility, Aphrodite is also known for presiding over marriages. Her public cult was generally solemn with an austere tone, though she occasionally watched over prostitutes in addition. Women have a powerful Aphrodite archetype to govern their love and beauty, sexuality (sensuality), creativity and procreativity. The realm of the lover exerts a strong pull on many women; as an impulse with her personality, Aphrodite can be just as demanding at times as Hera or Demeter (the other two strong instinctual archetypes). This is both because she forces herself upon them for women to fulfill creative functions but also so they may embrace their womanly duty which includes fulfilling procreation roles too. Of Aphrodite's mortal lovers, the most important were Anchises and Adonis. The two bore children that would have a huge impact on their world in years to come: Aeneas became one of Rome's founders by accident when he was taken from his home country Troy; while Adonis would be mourned every year at festival after being killed by wild boar during hunting an expedition. Among her symbols were the dove, pomegranate, swan, and myrtle. Aphrodite was so angry with Eos for falling in love with her ex-boyfriend Ares, that she put a curse on the poor girl. She had multiple lovers and gave birth to many children but never managed to find true love which is what came to fruition from Aphrodite cursing her. Aphrodite has many lovers, but her husband Hephaestus was also a blacksmith who created armor for men in battle to protect their bodies from harm. Her son Eros was an angel sent by Aphrodite with messages of true love between two people that caused them to fall passionately in lust or even become pregnant together. When Paris needed guidance on whether he should pursue Helen's affections, Aphrodite helped him make his decision when she encouraged him not just based on what he would get out of it (which seemed slim), but rather how much they loved each other; this led Troy into war against Greece because Helen didn't want it any more than anyone else did. Also known as the Trojan War. The goddess Aphrodite has always been seen as a personification of the deity who creates and rules over love. From her journey from sea to shore, she is characterized by her beautiful features that set all men's hearts on fire with desire for beauty. No matter what form they take, these women tend to have blonde hair or golden curls much like their Greek predecessor; however, this is not necessary in order to be considered an "Aphrodite." These gorgeous creatures are simply attractive people whose charisma makes them magnetic enough, so everyone wants them near at hand. Despite her many faults including jealousy and a bad temper that cause trouble with both mortals and gods alike, not even these can overshadow Aphrodite's desire for love. Meticulously sculpted from marble and adorned in flowing robes with flowers around her head, she takes on many different shapes depending on who's looking at her: For men to see beauty that they can't resist; for women-to feel their physical appearance isn't important but what lies within them. Her most well-known incarnation was when Ares ripped off Athena's helmet during battle and revealed Zeus' daughter without any armor or protection while all those watching cheered wildly because it meant victory would go to whichever side got possession of the goddess of war! She has been portrayed by artists through time not only as being beautiful but also powerful.

The Medicine of Breath

Pranayama is a practice that dates back thousands of years and has been used for its therapeutic purposes. Intended to elevate the life force, or Prana Shakti (or simply "Life Energy"), this ancient yogic technique can be practiced in many ways; find what speaks to you.

The 4/4 breathing technique is so called for its ability to balance out highs and lows. It starts by lengthening your inhale, then holding it in at the top of breath before finally exhaling into a longer than normal pause. You inhale for a count of four, pause, then exhale for a count of four. The key here? Don't rush! Repeat these steps three times or more until you can find that place between mindfully meditating and doing nothing but concentrating on your breath-work.

Box Breathing, Water Breath, Balanced Breathing - This technique can be beneficial to anyone who wants to reduce stress and come back down from tense moments as well as those with lung problems like copd and asthma etc., but it's also great when used simply for meditation purposes because this practice brings us up when we are down and down when we are up. Also known as balanced breathing.

To start sit upright in a chair with both feet planted firmly on the floor. Keep your hands relaxed on your lap with your palms facing upward.

1. Slowly exhale letting all the stale air from your body to release. Focus on the intention during this powerful exhale.
2. Slowly inhale and deeply through your nose to the count of four. Count slowly and feel the air fill your lungs, one section at a time until your lungs are completely full of air and the air is moving to your belly.
3. Hold your breath at the top.
4. Exhale through your mouth for the count of four, expelling the air from your lungs and abdomen.
5. Hold your breath on the bottom exhale.

Diaphragm breathing is a practice that has so many beneficial effects for your body. The diaphragm, which sits at the bottom of our chest cavity and separates us from abdominal organs like the stomach, spleen and liver, controls how well we take in air to fill those vital organs with life-sustaining oxygen. Diaphragmatic or belly breathing allows deep inhalations into this space without tensing up muscles in other areas of our bodies such as chests pectorals or abdominals- allowing more room for lungs to expand during exhalation. So, when you're feeling stressed out about work deadlines looming over your head? Breathe deeply through (or rather under) it.

1. Relax your shoulders and allow them to melt into the surface beneath you.
2. Put a hand on your chest and one hand on your belly.
3. Breathe in through your nose for about two seconds. You should experience the breath flowing through your nostrils into your abdomen, making your tummy expand. During this type of

breathing, make sure your stomach is moving outward while your chest remains relatively still.
4. Purse your lips (kind of like you're drinking through a straw) press gently on your stomach and exhale slowly for about two seconds.
5. Repeat several times.

Rib-Stretch Breathing is a different way of breathing that works with your diaphragm.

Stand up straight, arching back to loosen the chest and ribs. Take in slow breaths until you can't take any more air; hold it for ten seconds before slowly exhaling through your mouth while keeping yourself still - this helps decompress pressure on muscles from both inside and out. Repeat as necessary during exercise or high stress moments.

4-7-8 Breathing is an ancient yoga technique that helps you control your breathing. It can be done before bed to help lucid dreams, a deeper sleep and overall state of relaxation. The 4-7-8 forces the mind and body to focus on breath rather than replaying your worries from earlier in the day back at night when it's time for bed. This will put people into a natural tranquilizer like state where they're able to let go of their thoughts without getting worked up or upset about them anymore; this removes any anxiety caused by thinking too much.

Lie down comfortably on your bed and take a deep breath. Let go of any tension in the muscles as you exhale completely through your mouth, making a whooshing sound (ahhhhh). Close your lips and inhale silently for four counts through your nose then hold that breath for seven seconds before following up with another big sighing exhalation followed by an eight-count inhalation to complete one cycle. Repeat this exercise five to ten times while counting mentally or using an app like Insight Timer to time it at about ten minutes total length.

August 17th,

Thank you for the exhale. The knowing of my breath being magic – being medicine. Carrying me subconsciously when I can barely hold myself up. Thank you guides for revealing to me all I need to know. thank you guides of the highest truth and compassion for writing through me. I am in gratitude for the changes and life shifts happening at such a sudden pace. I trust the process as uncomfortable as I may be. I was feeling so stuck in this unhealthy cycle in which I tried to depend on self-will, and I could not. I thank you for gifting me the opportunity to change. To change directions even at this later stage of life. I will continue to stay guided with confidence and that I do not need to clench so tightly to the steering wheel. I am ready to openly surrender and live the rest of my days within beauty and grace. To live the purpose, I was designed for. I know some day I will feel a clearer guidance – for now thank you for your support and steadiness. I choose to be the warrior you created me to be and I let go of the victim who has prisoned me for so long. Life is no longer happening to me – it's happening for me.

—Courtney

The Heart Chakra

The heart chakra is crucial for emotional power and love. The color associated with this center, green, can also symbolize the earth's natural landscape as well as a place of deep healing in many religions across history. In Sanskrit it is called Anahata which means "unhurt or not wounded." This center teaches us to feel our emotions without judgment and that we are all one being - connected by unconditional love. Now the juicy part... How can we tell if it's blocked?

- You've been dwelling on a past relationship, missing the toxic sex or thinking they were the "one." Not feeling satisfied in your current state or relationship.
- Loneliness or feeling trapped.
- Depression and anxiety.
- Finding it hard to connect or feel empathy.
- Feeling shy in social situations.
- Noticing old baggage and trauma re surfacing.
- Trust issues.
- Feeling resentful or holding grudges.
- Procrastinating with relationships or struggling with commitment.
- Pushing yourself to the bottom of the list - feeling not enough or "worth it."

The heart chakra is the strongest of your body's energy centers. As such, it can be one that drains you and provides challenges in balancing out emotions with physical health. You may experience some physical dis-ease (high blood pressure, insomnia) when this center becomes imbalanced or overwhelmed by external factors (immune system function).

How to unblock this area?

Of course, I am an advocate for crystals and some of my favorites to bring into heart chakra healing are jade, green calcite, green aventurine, rose quartz, and amethyst. As we have covered in recent chapters - food and nutrition contribute a huge part in unblocking our chakras. Some of the absolute best heart chakra foods are...

- Green foods - kale, limes, bell peppers, spinach, salads, green apples, broccoli, and thing green goes!
- Cozy soups - Just as when we are in our flow cycle - soups warm the soul and a good hearty soup can rejuvenate and restore your emotional state. (They say chicken noodle soup cures all.)
- Rich vitamin c nutrients - you can get creative here and incorporate oranges, strawberries and other high vitamin c foods into your morning green smoothie.

Heart opening yoga poses like camel, bride, puppy pose, wild thing, half-moon and dancer's pose can be physically therapeutic for heart afflictions. They often make us feel cramped and hunch-backed, as if we are trying to shield our hearts from the world around it. But by suspending yourself in a deep twist or bending your body with hunched shoulders you will allow space for new movement that is just waiting to happen.

Heart Center Meditation

Sit up in a comfortable position. You want your spine straight, shoulders relaxed and chest open as you inhale to press the palms together lightly at heart level. Soften or close your eyes for an energy-boosting session of meditation that will leave you feeling refreshed and rejuvenated.

Can you feel the heaviness of your eyelids as they start to close? Can you hear yourself breathing deeply and steadily, inhaling oxygen and exhaling carbon dioxide with each breath. The sounds around us are muffled out by our mind's own silence. Let go for just this moment so we can explore what lies within ourselves together.

Close your eyes and imagine the center of your chest as a glowing orb- warm, radiant energy. As you rub them together in front of it, feel how this warmth is growing stronger every second. Place one hand on your heart and another on stomach to sense its comforting power coursing through you.

Place your hand over the middle of your chest. Take a deep breath and imagine that you're drawing in light from all around until it manifests as bright green energy right there on top of where you can feel your heart beating inside, just out for to touch. With each exhale, envision this light getting brighter with warmth and love flowing through every single cell in both body and soul.

Imagine your heart to be a big light. You can see the bright energy of this love emanating from its center and filling your body with warmth, safety, and security. Imagine that you are being held by it like a mother would hold her child—only infinitely more protective than any human could ever be for another person in need. As you breathe, use the mantra - "I love myself and I forgive myself, I am as meant to be."

Allow your heart to continue opening while radiating with positive energy that will envelopes all those who surround you. I love myself and I forgive myself, as it's time to end my journey. Allow the Universe in so you can feel all its energy around you, into infinity. After you feel completely soaked with heart chakra energy, gently release the palms by your side. As if reaching for the heavens on inhale and touching earth as we exhale, connect to both worlds through this exercise. Take a moment or two before opening your eyes & moving on with the rest of our day.

Manifesting through Self Pleasure

Now we're getting spicy! I know it sounds a little cray but hear me out - We can manifest through our heart chakra in several ways, and the simplest one is to focus the climax of your sexual energy toward the center of your chest.

Have you ever noticed how exhausted you can be after experiencing a powerful orgasm? The buildup of energy as we reach the peak is the power that has been created. It's certainly hard work and an additional natural melatonin right!? Next time you masturbate or have sex, pay attention to what it feels like at this point in your experience.

Clear your mind and allow yourself to feel the energy move through you. Once you can tap into this feeling, it's easy for someone to get intentional with their purpose in life. Imagine how great that must be -- all your desires being charged up by the orgasmic experience? Picture a blast of green light shooting out from between your chest as an intense climax runs throughout every part of your body: Focus that beam on what matters most--from who we should become or where our future might take us, right down to how we want ourselves and others around us to feel on any given day--and see these wants manifesting themselves before they are even spoken aloud.

Clear away thoughts so there is room for clarity when experiencing pleasure during masturbation.

The powerful energy you created through your pleasure becomes the catalyst for manifestation. You control where that creative and potent power goes by controlling what thoughts are in your mind. How amazing is this?! Remember, sexual energy can be used as a tool to create whatever we want.

I know it's hard to start this practice, but the more you do it and fall in love with yourself.

Closing Affirmations

A woman can be many things. The lover is the most instinctive feminine archetype and a powerful energy that empowers to create, transform and attract in all aspects of life. As you go through your day think about how she embodies these qualities within different situations as they come up for you-whether it's lustful or love driven thoughts, desires or actions; whether its beckoning someone into an intimate conversation with her magnetic charm -or even when creating something new out of nothing from scratch.

I am spirit manifested in beautiful form.

I am connected in love to all that lives and all that breathes.

I am the expression of love.

I am limitless.

The entire universe exists to support me in physical form.

My timing is divine and perfect.

I am connected to my highest self.

I serve from a place of highest good.

Love flows to me like the river.

I am calm and centered.

I am here and now.

I am peace, forgiveness and healing.

The Queen

The Queen is the ultimate leader. The soulpreneur, who everyone seeks for advice and guidance; she's a woman of honor with loyalty beyond reproach. She may be regal in her demeanor but not one without desires or needs: though they are few, all demand nothing less than total devotion - even if it means marrying someone else. Powerful men attract her like honey attracts flies because these types can offer what most women want out of life: stability as well as complete dedication. With a smile on her face and kindness in every one of her words, she's the one who can get any girl to be happy. She organizes meetups for all her girls, so they never have to feel alone or like an outcast. She is compassionate, inclusive and she rules in a space of kindness and gratitude. She can be both soft and firm, which is perfect for those around her. They respond with loyalty and respect because they know that she's a woman who stands out from all the rest. The Queen never wants to blend in or get lost within any crowd; rather, she sets trends by being different than anyone else could ever be expected to become. The Queen is both chosen and created. The Queen is a doer who knows her worth. She never sits back and lounges around watching the world go by on tiktok or social media - she gets things done, one day at a time. The queen has trustworthy team members to help in when needed while being an excellent delegator as well. The Queen archetype is one that we empower through our own maturity and growth, as it guides us to claiming full expression. The more mature you are the stronger your ability becomes to receive things from others in a way where both sides feel like they have received something worthwhile. No matter what circumstance you find yourself within, always be careful about how much of this energy can come into being without taking away from another side's empowerment. Queen/Leader Archetype: Selfless & Wise—incorporates the Lover, Mother, and Warrior. Authors, humanitarians, mystics (or shamans), politicians, queens [from Cleopatra to Queen Elizabeth II], saints [such as Joan of Arc or Saint Theresa] and scientists such as Marie Curie have all been classified under this type for their respective contributions in a wide range of fields.

The Shadow of The Queen

The shadow can get quite dark and the queen who craves the position of power and control and she doesn't care whose expense or feelings that comes with. There are many types of Queens, but the most common ones have a certain "feel" to them. You may know her as The Imperious Queen or even by other names like Silent Queen and Ice Queen - if this is you then your reaction to the queen might be met with sorrow, dismay and sometimes fear. The Queens temper can go from zero to one hundred just as fast. She has no problem transforming a small incident into pure rage and the need for revenge, but she always holds her tongue because of how much power she wields in comparison to those beneath her. She can be judgey, shallow, vain, and very vindictive. She can view sex as a chore instead of pleasure and struggle with setting boundaries. Queens can lose their identity in relationships and stay in abusive situations for the sake of loyalty and commitment. Everybody has their own take on what it means to be the archetypal Queen, but one thing's for sure - the archetype can have many different facets. For example, Lewis Carroll's Red Queen from Alice in Wonderland is very challenging and full of rage and danger when she shouts, "Off with your heads!"

When in balance: The Queen is a powerful archetype that can lead you to assert your power, take charge of situations and act with benevolence. She's loyal, compassionate and inspiring.

When out of balance: The narcissist is a fascinating and often dangerous character. They find themselves superior to everyone around them, the powerful queen that everyone should respect.

"Narcissists are very sensitive, oftentimes overly so," psychologist Dr. Nicolle Wahl said in an interview with The Daily Beast earlier this year. "They react more strongly than others when criticized about something they may not be aware of doing wrong... You can see it as being victimized by your own ego: you're too important for anything bad happening to you."

The main wound: Within the wound, the Queen can be shallow and image conscious. She is prone to judgment (of herself and others) as she strives for perfection, which stems from feeling vulnerable when someone has something that she desires. When threatened by other women or jealousy of what they have obtained without effort on their part, the Queen becomes vengeful in a way reminiscent of Snow White's stepmother who showed no mercy towards children just because they were born with beauty inside them.

> "Sacred Feminine, I give myself over to you, to be a vessel and emanation of your love. Your will is my will."

Hera

Story time of the Greek Goddess Hera. Grab a cup of tea and get cozy. Hera was the wife to Zeus and the Queen of the Gods (she was also known as the goddess of marriage and birth in Greek mythology.) She was the daughter of Cronus and Rhea, a mother of Ares (God of War), Hebe (Goddess of Youth), Eileithyia (Goddess of Childbirth.) These children were all with Zeus but here's the twist - Hera had a child on her own whose name was Hephaistos (God of Metallurgy) she did this to retaliate against Zeus for having Athena. We're getting steamy now... Okay so Hera was not all rose petals and petunias, she threw her son Hephaistos from Mount Olympus because he was ugly, and he came crashing to earth and became lame. He got pissed (I am sure I would too if my mom threw me off Mt. Olympus and my dad threw me from Heaven, I mean helllooooo, can you blame the poor guy?) He decided to imprison Hera in her own special thrown. The only way he would release her was if she hooked him up with the sexy Aphrodite in marriage. Hera was constantly in battle with staying loyal to Zeus while he was off being freak McNasty with all the other Goddesses. As any queen in shadow her go to was revenge. Leto (one of the many) was so punished that Hera cursed any land that gave the pregnant goddess refuge. Since Hera's daughter is the goddess of childbirth, she forced her to make Leto wait nine months to give birth to her son Apollo. Hera's jealousy continued to overtake her as Zeus continued to ho it up. We have Io (who was one of Hera's priestesses and a former princess of Argos) and she turned the poor girl into a white cow and then took her (as a cow) and set the one-hundred-eyed Argos to guard her. The list goes on for miles, but Hera went to great lengths and was above and beyond pissed about Hercules. Zeus had a little get together with Alkmene and along came Hercules. Hera delayed Hercules birth so that cousin Eurystheus could claim the throne of Tiryns. It gets better - she then sent snakes to kill the infant while he slept. Hera was primarily responsible for the "monsters" you hear of Hercules having to fight in his stories. You get it right? Hera would stop at nothing to get her revenge on Zeus and his player ways. She felt betrayed and could not release her loyalty to him.

The Crown Chakra

This is for sure one of the most complex connections because the Queen is a composite of archetypes and resonates with the four lower chakras. (Root, Sacral, Solar Plexus and Heart.) Once we activate The Mother, The Lover, The Huntress and The Healer we release the secret password to unlock the vault of The Queen.

The Queen herself comes from the seventh chakra (our crown). This is when all parts have become unified, and all the energies work with spirit.

The Crown chakra or Sahsrara is the bridge to the cosmos. Our divine connection. The color of this chakra is violet, and it acts as our center for spirit, enlightenment, wisdom, universal consciousness and connection to higher selves.

How can we tell if this is blocked?

- Rigid in thought process.
- Limiting beliefs.

- Lack of clarity or purpose.
- Dissociation from the body.
- Detachment.
- Psychosis.
- Feeling ungrounded.
- Fears and emotions, we are clinging too.
- Stiffness.
- Achiness.
- Headaches.

We can also have an overactive crown chakra which may come across as spiritual addiction (yes, it's a total thing) Remember the law of polarity. Balance my friend. Also, can come across in apathy, self-destructive behaviors or overwhelmed by new information coming your way.

How do we unblock this area?

- Stillness meditations where you sit in silence and see what comes to you.

(This is called a practice for a reason and takes time, just do your best to be the observer and not attach to your thoughts but rather let them float by.)

A book that changed my life when it came to the crown chakra was by Ram Dass - Be Here Now

"There is a voice that doesn't use words. Listen."
- Rumi

- Listen to podcast and read books that make you crave more. Be the student and just take it all in.
- Gratitude practices several times a day. When we are in gratitude, we are present and not worried about the day-to-day hustle. It gives us a sense of joy and connection to something greater than ourselves.
- Break the rules and question everything you have been "taught." Begin to question why with all your beliefs.

When a Queen walks in the room - everyone stops and stares. It's respect, empowerment, a let me fix your crown type of energy that you are so drawn to you can't help but stop and stare. Queen embodiment is an attitude and confidence that every person has within them. It starts with a commitment to stand in your freaking truth. Speak what's on your mind unapologetically and know you have nothing to prove to anyone. She has a collective mindset, a vision to change the world for the better. She knows what she wants and passionately pursues it without a care of what others may say or think of her. She shows up as a leader and leads others towards queen embodiment. She is authentic and has a strong sense of her body and feminine power. So, what exactly does the Queen need for her feminine release? The sacred feminine is made up of four archetypes: the mother in North, Amazonian woman in East, lover or seductive angelic being that embodies sexuality and pleasure in South and a balanced energy bringing intuition (Medial) to West. The center archetype - Queen – represents wholeness as well as women's full potential when they are initiated deeply by embodying their true nature which is pure awareness alive and awake within an inhabited body with its instinct towards fulfilling what it means to be truly meant for her entelechy.

"I don't chase I receive what's meant to be will come to me."

The Queen can be very easy to fall into chasing after what she wants from being so passionate and driven. She can fall into masculine energy and it's one of her downfalls. The Queen archetype is both the dance and stillness, embodying opposites. She brings balance to everything with her presence as a living embodiment of paradox. The queen embodies all feminine archetypes - she's bright while also embracing shadow in herself even when it may not seem like an obvious choice.

Imagine for a moment what it would be like to live at peace with your humanity. The Queen has learned that her human conditionings can't be avoided, but they don't have the power she once gave them. When one arises in her consciousness now, instead of getting caught up and believing its story or engaging it mentally as "business-as-usual," she sits quietly until all thoughts dissolve on their own accord without any effort required from within herself whatsoever.

She also practices various methods for working through these things when prompted by life's experiences; including meditation and contemplation on impermanence - death is not an enemy but something to see clearly. She is a money magnet by nature and needs to step into that state of receiving for full emergence. As we work on embodiment of Queen energy, we need to take time to manifest and let go of the control with the how. As the Queen one of the biggest down falls is being able to release control of the situation and this is where true empowerment and magic comes into play. Rather than bound up in dualistic thinking, she has learned to hold the conflict of opposites within her own container and endure the tension until awareness pops into non-dual spaciousness. She is willing to feel all feelings because they are just a part of life.

Queenly women are strong, independent beings who wholeheartedly embrace their humanness. They serve as priestesses of the Sacred Feminine and remind us that we are both body and soul, human and divine in a woman's body. We're born into this world with three fundamental life tasks: to love ourselves fully; to honor our bodies by valuing them through good health practices like eating nutritiously which is self-care for our physical selves; nourishing others with kindness (bonded relationships), nurturing skills such as cooking or knowledge sharing (giving); feeling worthy enough not just physically but emotionally too so you can be vulnerable without fear or shame - it's about understanding yourself before being able to understand other people.

Even when uncomfortable or uncertain about what will happen next, it's worth it for that one moment where everything falls away. She also has a desire to block off sexually when she is in masculine - to step into feminine she needs to explore her sexual power and dive deeper into her own body. It keeps her joyful and energized with enthusiasm. Over the next few chapters, we will work on embodiment as a collective, manifesting techniques and self-empowerment vs. victim mentality to truly embody the archetype of the Queen. I encourage you to take your time and find what feels right for your personal practice.

Manifesting is all about becoming and believing before you see. Using archetypes, such as the Inner Queen archetype, is just a clever way to trick our brain into harnessing that powerful confident feminine energy. The Queen knows her own power–and she also knows just how important it is to receive exactly what she wants. The most beautiful thing about the queen, however? Her patience: not something many people would expect from such a powerful being! She understands that sometimes life will throw you some curveballs and it might take longer than expected for things to fall into place, but no matter what happens-it's always worth waiting until they do.

What would your life look like if you invoked your Inner Queen?

Manifesting

Archetypes are useful because they're shortcuts to accessing different types of energy. Law of Attraction is all about being aware and control the type and amount of energy you emit - for what we put out, it's always going to be drawn back in one way or another. Imagine your life like a garden: whatever seeds you plant will grow into plants that produce fruit with similar qualities as their parent's fruits – if both plants have apples on them, then so do both gardens. Archetypes can help us tap into positive energies such as love when needed most; whereas negative emotions come from our own personal experiences- which inevitably attract more negativity towards themselves. The power to consciously attract what you want into your life can be yours if you choose the energy of an archetype. The more we can co-create our lives here on earth, the better quality of life that is. It's up to each individual and their own self determination as well as willingness for change in order to create a world they want.

Know the what behind the why.

The human brain is a phenomenal thing. We can use it to manifest anything, but sometimes we're not clear on the "what" behind our desires for what we want in life. If you don't know why you want something and how that will make your life better, then of course there's no way of knowing when or where those things are coming from because they simply won't show up at all. It gets even more complicated with money since most people have an idea about so many different aspects such as time freedom (to do whatever I want), travel opportunities, etc., which brings us back around to being specific about exactly what we desire out of this situation--and having clarity over both them AND their purpose becomes important. We are all cultivating experiences, it's what we thrive for in this human form. So be as specific as possible with exactly **what** you are cultivating.

Know the why.

Do you ever wonder why the things in your life happen? When people ask me about how I stay motivated, my answer is always simple: "Know WHY you are doing the actions you do daily." When we know our motivation behind the reasons that make us strive for success and happiness, then it becomes easier to accept any sacrifices needed. We must become clear on why we want this manifestation. How will it serve our highest good? The highest good of the collective? Will it cause harm in any way?

Who Benefits?

The more people who benefit, the better. For example, I want to help as many people as possible discover their unique gifts and talents; discover just how beautiful and powerful they really are; find out what it is that makes them a master at peace and healing within life. Who benefits when you have these things happen? Who will benefit once your manifestations are fulfilled? Is it only yourself or do any other people get involved with this?

Feel all the feels.

Manifestation is the process of creating something from nothing. In this case, manifesting your desires and achieving them by tapping into emotions. For example, if you wanted to create more money in your life then you would need to tap into feelings like excitement or fearlessness when it comes time for making financial decisions such as buying stocks or investing in a business venture that could be profitable but risky at the same time. If it's joy or happiness we are cultivating, how can we experience these emotions right now at this current state in time. We must tap into the emotion as if we have already arrived. Know that anything you need is already created for us and it's only a matter of time until we open our eyes wide enough to see them within ourselves. It's just like Wayne Dyer said: "We have everything we could ever imagine at hand because nothing exists outside our own consciousness. Everything that is created in the universe is here already. We are not really creators as much as we are recombiners of everything."

Gratitude

There are many ways to be grateful in our lives, but we forget how easy it is. We can always find gratitude by changing our perspective, says Gillian Deacon from Oxford University's Department of Experimental Psychology. "It doesn't have to wait for a special occasion or go looking for something new," she writes on the American Psychological Association website. There is no prescription because all you need do is take notice and choose. Gratitude is a powerful and positive input to our mind-body system that leads us not only towards psychological well-being, but also physical wellbeing. In the simplest form of gratitude as an attitude or mood it can lead you into more creativity in your thoughts which will then result in new pathways for brain patterns. The practice of this state has even been found to change gene expression within 100 trillion cells by creating new ones with grateful thoughts alone. How awesome sauce is this?

Visualize and Meditate

Queen energy does not chase. She handles her business and then patiently waits, knowing the fruit of her labor will come when it is meant too. Take time to visualize all the details of your manifestation. Who are you with? What are you wearing? Where are you? Tap into this space daily.

LET GO

You are not running the show. It is not your business to worry about the **how.** The queen archetype knows that she doesn't have to do it all on her own and has a team by her side. She understands the worth of time so delegates tasks when possible, knowing what is meant for you will come your way if you don't go looking too hard. Release attachment to any outcome and allow it to flow effortlessly to you.

And so it is.

> If she builds networks, only to sever them at the tiniest hint of betrayal, she's a great villain. If she sees her power in ruling over others and telling them what to do, or manipulating them into it, rather than asking them because she understands their strengths and delegates accordingly—she's a villain.

As you move away from the princess archetype, your vision and intuition will grow. You'll be able to discern what is really going on in a situation – not just how it appears at first glance. Eventually, this heightened perception will make you wiser than the princess archetype with limited knowledge of the world and its workings; they can only see one dimension while you have learned to look for many more factors when trying to understand why things happen as they do. As someone who has reached adulthood but never stopped desiring goals or lost her fascination with life's possibilities (nor given up hope), all those moments where others may have doubted themselves seem like opportunities instead - ones which nurture creativity. You are a Queen, as you build your Queendom you extend your energy to others. Your deep healing power is deeply nurturing and loving in nature; the queen exudes confidence while being self-aware of her own actions. She builds up her queendom through teaching others by example what she has learned herself along life's journey with love guiding every step taken "the way home always leads back to yourself."

Self-Empowerment

Personal empowerment is about taking control of your own life and making positive decisions based on what you want. It's closely linked to attributes like self-esteem and self-confidence, but true empowerment comes when you convert intention into action. You may feel like you're on your own at times when it comes to achieving personal empowerment. But what really is the point of living if we can't share our successes, and help others achieve theirs? Empowering ourselves means empowering those around us too. When we are connected to our higher self, the cosmic crown chakra of God, it is difficult not to feel joy.

Empowerment: The process of becoming stronger and more confident, especially in controlling one's life and claiming one's rights.

When we live in harmony with that which connects us all -the universal consciousness- a sense of peace and belonging becomes part of who you are. When you're operating from your highest level -your connection with what's greater than yourself- there isn't much room for discomfort or negative emotions as everything else seems so trivial by comparison. Feeling entitled is not the same thing as feeling empowered. A person who feels entitled has a problem because they think that benefits and privileges should come to them automatically, without any work or effort on their part. On the other hand, an individual who feels empowered may have had to apply themselves for success but are able to recognize what it took from hard work, reflection and working as a collective.

I'll never forget the moment I felt permission to empower myself. My entire life, I had walked around people pleasing and saying yes to anything that came my way because of a sense of obligation--I owed everyone everything. But as an adult, not being able to feel empowered was starting to wear on me immensely; it made me less confident in who I am both inside and out while also limiting what kind of person others saw when they looked at me. I was timid and in constant fear of being "exposed" for my past. I refuse to fear my past and secrets. I know that they are the things which make me a <u>fucking queen</u>, able to connect with others who have similar experiences as well as teach them how incredible they truly are despite their flaws. I was sitting in a therapy session with Julianne and explaining how broken I was and begging her to fix me. (You think I am being dramatic, but it was really a pleading matter here.) I from the bottom of my heart thought that I was damaged goods unworthy of anything or anyone. We had just finished working through the mother wound and I read her my first letter to my dad.

> "Vulnerability is the birthplace of
> innovation, creativity and change."
> - Brene Brown

Her eyes widened and she said, "I thought this was stemmed from your mom, but this is just as deep with your dad." I explained all the ways I had gone wrong and ruined relationships, how much I owed them, then she interrupted me. "You do not owe them shit." I was taken back. I continued on my hysterical word vomit, and she looked me dead in the eyes and told me to stop. Her eyes filled up with tears. I've never met anyone more empathetic or genuine in my life. Her personality is less than fluffy, and she calls it exactly how she sees it – the good, the bad, the ugly. She's real. I appreciate that. She was silent for a moment and then told me it was time for me to "put my big girl panties on and take my power back." I was to write a declaration letter claiming my power back and releasing fear from my father's hold.

COURTNEY HANSON

Dad,

I'm 33 and for my entire life I've allowed you to control or push your perspectives on me. I've felt guilt, shame, less then and like my actions defined the rest of my life from my past. There is rarely a conversation brought up without mention of my past or how much damage and harm I have caused to so many people. Dad you are wrong. Your perception is wrong, you are bitter, you are hurt and I was a safe punching bag incapable of standing up for myself so instead I acted out. Just so you know the way you parented me and treated me as an adult was half of the reason I behaved and rebelled as I did. You never let me be my own person and when I was it was wrong or looked down upon. You called the police repeatedly on me, you called me names, you compared me to my mom, you always made me feel an inch tall. The control and lack of freedom made me feel suffocated as a teenager. I am sorry for lying in court to get away from you, but I was desperate to break free. I remember sitting in my room goal planning how to afford to move out on my 18th birthday since you wouldn't let me get a job and refused to get me a social security number. You made me incapable of any sort of self-discovery, you know all I ever wanted was for mom and you to love me. Its crippled me most of my life and I didn't even realize how much self-hate I had developed towards myself, but you know what I don't need your approval anymore. If you don't agree with a choice I make - to bad. If you think I should parent differently - I am breaking generational curses. You hate my husband, I don't care, you have no pedestal to stand on when it comes to relationships. My point is - the control ends today. If I don't like how you're speaking to me or my family, I am going to stand up for what I believe is right. Today I take my power back. I have forgiven myself and am done seeking your approval. I apologize for the hurt I've caused you, but the truth is - I didn't ruin your relationships - you did. I didn't make you lose friends - you did. I was being a selfish teenager who didn't know how to cope or think rationally because I was never allowed to feel. I no longer want to hear about your personal life - I want a healthy relationship with my dad, and I will set every boundary and love myself enough to know I deserve better. I will not play the childish games and mind fucks any more. You will no longer damage my children in any way. You have hated everyone I have ever dated; you say you will be shocked if Cameron and I work out and when you strip it all away - You taught me what a relationship was. You put down women, you were always sexist, and name called, and you put every relationship you've ever had in front of me. I stayed in shitty relationships because I felt not worthy, or I just wouldn't commit at all because I thought I didn't deserve to be loved. That I should pay my karma by being a single mom, by feeling lonely by putting myself through the pain you made me feel I put you through. I am choosing to be free every time you tell me how much money I owe you or how rottenly behaved my kids are I will immediately end the conversation. You do not know what it is like raising three young children and you do not know how to raise a child with special needs or what that feels like as a mother. You can keep your opinions to yourself. I won't deal with the snarky little remarks anymore about how you always wanted to study what I am in school but never had the opportunity.

You won't call me names anymore to attempt to hurt my feelings or put me in my place. You won't belittle me or my family. Today it all stops. All the bullshit, all the manipulation, all the guilt, all the shame - it ends here. The bondage and ties I've been held down from for so long are done. I will be free. If you want a place in my life you will be loving, kind, peaceful and civilized. The vulgar language around my children fucking stops - you will respect my boundaries. I am no longer scared of you or your threats of how you'll take things or hold money over my head. It's just stuff. I hope you heal whatever makes you bitter and learn to open your mind and see other perspectives, but it is no longer my load to carry. I forgive you and love you, but I choose to be free, healthy and happy. I no longer will live in the past with you. I am closing the door.

- Courtney

I closed the journal after reading and looked her dead in the eyes nervous as hell for her reaction. She was about to jump out of her chair over the brown desk and high five me. "You didn't sound like a five-year-old. You just empowered yourself girl, you just took your freaking power back." Every other letter I had written to my mom or dad I subconsciously would raise my voice about five octaves and go into this scared little girl voice. Timid and terrified. Her exact words "You just sounded like a bad ass bitch." It hit me right there. **I AM A BAD ASS BITCH.** I am not my past I AM HERE. Right freaking here, right freaking now. I can fly and can love people from afar. I am not tied to toxic behavior. I have chosen to stop it myself but can choose who is in my life?! Mind…Blown…Queendom foundation laid.

Embrace:
hold (someone) closely in one's arms, especially as a sign of affection.
accept or support (a belief, theory, or change)
willingly and enthusiastically.
noun
an act of holding someone closely in one's arms.
an act of accepting or supporting something willingly or enthusiastically.

"Most people don't listen with the intent to understand.
they listen with the intent to reply."

Holding Space

A queendom is not run by one person. The Queen energy knows how to delegate and thrives when working in sync with others. The act of holding space is not just a beautiful gift to others, but it can be an opportunity for self-exploration. When we hold space with another person, there's more room in our hearts that allows the other individual to explore themselves and their emotions without feeling judged or uncomfortable. It really does make us grow as individuals because when someone reaches out to you at such times, they are offering up something intensely private about themself which shows how much faith they have in your character and capacity as human beings. It creates a sense of safety for everyone involved. Holding space is a spiritual practice within itself. It brings us back to the collective and knowing we are all interconnected. Holding space is a practice of accepting others without judgment. It does not mean taking up personal space or being critical; it means staying open and receptive to what's happening around you, wherever that may be.

To learn how to hold space, it's important to let go of your ego. One step on the path is learning how you would react if someone else were being spoken down about in a public forum by listening for thoughts and feelings that arise when this scenario plays out inside of us. The less we judge ourselves or others, the easier it becomes for our egos do not get involved with situations which can cause division between people who are trying to come together under one roof while sharing their truth; holding space open authentically through love instead of fear. The practice of holding space allows me to trust that the person I am with has all the answers they need. It's about creating a safe environment so people can get in touch with themselves and their feelings, which creates profound insights into who we are as individuals.

I always had this need to know instead of the need to ask. I would get anxious if I couldn't be in control – like to the point I would feel the need to interrupt someone so I wouldn't lose my thought because it was just oh so important. When I began letting go, profound healing happened within my personal life by allowing exploration without feeling like a victim. While in a yoga training, I was given guidance from a mentor to allow the experience of exploration rather than feeling like it is necessary for me to have all the answers. He explained the power of asking questions and just listening. "If you don't know what to say, ask another question." The Zen Peacemakers Foundation runs "Bearing Witness" retreats where the sole practice is to sit with others in their suffering and allow our discomfort to arise. Krishna Das, who sometimes attends these retreats, describes it to "clean your heart of fear." He explains: "When you bear witness to another in their pain or suffering, many emotions arise but the goal isn't indulging them; rather we're supposed to recognize them and then process through them until we can be present for comfort." Deepak Chopra is a spiritual guru and author who believes that self-awareness leads to growth. "Whether it's awareness of the body, awareness of your relationships, or even just being aware how you feel when someone says something hurtful" he explains "I think the key to transforming your life comes from being able to recognize yourself." When you are in an environment, consider not just what is there but also how you can embrace it with your awareness. Explore the physical space by noticing where things and people are located as well as their meaning to one another; explore emotional spaces through conversations that flow freely or a sense of shared responsibility.

Listen.

One of the most important things to do when talking with someone is listening. When we're in a discussion, it can be easy for our minds to wander off and think about what we want to say next. This may not allow us as much time or opportunity for them if they are trying express themselves fully; instead, try focusing on understanding their side first without worrying too much about your own response until later - this will help you get more out of any conversation that you have together. If your mind is wandering during the conversation, focus on repeating back to them what *they said* instead of what *you want* to say.

Detach from the situation.

It's human nature – we want to be in the mix of everything. A friend is telling us a story and our subconscious is conjuring up all the experiences we personally have been through and can relate. We put ourselves in their shoes and talk about our experiences instead of listening to their personal story. It's always easier to understand something when you can relate it back to yourself. Resist the urge of inserting your own experiences in this situation and focus on being there for that person instead. Allow them to experience their own truth instead of forcing yours upon them.

Allow flow.

When we give someone space to be vulnerable, they may not know what's going to come up. It can be complicated and confusing or even conflicting so instead of fighting the feelings that want to come out for them, encourage it and allow room for the other person by giving positive reassurance when these emotions surface. It was a late summer evening, and I felt so small underneath the grandeur of the mountains. The only compared feeling was like a speck of dirt on an otherwise perfectly white sheet of paper. The sun set perfectly across Lake Tahoe, it was so orange and bright that the reflection shimmered across the mountain tops. As it disappeared behind me in my rearview mirror I began to sob. It had been three months since I started sobriety- this time being with absolute clarity. Tears streamed down my cheeks from sheer joy at finally feeling alive again; The golden light of dusk seemed like an epiphany-the proof that life goes on no matter what we do or how much it may seem otherwise at times. It made me feel grateful for space, Mother Earth's embrace, and even the chance to experience these emotions fully. The first time I was conscious of my emotions flowing, it felt like a huge release. I had never allowed myself to feel emotions before that moment that weren't centered around drama. How much freer I can be if only give myself permission from within.

- I am a masterpiece.
- Creative energy surges through me and brings me to new brilliant ideas.
- I am abundance.
- My ability to conquer my challenges is limitless.
- I am forgiving.
- I am multifaceted.
- I am fearless.
- I am free.
- I am worthy of the purest love.
- I am compassionate.
- I forgive myself and set myself free.
- What I focus on grows. I choose wisely.
- I am the queen of my life.

The Sage

The Sacred Sage is the most powerful archetype of wisdom. She takes all that has been learned and gifts it to others so they may find their own truth, as she did. For this to happen, the sage first must reach a place of understanding her inner masculine and feminine energy in balance together - without either one overpowering or suppressing the other. The wise woman within each person knows what will lead them into growth both personally and spiritually; therefore, we should be able to trust ourselves enough not only listen when necessary but also speak our truths with confidence. The sage is calm and collected, but she has a deep understanding of men. In a love relationship, the Sage archetype needs their partner to be stable and predictable. They are looking for commitment in order to build comfort with someone special. The person they end up dating should also appreciate them for being thoughtful, but it is important that this doesn't come at the expense of social awareness because Sages enjoy playing to strengths more than anything else. She understands the masculine side to femininity in humans as well as what it means for them individually. Men are often misunderstood because they have this duality that goes unnoticed by many people who only focus on women's needs; however, with her insight into both sides of life she can be more empathetic than most other couples would ever dream possible which leads to an intimate relationship where there is mutual respect. The Sacred Sage is the embodiment of balance, wisdom and understanding. She guides you in dark times with her grace and creativity that transforms darkness into light. Her immense presence allows for a deeper connection to our intuition which helps us understand others on their deepest levels without judgement or discrimination; she sees things from all angles at once while we're caught up in drama! The sacred sage integrates each aspect of human existence: physicality, emotionality, rationalization and spirituality- always with love as it's foundation. She can sense energy, whether consciously or unconsciously. Her intuition will let her know when something feels off in a room. Carl Jung believed that the sage archetype could take many different forms in our lives. The most common form is a teacher who plays an integral role on the hero's journey from start to finish, and this includes both people as well as other symbols like insights, dreams or life lessons learned. The sage is a wise older woman who helps the hero in his quest to find himself. They offer measured advice and guidance, letting the hero choose their path towards destiny while still giving them help on where they should go next. The sage archetype is one of the most important archetypes in personal development because it seeks truth and enlightens our path to individuation. It implies asking questions to self so that we may understand ourselves better, generate insights into life, discover new perspectives, and find actionable solutions. The sage archetype is a powerful, strategic role that women have been embodying for centuries. The sage's virtues are strategy and emotional objectivity. She has discipline too: she can think of outcomes before they happen. The sage archetype has the burning desire to understand all mysteries of life. They are curious and eager learners who want to share what they learn with others in order rid them of ignorance, fear, and confusion.

> "One does not become enlightened by imagining figures of light, but by making the darkness conscious."
> - Carl Jung

Greatest Strengths: The Sage is a deep thinker who loves to learn. The Sage's favorite subjects are ones that will help her in life and those with social implications. Her thirst for knowledge has made it her goal to know everything there is about the world, as well-rounded of an education as possible being very important to the sage personality type. Though she may not be interested in learning things irrelevant to her interests, if something new comes up he always finds herself wanting more information on what this topic entails so that she can have a better understanding of it all. She is curious and highly intuitive.

The relationship between the Crone and Sage

The Sage is a wise woman, the Crone an old one. The two are related archetypes and often overlap in their purview- they both carry wisdom across cultures and generations alike without prejudice or bias for either age of life. A Sage is not a spell-caster, but rather the carrier of wisdom about life choices. The Crone too, carries female wisdom in the form of motherly advice and maternal care that cannot be matched by any other energy type. A sage will know when you need them more than anything else because they are able to counsel without conditions or personal agendas which can make for an unbiased perspective on your situation whereas a witch may bring her own agenda into discussion with little regard as to what best suits you personally. A wise woman also known as "the crone" has been seen throughout history carrying feminine knowledge in a more mystical way. Wisdom is often confused with intelligence, but the two are not interchangeable. While wisdom comes from a deep knowledge of something and can come from sources other than books, intelligence is frequently dependent upon studying to acquire it.

The Shadow

The sage archetype is associated both with wisdom and knowledge. Yet, there are two different aspects of the sage's approach to life that we can't ignore: attachment and detachment. The shadow side of this wise woman may be seen in situations where she becomes dogmatic or critical when confronted by new ideas--even her own! On the other hand, as a non-attached being who sees material things more objectively than those caught up in them, it might seem like sages have little interest in society at all when they avoid forming bonds with its members--but one thing which distinguishes these individuals from their peers is an allegiance to abstract principles such as truth (as opposed to social rules). In the shadow of sage, we tend to be critical and make judgments about our thoughts, feelings, actions. We label them as good or bad and right or wrong. Despite the need for physical activity, Sages can still be a bit lacking in terms of health. This is because they tend to focus more on learning and intellect than exercise which takes away some time from leading an active lifestyle. Meditation is an excellent means of self-discovery. By meditating, you can better understand yourself and how your personality fits into the world at large. (At an emotional health level Sage's need this in their life.) With it's important that sages incorporate daily exercises into their routine so as not lose out physically. Sage's can project themselves in a light of arrogance by looking down upon others for their lack of knowledge but are stubborn when it comes to opinions which might conflict with theirs. Despite being rich in both intelligence and experience they struggle immensely when taking action.

When to call on her

Your mind is in a tizzy. You feel as if there's no clear path forward, and you're desperate for information that can help make sense of things. To become a sage the first thing we must do is learn to unlearn. To embody this archetype, you need to be willing and open-minded enough any life experiences that allow you see things with new perspectives. There are many ways to figure out your true passions and connect with the wisdom within yourself. A great place to start is by asking: what do you want? Where can I find my platform, or voice so that it stands for me rather than others? When we tap into this self-awareness, along with bravery as a result of experiences gained from overcoming obstacles in life - anything becomes possible. Just like explorers are driven to discover new lands, sages drive themselves towards self-discovery. However instead of heading out into the unknown outside and discovering new landscapes, these people invest their time in looking within for answers that will help them uncover who they truly are. All their wisdom and power are useless if they don't act. This type of person possesses a lot of information about the world but isn't motivated to act on it. In this chapter, you'll learn all about taking action - specifically how to keep up your momentum. Most sages are curious about the why behind momentum and action. To understand how to apply the Law of Attraction, it's important to know why we must act for our thoughts and feelings about something manifest. Using spiritual laws as a guide is not only applicable when trying to create an abundance mentality; they can help us operate from wholeness with unconditional love so that we attract what serves our highest good without judgment or expectation on how things should be. Many of us have worked to disconnect from our bodies over the years to tame, control and separate ourselves. We must release this stuck energy within us so we can reconnect with our bodies and feel at peace within them. This allows the vibration of Her to rise fully inside each one of us.

12 Spiritual Laws

1. THE LAW OF DIVINE ONENESS

The law of divine oneness connects the whole human race and nature to one infinite energy source. When we give happiness, we receive equal kindness in return because this is how balance and stability are kept with the Universe. Everything is connected through vibrational energy. Every atom inside of you is connected in some way to the rest of universe. This means that everything we do has a ripple effect and impacts the collective. Energy can't be created or destroyed, but only changes from one form to another. This means we interact with everything inside the universe through our vibrations, including other people. We are consciously unaware of how much communication takes place in this way; it turns out that only 7% of what we communicate verbally actually matters. 38% comes from tone and body language, while 55% comes from non-verbal signals like energetic presence or a person's "vibe." The universe is a self-organizing system that responds to our thoughts and feelings. The divine oneness connects everything in the universe, so if you desire good things, it's only natural, they'll come your way. But what exactly does this mean? Our desires, beliefs and behaviors will be aligned when we think positively because positive energies are drawn into our lives. When you speak or act with negative energy nothing, but bad experiences can happen; like attracts like.

2. LAW OF VIBRATION

The Law of Vibration states that everything in the universe is constantly moving, which we refer to as vibration. Everything vibrates at different speeds or frequencies depending on its makeup and characteristics. The waves of energy never rest. They move up and down like little ripples in a pond on top of water, always moving back and forth rather than staying still or standing still. These are also known as frequencies and vibrations. Everything vibrates at a certain frequency, and therefore we can only hear certain sounds or see certain colors. As the vibration increases, one perceives lower-pitched sounds until they become high-pitched, and we no longer can hear them. The same goes for colors we start at darkest red (low vibration) and flow through the rainbow until the color reaches its peak to ultraviolet or infrared which is beyond our range of vision. (Violet is also the color of the crown chakra.) In the Fifth Dimension, things like thoughts and emotions are considered to only be frequency. There is no meaning assigned to anything there because everything can change depending on what level it's at. By aligning our bodies and behaviors with source, we can cultivate a sense of inner harmony. We do this by choosing options that are aligned with the way in which source works within us. We can create internal harmony through alignment between our body and behavior. By doing so, we're able to maintain consistent patterns as they relate to how spiritual forces work inside ourselves. When you feel negative emotions, your frequency is lower than it would be if you felt positive emotions. This means that people with low frequencies are attracting other individuals who have similarly low vibrations and vice versa. The Law of Attraction states the higher vibration attracts like energy because we all exist on a spectrum between high vibrational beings to very little or no consciousness at all. The amazing part of this all is you have the power to choose.

3. LAW OF CORRESPONDENCE

"As above, so below; as below, so above."

The Law of Correspondence is a law that can be difficult to comprehend, but very interesting and deep when learned. It's directly related to the foundational Law of Divine Oneness. The key idea here is that patterns repeat throughout the universe (the macrocosm), like prominent ones on an even smaller scale (microcosms). The Law of Correspondence is that our current reality reflects what's going on inside us. This basically means, for example, when we encounter problems in relationships it can show us something about ourselves and prompt healing within. Life will always mirror our inner state, so if we feel bad about ourselves the world around us feels chaotic. If at peace with oneself then life flows smoothly and harmoniously without any problems or disturbances to deal with. Life is not happening *to you*; life is simply a reflection *of you*.

4. LAW OF ATTRACTION

> "Watch your thoughts, they become your words; watch your words, they become your actions; watch your actions, they become your habits; watch your habits, they become your character; watch your character, it becomes your destiny."

The Law of Attraction states that positive attracts positive and negative attracts negative. With this law, we are like magnets with thoughts attracting what is in our minds into the physical world. We must know exactly what it is that we want or else there will be no result for manifestation through thought alone because you must focus only on positivity when applying The Law of Attraction. It's a relatively simple principle but one which can prove difficult if not applied correctly over time since its application changes from person-to-person according to their own experiences and limiting beliefs.

5. LAW OF INSPIRED ACTION

The law of inspired action tells us that we need to take physical actions in order to manifest our goals. We are spiritual beings having a human experience on this planet, and so taking the right type of action is required by our bodies for manifestation. Thoughts and visualization are forms of ritualistic behavior, but they do not have any real effect without an accompanying act. Inspired action comes with an electric and spirited energy that makes one feel invigorated. It is naturally flowing and easy for you. When a nudge hits, it feels like your body knows what to do without thinking too much about the next step. To differentiate between an ego-based action and a Universe-inspired one, start by checking in with your intention. Is there selfless intent behind what you want to do? Does it bring value or opportunity for someone else? Or is this about seeking approval from other people because of the reaction that they will have when you make them happy? If yes, then it's coming from your ego not the universe! When you allow something to happen, inspired action comes. When looking for answers and trying to figure out how things will play out before they even occur, ego-based actions arise. Inspired action feels good because it allows the natural flow of life without attachment or reliance on any specific outcome; therefore, there is no fear involved in doing what needs done when inspiration strikes. Ego-based actions are based in fear.

6. LAW OF PERPETUAL TRANSMUTATION OF ENERGY

Everything in the universe is constantly evolving or fluctuating at an energetic level. A thought predates every action with thoughts themselves having the power to ultimately manifest itself as physical reality via energy moving from one state into another. This law states that all forms have a tendency towards change and materialization — often referred by many as "the process". When you have a thought, idea or emotional connection this energy within your body takes on form such as images before it finally becomes something more solid like an object, we can touch around us, aka matter.

Perpetual – Never ending.
Transmutation – Action of changing state.
Energy – everything that is around us.

If you are unaware of what it means to be poor, or live-in poverty, would this area still exist? No. Because the idea – your thought surrounding being poorer than others - doesn't come into fruition because our infinite cannot be contained within a finite state. If we desire abundance yet feel unworthy due to self-doubt and insecurity; eventually we will sabotage ourselves since subconsciously these messages tell us not to do something which can further progress oneself towards success. We have an endless power as human beings when creating change through thoughts and things that emit energy such as objects around us. 80,000 thoughts race through our minds every day. 90% of them are repeated on a regular basis and tend to be negative when they appear unannounced. If you don't want these controlling thought patterns that negatively influence your mindset in the future, it's essential that you're conscious of their presence now so as not to miss out on opportunities for happiness and success later down the road. To do this successfully, we must remove any negativity surrounding us by replacing those limiting beliefs with positivity rather than accepting what may seem like fate or destiny at first glance because if we continue having such thoughts about lack, fear etc., then more energy will follow suit which means even more feelings of discontentment can creep up too. There is a correlation between Spiritual Growth and the Law of Perpetual Transmutation of Energy. The more you grow spiritually, the less energy will be wasted on things that do not matter in life such as negative relationships or materialistic possessions.

7. THE LAW OF CAUSE AND EFFECT

The law of cause and effect is the idea that every event in our lives has a specific reason or causes behind it. It's often referred to as 'the iron law of the universe'. The premise suggests that everything happens for a reason; there are no accidents, we live in an orderly world governed by natural laws. Karma is a law of cause and effect that states every action, positive or negative, has an equal reaction. Karma is a Sanskrit word that means action, work, or deed. It refers to the sum of all deeds one has done either in this life or previous lives. Nothing is a coincidence; everything has its roots based on time and place of events that occurred before it happened to bring about this moment we're experiencing now or any other moments from past experiences which eventually made us who we are today.

> "Every cause has its effect; every effect has its cause.
> Everything happens according to law, chance if but a name
> For law not recognized; there are many planes of causation,
> But nothing escapes the law."
> - The Kybalion

8. THE LAW OF COMPENSATION

What you give, so shall you receive. The law of compensation is important because whatever we do will result in a level of reward equal to what the deed entails. It doesn't matter if it's physical or psychological; every action produces an outcome that returns as its opposite: hatred creates love and vice versa, resentment brings joy while joylessness causes pain – everything has balance by way of influence on our emotional state which ultimately affects how well we're able to serve ourselves and others around us through compassion. When you understand that every action has a reaction, the world will start to reward you. Often, we associate compensation with money or material things. When we talk about this universal law it covers all forms of blessings in return for your contribution to the world regardless of how much they are worth monetarily speaking and without any sort of bias towards one thing over another. The crux is whatever good comes back into your life right now is equal proportionally what was put out there by yourself. Nothing more than what came at first can be expected later on unless an adjustment occurs somewhere along the way but even then, still no less contingent upon its own merit when eventually able to balance itself properly again.

9. LAW OF RELATIVITY

The Law of Relativity states that nothing is good or bad until you compare it to something else. A person, emotion, action isn't judged as being "good" or "bad," but rather compared with others around them. This law teaches us to put our problems into perspective by comparing them with others. It doesn't matter how bad we perceive things are - there's always someone who has it worse off than you do. So, everything is relative and that needs to be kept in mind. Most people would think that everything in life is just as it seems, but they are wrong. Life has no meaning until you compare things to something else or give them a certain perspective.

> "In form, you are and will always be inferior to some, superior to others. In essence, you are neither inferior nor superior to anyone. True self-esteem and true humility arise out of that

realization. In the eyes of the ego, self-esteem and humility are contradictory. In truth, they are one and the same"
-Eckart Tolle

10. LAW OF POLARITY

The law of polarity states that everything has two poles: good and evil, love and hate. It is what allows us to appreciate the world around us-the positive as well as the negative aspects. The difference between the extremes of one thing is called polarity, but there are degrees. There aren't any absolutes because this law states that these opposites are simply different manifestations of a single idea and cold doesn't stop being cold at some point; it's all on the same pole! Think about how every adversity carries with it an equivalent or greater benefit; for example, you learn from your mistakes so they're not in vain. Newton's Third Law of Motion teaches us those forces come in pairs: negative and positive, action and reaction. You can not only nurture certain energies within yourself, but also use the law of polarity to draw other energy towards you like a magnet. When we talk about polarity, it is often confused with duality. The two words sound similar and are very easy to mix up when used in everyday conversations or writings. However, polarity means that the opposite poles of something come together as one whole unit rather than just having a single pole manifest while another suppressed like what is found in duality. This concept can be seen throughout nature where there exists Yin and Yang which represent opposites coming together as not only complementary but necessary forces for life on earth to exist properly such as light being essential for dark, order needed for chaos.

11. LAW OF RHYTHM

The Law of Rhythm is focused on movement and states that all things come in cycles. Everything in existence is caught up in a dance. A constant swaying, flowing and swinging back and forth between right to left or growing to dying.

"Everything flows, out and in; everything has its tides; all things rise and fall; the pendulum-swing manifests in

everything; the measure of the swing to the right is the measure of the swing to the left; rhythm compensates."
-The Kybalion

The law of rhythm is like the ocean; it's a constant state of ebb and flow. Sometimes we're on an upswing, sometimes our lows can be low, but this is just what happens to us when following our biorhythm. By recognizing where we are in that moment--up or down-we have more agency over how things play out rather than being pushed wherever they go without much control.

12. LAW OF GENDER

The Law of Gender has nothing to do with your sex. It refers to the two major types of energy, yin and yang. This is like anima (feminine) and animus (masculine). We must find a way to balance these energies for us be happy authentically within our lives. Feminine energy is very giving, receptive and passive. It likes to guide itself inwardly and intuitively rather than act outwardly like masculine energy does. Masculine energy makes up our conscious mind as it's the power of will, determination and determined thinking. Each personality trait has its own value but together they make a complete person so one should not be neglected over another because both sides need to work hand by hand if you want your life journey full of successes on all ends. The Law of Gender states that every seed takes time to germinate, and its resulting physical form or results are a product of the right timing. We want everything NOW – we want results yesterday - but nature is part of a cycle where patience will get us much further in our process than impatience ever could.

Understanding Polar Energies

The sage archetype is an example of the balance between yin and yang energy. Yin represents the earth, while Yang symbolizes heaven. Both oppose yet complement each other, causing one to be dependent on another for existence—yin-yang translates to "dark-bright". The sun is Shiva the moon is Shakti. This life force energy exists within all living things including human beings; it reflects our feminine side that balances against a masculine aspect in every person's psyche or personality structure--it can also manifest as duality when we must deal with good versus evil forces in our everyday lives.

The first reference to yin & yang dates to 700 B.C., in the I Ching or Book of Changes, one of China's most iconic works of literature. The dynamic between these two forces is said to be responsible for all changes: Yang represents energy from heaven and Yin symbolizes movement on earth; they are considered opposites that create each other through their existence together as cause and effect. Yin energy is the passive, feminine side of this polarity. It is associated with, darkness, earth and water. In the body yin feels cool or cold and heavy.

Excess yin may express itself through dry skin, slowed pulse rate, lethargy/ fatigue overall feeling tiredness all over, so an individual becomes immobile for long periods of time not really caring about anything. Yang energy refers to active masculine qualities such as air, fire, activity, and expansion in our world. This can be expressed by hot tingling sensations, excessive expression and would include things like dried out skin, accelerated heartbeat, irritability and restlessness. To reach enlightenment, one must unite the masculine and feminine principles.

Shiva is a symbol of consciousness, while Shakti represents power and energy. Shiva and Shakti are two sides of the same coin, one is female while the other is male. Each side represents a primal power that comes together as all-in-one divine consciousness.

In many pictures these two forces come in different shapes, but they always share similar features such as both being half an image each - Parvati on the left often depicted with feminine qualities and Shiva on right depicting masculine ones. Energy and consciousness are both necessary to cause anything in the universe. Energy alone cannot do much, but together with consciousness it can create richly complex systems like life on earth. In turn, without energy there is not enough "oomph" for a force such as gravity or electromagnetism that affects how everything moves through space-time; however, by itself it's just potential until something else changes its state of being whether into motion or shape (e.g., lightening).

Consciousness lay dormant within all things when they're still at their most basic level: atoms/molecules/energy whizzing around aimlessly waiting for other forces (like electricity) to give them purposeful direction so then they may interact meaningfully with each. Our world has been flooded with masculine energy and a lack of feminine energy which is why the rise in feminine energy is so important. To create balance, we need to understand that yin (the female principle) and Yang represent the basic building blocks of male/female energies on Earth. This isn't just about gender roles but instead speaks to our overall outlooks as well as how we view others- it's all connected. Yin represents nourishing nurturing principles while Yang shows up often for things like structure and boundaries. The earth has suffered too long from an excess dominance through masculinity without sufficient nurturance or creation coming into play by the power of feminine energy. The masculine likes to "do."

The feminine craves just being. In order to begin nurturing your feminine energy, one of the best ways is by remembering to slow down. Taking breaks from our busy lives and allowing ourselves time for rest is important because it allows us to awaken our own power and strength within while also shedding whatever no longer serves us- which could be a taboo topic in society today. We should honor our cycles as sacred rather than making them into something shameful or dirty, we can use these times as an opportunity where we reset ourselves with some much-needed personal reflection too.

How am I using my voice?
_____
_____
_____
_____
_____

What do I want in life?
_____
_____
_____
_____
_____

Why do I want this?
_____
_____
_____
_____
_____

Athena – Goddess of Wisdom and Craft

The woman with the qualities of Athena is a keen strategist who can easily distinguish between emotions and the task at hand. She usually prefers male company to female, so she may often experience kinship issues with other women. This woman will be poised for power and could potentially empower society on a political, intellectual or creative level. Athena women are drawn towards successful men, typically heroes. According to the author of Athena Woman, an important part in understanding a woman's personality is realizing that no two people are exactly alike. In fact, she argues that there are four distinct stages and types: Aphrodite women who love beauty; Artemis women who value independence; Hestia women whose priority it is family life; and then Athena which was what interested me most because this type has difficulty living spontaneously or empathizing with other people's experiences. However, while reading I realized how every person may be similar, but they all have their own unique traits as well. For example, when talking about empathy toward others some can understand someone else's perspective very easily whereas for another person it might not come so easy at first glance according to their own personal experiences in life.

Athena was the daughter of Zeus, birthed without a mother and emerging as an adult from his forehead. Being favored by her father, she had power over other goddesses such as Aphrodite who could not dominate Athena or violate her like many others would try to do. With birds being associated with this war goddess including owls which became famous for representing Athens itself due to its own symbols throughout history; Athena is also associated snakes. It is said that Medusa was once a beautiful priestess of Athena who broke her vows. Outraged, the goddess turned her into an ugly hag with writhing snakes for hair and greenish skin.

Occupations associated with Athena include academia, architecture, business and security. She is also known for her skills in diplomacy; she was the goddess of peace after all! The Greek Goddess of wisdom can often be found acting as a mentor to many people who need help understanding things like philosophy or technology. Athena, the Greek goddess of wisdom and warfare is compassionate in her pursuit to know truth. However, she has a healthy fear of deceit which can make her skeptical about people around them; once they lose trust in someone it's unlikely that their relationship will be restored.

"Only-begotten, noble race of Zeus, blessed and fierce, who joyest in caves to rove: O warlike Pallas, whose illustrious kind, ineffable, and effable we find: magnanimous and famed, the rocky height, and groves, and shady mountains thee delight: in arms rejoicing, who with furies dire and wild the souls of mortals dost inspire. Gymnastic virgin of terrific mind, dire Gorgon's bane, unmarried, blessed, kind: mother of arts, impetuous; understood as fury by the bad, but wisdom by the good. Female and male, the arts of war are thine, O much-formed, She-Dragon, inspired divine: over the Phlegraean Giants, roused to ire, thy coursers driving with destructive dire. Tritogeneia, of splendid mien, purger of evils, all-victorious queen. Hear me, O Goddess, when to thee I pray, with supplicating voice both night and day, and in my latest hour give peace and health, propitious times, and necessary wealth, and ever present be thy votaries aid, O much implored, art's parent, blue-eyed maid."

— **Orphic Hymn 32 to Athena (Greek hymns C3rd B.C. to 2nd A.D.)**

Breaking free of suppression

If we want to live a healthy life, it is important for us to step into our stillness. Every woman's expression of the divine feminine is unique and beautiful in its own way. We spend our lives either fighting against what is expected of us or embracing it without enjoying the process. Instead, we should live our own truth and not follow a different path just for the sake of acceptance from others. We will never connect to our highest selves from the space of "I'm not enough." You cannot awaken your Divine Feminine Energy until you learn to accept and love yourself just the way you are.

Dhar·ma

/ˈdärmə/ **The eternal and inherent nature of reality, regarded in Hinduism as a cosmic law underlying right behavior and social order.**

(Buddhism) the nature of reality regarded as a universal truth taught by the Buddha; the teaching of Buddhism. An aspect of truth or reality.

We all try to pretend that the dominant masculine within us is whole and complete on its own, but it can't be. Like I said at the beginning of this chapter, our divine feminine and masculine were created as two halves of a whole from which we are born into existence. When you feel profoundly happy, think about the crystal-clear purpose that lives in your heart. Think about how to impact the world by living out this clarity of focus and letting it guide you. Your Higher Self is the part of you that transcends your physical form and contains unlimited potential. It excites you with inspiration, guides you through intuition, and teaches you via insight to make better choices in life. She is unlimited and eternal.

In a state of separation from Higher Selves, it may seem like an impossible task to connect with them. But this is not true at all! In fact, you are connected by something more than just the physical self - your energetic consciousness-self. All though we live in a physical realm the energy may feel lost, but it is always present within us. When you inevitably experience some sort of trauma within your life, it is your choice whether to become upset and live in a state of unhappiness or observe the situation without judgment from within - from a state of pure awareness. This ability that helps you remain calm amidst chaos is known as Higher Self.

This is your intuition and knowing - any time you receive a feeling or premonition that cannot be explained, it means your Higher Self wants to communicate with you. Your dreams are the only time when your brain is relaxed enough to still function like during waking hours, but you're in a completely different state of consciousness.

Your Higher Self speaks with you in your dream state – the realm of your subconscious. That's when all mental constructs strip away and seize to control reality. It's known as REM (Rapid eye movement) where brain activity is active like during waking hours, but body completely relaxes instead. During your dream state, you connect to the Higher Self every night to obtain clues and gain insight on yourself. So how do we begin the decoding process of our subconscious through a dream state? The answer to this question can be found in understanding that dreams are symbolic representations of oneself and their deeper thoughts.

In a dream, I was running around in panic trying to protect my children from the villain destroying our city. The villain used carbon monoxide as gas and explosions filled every corner of where we lived. My husband worked during this time so it seemed like there would be no way out for us unless we boarded an airplane that happened to appear while avoiding all these tragic events happening beneath us. I was alone and had my children to protect. We boarded the plane and beneath us watched everything burn down. I held my crying children and felt this deep sense of despair and pain. As I awoke from the dream, my body was still in shock. Even hours later, when waking up to a new day and getting ready for work; this wasn't just any dream that could be forgotten by breakfast time - it had an impact on me. And so as soon as I opened my eyes within seconds of awakening...I began writing down everything about what took place during those vivid moments before being catapulted out of sleep into reality once again: The explosions were filled with fiery hellish flames! It reminded me of Dante's Inferno – this carbon monoxide smell permeating throughout my senses. My body still felt adrenaline flowing through it like electricity, it all felt so real.

My morning meditation yielded some interesting results. I began decoding this dream and couldn't believe the events that occurred in my subconsciousness. I pulled my dream book out to search the meaning of carbon monoxide. This is what it said: dreaming about carbon monoxide poisoning represents how negative elements can make their way into your mind without you even realizing, symbolizing an unconscious fear or feelings that a relationship could be too easily contaminated and negatively altered. I went deeper in - running away from fire means you are hiding from something, an event, situation or someone. To run away from fire also indicates your stress, anxiety and insecurities. You tend to easily panic even the slightest circumstance because of your fear that everything will go wrong for you all at once if it isn't going right already.

My highest self-had to communicate with me in my current life situation. What was I trying to tell myself? My oldest child is still dealing with a lot of the trauma he had faced from his early years. He often expresses and externalizes hate towards me, my husband, as well as his siblings because I will not leave them or divorce him. Questions like "when are you going to leave" started arising more frequently. I was heartbroken but noticed a pattern of protective mama bear to loyal wife. I myself on this healing journey could not distinguish the difference between where my loyalty should lie; inside, I would get mad at my husband and start mentally planning our divorce; it was affecting how I treated everyone around me so much that even in dreams, there were signs of self-sabotage! I felt like I couldn't do anything right within my relationships, so to feel better about myself and make a change for the future I placed all of my time into work.

The wrong or right button seemed hazy.

During meditation, I came to the realization that I had fallen off heart-centered parenting. Subconsciously, my resentment for how chaotic life has been caused me to hold everyone else responsible except myself. As a result, instead of empathizing we were all on this journey together as a family trying to heal from trauma and grief - which is what we all needed in our lives at this time -- I became snappy towards them when they did not meet expectations or follow through immediately after asking something. This was my body trying to tell me that I needed more balance in life - My soul was telling me to slow down and come back home.

Every single character in our dreams represents ourselves. For example, when we dream about the person who was present during a certain time of life, this is how your Higher Self tells you that there are some events from then you haven't learned from yet. The nightmare scenarios also represent fears to be released through nightmares – these draw attention because they might mean something more serious than just fear itself is present.

Dreams are the messages from a deeper part of our minds, and so we need to analyze them in order to gain wisdom. In our psyche, there are 3 phases: the conscious phase (our normal waking state), repressed unconsciousness (where we keep memories that still affect us today but we have trouble remembering because they may be too shocking or painful to deal with directly) and finally archetypes. Jung believed dreams reveal these different aspects of ourselves which is why it's important for us all to understand them better. It's like the part of you that makes your heart pound, but it is not available to conscious thought.

Conscious Mind (1% of total psyche)
Subconscious Mind (5% of total psyche)
Unconscious Mind (94% of the total psyche)

Some dreams are more intentional than others. Our higher self gives us messages to help guide our energy in life, and it uses animals or symbols that the unconscious mind is familiar with so we can understand what they mean. By dismissing these visions and dreams, we are missing out on the valuable guidance they can provide.

Instead of sleeping through your dreams, start writing them down. Dream journaling is a great way to learn more about yourself and your subconscious. Start by keeping it beside you when you sleep, you won't forget because everything will be right next to where you lay your head down.

Your higher self and spirit often try to get your attention with signs in the physical world, which can help you connect with your soul's wisdom. These signs can be visual like ladybugs or birds found in unusual or significant places, they could also be sounds like a special song playing at exactly the right moment that invokes memories of times past; scents such as food, flowers or cologne are also common. Regardless of what we call it, our deepest and most Divine essence is the Higher Self. In various spiritual traditions throughout history, this has been called many things including Soul or Christ-consciousness. The Higher Self remains unchanged regardless of any name assigned to it by different religions around the world.

When we resist life, it's like trying to push against a wall. When our thoughts are not in line with the truth of what is happening around us--the result is that there will be negative feelings and emotions until eventually those walls cave down on top of you whether physically or mentally. Non-resistance doesn't mean being a doormat (it's important to create boundaries and say no). It honors reality – when your mind aligns itself with this philosophy toward life, ultimately access lies within reaching your Higher Self more easily as well by allowing everything—including yourself–to flow freely through things without resistance from either side.

Mirror work is a profound healing modality. This method was originally developed by Louise Hay to get in touch with the inner self, and it helps us develop our relationship with others as well as ourselves.

Go to the bathroom or living room and look at yourself in a mirror. Hold gentle eye contact for five minutes, like you would with any friend who is telling an interesting story.

Now take ten minutes to write about what came up for you. Maybe it was awkward, maybe you were resistant or uncomfortable, maybe your mind wandered away from the task at hand. Whatever comes to mind just let it flow.

_____
_____
_____
_____
_____
_____
_____
_____
_____
_____
_____
_____
_____
_____
_____
_____
_____
_____
_____
_____

I come to you with wisdom and learning as well as teaching. I fear ignorance, or that others will see me this way. You don't need to be nervous about what you know—you have the tools necessary for proceeding with confidence and courage! The shadow of a judge is someone who uses their power over others while simultaneously elevating themselves above them; true power does not need validation by any means.

I seek spiritual enlightenment.

I look for the gift in the moment.

I am a non-judgmental observer.

I am grounded in peaceful wisdom.

The Call to Sacred Archetypes

We are living in an age of the return to feminine energy. The divine masculine has dominated or so long and women have lost touch with their power. This is slowly changing as more people start waking up to what they've been missing. A divine feminine archetype is when a woman embodies the highest expression of her self-love, courage, grace and wisdom. By focusing our attention on these personas, we are awakening the expression of these universal qualities within ourselves.

There are seven archetypes according to Jung that represent this awakening, which we have covered: Maiden, Mother, Huntress, Queen, Mystic, Lover, and Sage.

Each one represents a unique perspective on not only femininity but life itself - these powerful female archetypes are inside you just waiting for the right time of expression. There is an infinite number of archetypes that a woman must embody in order to grow within her feminine energy. Some people only say the Maiden, Mother, and Crone as these are typically identified upon research; Jung says there are seven; however, I believe there's so much more for us women to understand about ourselves through different life experiences.

You can call on each archetype during different stages of your growth, but you probably have been identifying with at least one from each stage already. Archetypal embodiment is so life changing because it allows us to remove the mask and reveal our desires and goals.

Understanding our story and shadows allows us to gain access to unrealized potential, increase empathy for others, serve the collective good at large, tap into emotions of which we've never been aware before--and stop habit patterns that have developed throughout time itself.

When we understand that each of us has access to the full human potential and know how to awaken these qualities within ourselves; we are empowered by this knowledge in creating lives and worlds that align with our deepest desires. We can then tap into abundant healing for not only ourselves but also the planet.

So, what is collective consciousness? Collective consciousness refers to the set of shared beliefs, ideas, attitudes and knowledge that are common among a social group or society. This concept can manifest itself in various forms such as gender norms concerning how people dress and act; laws which socialize people into what's right and wrong for their country; rituals like parades on holidays or weddings. In the simplest terms it's a sociological construct that helps us understand "our role" within society.

Humans are unique in their ability to access the energy of everything around them. We have been hunters and gatherers for most of our existence, we have had to operate from a survival system - but now we can connect through fractals with everyone else on this planet. Our collective consciousness is one that has always existed within us- it's not something you need to search outside yourself or others for meaning; rather, think about how all things are connected by these tiny bits of energy called 'fractals.' Whatever you feel will be felt by everyone else because your thoughts create a type of interconnected web between people across time and space.

In today's world, we are fighting more than ever to connect with others. We're constantly being bombarded by new algorithms and information from social media that determine our "status" and who we think we should be online. We're constantly being inundated with messages about what to eat, how much exercise we need and why our bodies are failing us. We are being bombarded by advertising from different sources all the time. Instead of seeing people enjoying each other and connecting, we see them glued to their phones. We are deeply connected with what is happening in front of us but feel powerless because it feels like nothing can be done about the problem at hand.

Those who have heightened sensitivities will be able to raise their own vibrations and in turn benefit the collective vibration. By "those" I mean YOU.

For thousands of years ancient civilizations and indigenous cultures, including the Mayans, Hopi, Chinese, Hindus, Incans, and Aztecs believed that a collective consciousness exists in which shifts take place causing mass awakenings, this shift in consciousness is a period when humans can take control over our thoughts and actions.

People are now reconnecting to past traditions, beliefs, ideologies of our ancestors. This is known as the Age of Aquarius or the age of enlightenment that was predicted by Mayans. We are beginning to realize this collective energy and putting ourselves in a position where we understand we aren't separate from one another. We are craving connection, we are craving growth, we are craving oneness.

The Maya myth does not usually use language that suggests an end-of-the world scenario like many Western myths do - instead they employ beliefs about rebirth after it ends. The end of the world is a common fear that has been present for centuries. According to astrology, there are cycles that have occurred hundreds and thousands of times before. Additionally, these timelines are cyclical which means they will occur again in the future. We are in a constant state of re-birth and new beginnings.

The 5,000-year period is known in the Vedic tradition as Kali Yuga or Dark Age. Five thousand years ago, at the beginning of our acknowledged history, humanity had a direct window into the spirit world and began to move deeper into materialism which led them to forget their true spiritual nature also called duality. For us all to raise collective consciousness we must focus on freeing ourselves from belief systems that hold us back because it will only bring about positive change within society moving forward in time.

Deepak Chopra states in The Seven Spiritual Laws that *"The source of all creation is pure consciousness...pure potentiality seeking expression from the unmanifest to manifest. And when we realize that our true self is one of pure potentiality, we align with power that manifests everything in universe."*

We are freaking magical unicorns capable beyond what you have been led to believe.

-There is not one truth or reality.

The Healer

"Our efforts to heal others are only fruitful if we have first healed ourselves. This is because whatever wound that exists within us, will be carried over and inflicted upon those who receive our healing."

Today, the archetype of the healer and wounded healer are in restorative calling. A person with this type may be born or learn how to heal someone else. The effectiveness of healing is heavily dependent on their own belief in themselves as well as knowledge about it being effective for others who need help. An Enlightened Healer is first and foremost a self-healer who is humble, pliable, compassionate and caring.

They have deep wisdom about the healing of both body and soul. The true mark of an enlightened healer is their ability to create lasting change for patients they work with through either catalyzing or channeling it in some way. Healing happens in countless ways such as through caregivers, nurses or therapists across the world every day. Every culture from the earliest tribes of ancient man all through the ages to modern times, has an archetype for a Healer. This is because it's an experience that humans have gone through on some level since their origins; being hurt or wounded any way whether it be physical, emotional or spiritual.

Shamans are one of the oldest known healers.

Witches were also historically healers, especially in pagan religions where nature worship was easily incorporated into healing practices and health care. In addition to witches, midwives helped bring new life onto the earth, monks, priest, the medicine man, etc. She takes time to care for herself, which then allows her to extend that same love and compassion towards everyone around her.

Holistic medicine is the combination of science and art that focuses on healing all aspects of a person, including their physical health as well as mental state. The practice involves homeopathy (which uses highly diluted substances), acupuncture, herbalism, energy therapy techniques such as quantum touch therapies and therapeutic massage which involve various forms like yoga or aromatherapy to help heal different parts of one's mind body connection.

The Healer allows for the creation of genuine connections through love, grief and acceptance. She is an alchemist who transforms these emotions into something beautiful if we are willing to face them ourselves as she serves only as a space holder alongside us in time. This person is patient, present and compassionate - never forcing our healing but instead standing beside us when committed to doing so on one's own accord. The ancient and powerful archetypal energy of the healer often feels like serious energy.

The Healer knows pain, has an attuned understanding of its source and possesses a base knowledge that may be gifted or developed through experience.

> *"Healing may not be so much about getting better as about letting go of everything that isn't you – all of the expectations, all of the beliefs – and becoming who you are. Not a better you, but a 'realer' you. People can heal and live, and people can heal and die. Healing is different from curing. Healing is a process we're all involved in all the time. Healing is the leading forth of wholeness."*
> – Rachel Naomi Remen, M.D.

The Shadow: When a healer has too much power, they can do more harm than good. They oversee using their powers responsibly so that the patient doesn't get hurt. On the other hand, when healers doubt themselves or feel like they've lost faith, this is known as shadow healing and it's not helpful to anyone involved at all. The archetype of the shadow healer can become wildly overconfident when seduced by power. This person will claim to have a remedy that cures every ailment out there acting like they know best in all things. They might take credit for everything good around them even if this is always not true. The healer can choose to be either in God-type complex, projecting their own pain onto others and overextending themselves; or an over-giver who lacks self-care. They are at risk of feeling drained by helping people with nothing in return for themself. The shadow is taking responsibility for solving everyone's problems without being asked, leading the healer into danger of becoming overly involved with other peoples' issues while neglecting her own wellbeing. The shadow healer's cynicism has spread to everyone around her, which only creates more pain and suffering.

The Wounded Healer

The wounded healer and shadow healer are not to be confused. A person with the wounded archetype can transform her own pain into empathy for others, people who might have similar wounds or struggles as hers. In times of darkness this manifests in a bleeding heart that gives beyond their capacity when it comes to helping other people overcome these kinds of hardships too. She overextends herself and like the shadow healer becomes empty herself. This wounded healer energy reflects patterns and behaviors seen among healers, but in the light, they become rock-solid individuals who can provide just right remedies at exactly the right time without fail—The glue of the situation and a wisdom cultivated from personal experiences of her own. The wounded healer has a strength that is the ability to channel her own wounds through an awareness and detached state, which she uses to help heal others.

When I began my Reiki Master training, I felt like an imposter. Despite this fear of imposter syndrome, I followed my intuition and went through with the attunement for reiki mastership because it seemed to be what was best for me at the time. One of things my mentors taught me in NLP training is that in order to heal others we must first heal ourselves - which left me feeling quite conflicted about our ability to ever truly become healthy again after experiencing a traumatic event or life change.

If we are truly healed wouldn't that mean are journey is over?

I decided to take time and dedicate myself completely towards finding the answers I was seeking. All my hard work paid off, as I became certified in many areas that brought me closer to understanding this 'healing' energy we are all capable of tapping into.

However, while receiving these trainings, it still wasn't enough for what I needed personally - an answer about how healing works at our core level when everything else is stripped away from you except the raw self within us all waiting patiently for recognition.

We all heal differently.

For me, it came down to awareness of my pain and forgiveness. I realized that everyone's path is different- there isn't a magical way to forget your trauma, but you can come from a place of love and forgiveness instead! The definition of healed wasn't some miraculous combustion for anyone either; rather, healing was about seeing the truth in our situation and cultivating awareness as opposed to reacting with anger or letting ourselves be overwhelmed by thoughts on the past.

When my mentor said healed, it made me think of the word buried. No longer in existence. This was fear. Fear that the word healed itself was infinite. I knew the wound would always be there - but this was my superpower: The vulnerability that allowed intuitively understanding other women. I didn't want to forget or put a band aid on it because doing so would limit me further from being able to grow beyond my past.

I realized that the healing journey was self-love through acceptance rather than rejection by hiding behind fearfully and running away from what makes us who we are today. Our lives are more like a cycle of seasons, constantly going through rebirth and death. It's not on the physical level but rather an emotional one where we evolve ourselves by embracing our shadows and demons instead of disabling them.

As humans, some parts die while new horizons come to life within us all as mothers earth has her own cycles too. To me it really comes down to energy vibrations flowing from everything around us that heals or helps you grow into your best self. I have many dark sides but what keeps getting better is just understanding how much power there exists inside these negative emotions if only I am willing enough to let go off my inhibitions in order to embrace empowerment over disablement.

One of my biggest pet peeves is when coaches or therapist use the word fix. First off, no human has the power to "fix" you - this would be a shadow healer and secondly, you are not damaged goods. You simply had a soul contract to learn certain lessons and grow from trauma.

Shame is a sneaky little emotion. It lies to your soul and tells you how to hide instead of running toward yourself and your potential where connection with self should take place. Instead of going within we learn to run, to numb, to escape. Our perspective feels like walls closing in around us. Here is what I have learned though. Wherever you run - there you'll be. We may feel like we're broken, but these feelings are just temporary.

The real problem is our negative beliefs about ourselves that cause us to continue feeling this way repeatedly. We need new experiences for our thinking to change so that the belief doesn't have power anymore. This journey of stripping away all those false childhood beliefs begins with a rebirth into who you truly are meant to be on the inside - someone strong, confident, kindhearted. It comes back to love for yourself and others because that is what heals us. Being healed and operating from this space of love were one in the same path towards self-actualization which was an internal process rather than forgetting things or moving forward without remembering them.

We are not breaking. We are becoming.

Chiron

In Greek mythology, Chiron was a Centaur who was known for his wisdom and medical knowledge. He taught many heroes of the time including Heracles, Achilles, Jason, and Asclepius. Chiron was born with two natures, horse and man. His mother refused to accept him because of this dual nature so he had a deep wound that would not heal from birth. Abandonment. The mother wound. Apollo, the god of poetry and music, came to the rescue. Apollo adopted the infant Chiron and taught thoroughly in the arts, sciences, and mysteries that he would need to rise above his beast nature. He became one of the great teachers in mythology known for his wisdom and knowledge on healing different types of wounds. Centaurs by nature, were known for their riskayyyy behavior – drinking wine, chasing the ladies, partying it up. Chiron was different though - He escaped to live alone in a cave on Mount Pelion and over time earned respect as a healer, astrologer, prophet, and teacher. Chiron is an archetype used to describe humanity's need for spiritual transformation. He embodies lessons on bridging the gap between everyday life and spirituality. Chiron symbolizes our ability to establish a bridge that can bring balance back into our lives. One day, a man was hunting when he accidentally shoots a poisoned arrow at Chiron. The pain from the poison is unbearable and never goes away no matter what potions or herbs are taken. However, instead of taking his revenge out on this hunter with rage as most people would have done in that situation, Chiron uses it to teach others about healing, so they won't experience any more pain like him. Chiron was a centaur who, after being taken in by the gods, willingly sacrificed himself to save Prometheus. After nine days of suffering from his liver slowly getting nibbled at by vultures he was rescued by Zeus and placed among the stars forever. Chiron is the OG Wounded Healer. Through the unconscious yearning of the wounded self to become more conscious, an archetypal growth pattern toward Healed Healer is activated. Rumi also said, "If you desire healing let yourself fall ill." The "Healed" Healer is in a state of active integration. This means that they are aware of their own cycles and patterns, allowing them to respond instead of reacting when something happens. They let themselves feel curious about what's happening rather than just staying in an emotional state. They are conscious, they are aware, they fully understand the shadow and embrace it.

The Eight Archetypes of Healers

The Shaman: The archetypal force of the Shaman is the earthly, elemental aspect of healing. They will fiercely protect all that they believe in and being wounded almost always initiates their archetype to begin formulating itself within their unconscious mind. The root from which humanity's various spiritual disciplines have issued lies deep with shamanism as it connects them deeply to nature and its elements. The strengths of the shaman are grounded in the body, they conjure elements to honor both light and dark aspects of life. When the shaman is in their shadow, they feel fear and anxiety of death or endings. They also may be suppressing unexpressed feelings such as anger, rage, and even escapism to cope with what's going on around them. This Shaman archetype is associated with the Root chakra.

The Sensualist: The Sensualist archetype is not ashamed of their sexual or sensual nature. Those with the Sensualist as their Lead Healing Archetype are tactile, sensuous beings who have an abundance of creativity flowing through them. The primary communicator of the passage is touch. She deeply understands the intrinsic connection between sexuality, life force, creativity and embodied healing—she uses all five senses and has a "healing touch." The strengths that she flows in life with are gracefulness and being creative. There's also an appreciation for beauty as well as exquisiteness within her character. When the sensualist is in shadow, they may be feeling fear of intimacy and difficulty opening their heart. They might also feel manipulation through sexual allure or power/control issues which lead to shame about a deep rejection of one's own sexuality as well as helplessness playing out the role of being a damsel who needs saving from distress. These feelings can create dramatic behavior along with creative blocks that keep them disconnected from their creativity energy. The Sensualist archetype is associated with the Sacral chakra.

The Coach: The Coach archetype is direct, strategic and always has the goal in mind.

The motivator of them all, the Coach is a natural leader who thrives on empowerment, discipline and results. Masculine energy led by nature, primarily within their yang energy, the coach is linear thinking and action-taking. The coach archetype is clear and direct with their approach. You know what they are always thinking, because of this you also get a healthy dose of competition that will help motivate your team to work harder. Their solution-based mindset helps them craft better solutions for the problem at hand. When the coach archetype is in shadow, they lack purpose and direction. They are critical of others' work ethic, over-achieving to an extent that can be harmful for their own health or wellbeing. The Coach archetype is associated with the Solar Plexus chakra.

The Nurturer: The nurturing archetype is a person that understands people and all their greatness, both in good times and bad. Their nature makes them the 'mothering' type who takes others under their wing to care for them unconditionally like an embrace. The Nurturer Archetype is the first to put other's before themselves and hold a steady patience and compassion unknown to most. They are generous, compassionate people who naturally care for those around them as well as hold ethical principles that work collaboratively with others. When the nurturer is in shadow, they become self-neglectful and neglect others needs as well. They are also bitter with others around them who have unrealistic expectations of what it means to be a parent or caregiver.

Sometimes this can lead to unforgiving behavior because these individuals feel like nobody understands how difficult taking care of someone else's life may truly be. This falls very similar to the mother archetype in shadow. This Nurturer archetype is associated with the Heart chakra.

The Counselor: The Counselor is led by the truth -- whether it be the situation or a higher, more universal wisdom. They are naturally gifted at giving advice and guidance, as well as being excellent listeners. The counselor's tendency to "read between lines" comes from their ability to pick up on subtleties that others miss-- they tend to unbiasedly see both sides of an issue without getting caught up in emotions or personal bias. The counselor's true gift is being able to help people in a way that empowers them and makes them feel self-confident. In their highest manifestation, they can be seen as the helping partner you need when going through a tough time. The counselor archetype strengths are integrity, being clear and direct in communication with others, listening attentively to help people build relationships. When in shadow they can find themselves being gossiping or trying to be the bossy know-it-all. They need to practice listening and guiding others, not just talking about what happened with them when it is time for someone else's story. The Counselor is associated with the Throat chakra.

The Mystic: Mystics develop heightened psychic senses that allow them to see and feel truth beyond words. They trust in their higher force, are clear channels for guidance from Spirit, prioritize relationships with the divine above all else, and love anything esoteric. Their relationship with Spirit takes priority over everything else. The mystic archetype is a powerful one. They have conscious connections to Spirit and are deeply intuitive, which makes them excellent channels for prophetic messages that shut down earthly propaganda. When they become disconnected from reality, delusional people lose touch with the ground beneath them. This is the definition of shadow for the mystic. They forget we are living in an earth realm and require grounding and roots to fly. The Mystic is associated with the third eye chakra.

The Buddha: The Buddha healing archetypes are naturally drawn to meditation and balance, making them calm and centered individuals. They can ride the storms of any challenge with equanimity because they remain still within themselves despite external circumstances that may be otherwise chaotic or turbulent. The Buddha's peaceful nature is their most striking trait as they embody a heightened awareness consciousness which makes them understand challenging spiritual wisdoms deeply. This archetype has strong spiritual beliefs and enjoys solitary time to seek answers. They also have a higher state of unity consciousness which allows them to find inner strength within themselves. They serve the highest good of the collective and always have this thought in the front of their thoughts and actions. The buddha archetype may feel lost and introverted when they are in shadow, disconnecting from their personal emotions.

They can show a lack of self-care with disregard for the temple - referring to the body as "the temple." The Buddha is associated with the Crown chakra.

The Guide: Guides are extremely intuitive people who have an innate connection to the greater cosmos. As they lead others on their own path of soul fulfillment, Guides trust in serendipity and a higher power. They're big picture thinkers with visionary natures that help them tap into unlimited wisdom from above. Their strength lies in their understanding of the "big picture" and how it relates to individual needs. They are also brave enough to walk through life following their soul's truth, not afraid or ashamed of being different from others around them.

The key strengths that lie within someone is often best seen when they take a step back and look at themselves as an outsider would view them --- without fear or shame over who they truly are inside. When the guide archetype is in shadow, they become overwhelmed and create a God complex. They think that no one knows as much as them and do not like to be questioned.

Each archetype contains different healing modalities like herbalism, crystal healing, energy work and health & wellness. As a healer there is nothing more important than developing yourself as you continue your path of self-discovery to uncover the most useful practices that will appeal to your unique identity which shapes an archetype. Give yourself time, permission and space for further exploration into all things related to healing. In ancient culture, wisdom was shared from generation to generation enabling rituals and healing. Recently there has been a resurgence of this connection with the planet which was lost over the past five hundred years. We are all aware that there is much more to our health than just the physical body. Our minds, hearts and spirits must also be aligned with ourselves for us to feel happy and healthy. So often we forget these aspects of life; but without them being present within oneself it will lead towards dis-ease rather than wellness or wholeness. In a world of disconnection, we need to embrace the wisdom that our ancestors have for us.

Ancestral lineage healing

Ancestral lineage healing is a ritual process that empowers you to connect, repair and nurture relationships with your own wise and loving ancestors. Inherited burdens and the full embodiment of your gifts are transmitted by way of family lineage. The process involves uncovering inherited problems, transforming them into positive energy for yourself, and then passing on that same positivity to future generations through those roots you've uncovered along the way. When I first began ancestral healing, it was difficult to know where to start. It all just felt so vast. Everyone in my family had lied about our history so much that the information felt overwhelming and untouchable. It was like this big lock box of secrets I craved to uncover. The inner Nancy Drew in me was ready to go to work. Ancestral healing is a process of recalling and acknowledging the pain that our ancestors have gone through, while figuring out how they overcame it. This healing is gritty and raw. You will be challenged to find the root of your pain, the patterns that trigger you (blocks) as well as coming towards understanding and forgiveness for our ancestors' past experiences.

Releasing Ritual

By ritualizing the release and redirection of these patterns, we can begin to integrate lessons into our daily life. This will be most effective if done during a full moon, when intentionally releasing old cycles are powerful.

What you need?
Sacred Flame (candle, fireplace or firepit)
Affirmations
Glass of Water to Drink

*Offering to the Ancestors (tobacco, cedar,
or a dried plant that is sacred to your lineage)*
Ancestral Music

Burn this plant offering with an intention to heal the wounds in your family and open yourself up to receive support from your ancestors. Know that you are supported by them in this endeavor and feel their love for you.

The fire's destruction is a form of transformation, making room for newness. Let your affirmation integrate into the cells and permeate your being to make space for something better in life.

A glass of water absorbs its surroundings, including the intentions you send to it. By directing your affirmation again but now toward your drink and drinking from that same cup with intention in mind, you allow yourself to fully internalize this message into your life.

And so it is.
With love and gratitude.

"Every cell in my body vibrates with healing energy."

"My body is healing, and I feel better and better every day."

"I send love and healing to every cell within my body."

"I enjoy radiant energy from within."

"Within and without I feel balanced and healthy."

"My body is whole and healthy."

The Creatrix

sov·er·eign
possessing supreme or ultimate power.

The Muse archetype is sometimes known as the Goddess or Creatrix. She's an artist, writer, poet and storyteller who helps people unleash their authentic selves without fearing external judgement. The muse gives rise to desires while bringing about new ideas that can help protect lives of all kinds. Her dreams are full of courage because she trusts so deeply in her connection with nature itself. The Creatrix is a master manifester and protector of the magical realm, she understands that without darkness there is no light. Overflowing with ideas, everything she creates originates from a deep place within and are true expressions of her soul. She shows up with honesty, integrity, purposefulness - understanding this to be pivotal for co-creating in harmony with the divine. A true Creatix is a woman who weaves her highest multi-dimensional soul truth and perpetually is inspired by the masculine. She co-creates ultimately with the King principle in order to achieve ultimate success. She builds her Queendom through operation from higher self. The Creatrix assists you in manifesting your abilities. She is deeply connected to the moon cycles and honors her body with some R&R when needed. Even through dark tribulations, she knows everything that happens TO her is happening FOR her not IN spite of what's going on around her. Some goddesses that represent this archetype are Aphrodite, Rhiannon, Ishtar, Astarte, and Saraswati. The Creator takes great care of their mind, body and spirit - they know it's all their temple for them to explore life fully within. They flow like water whenever possible never worrying about where or how far they go if something is cultivated by the experience.

Creatrix Strengths: The Queen of her own Universe, the Creatrix has a strong understanding of the collective consciousness and is driven, creative, a visionary and vulnerable. She's passed through phases in her life with an innate need to "compete" where she wants to leave behind a legacy for other women too. She understands her place within this world as well as its importance across cultures. The Creatrix has a deep desire to lead others on journeys that will change their lives forever; empowering them not only financially but also emotionally- inspiring them to never give up even after failure. She knows true greatness lies beyond these moments.

The Shadow: The "shadow" in psychology refers to an unconscious part of one's personality made up by repressed experiences, instincts and natural urges as well as those aspects excluded from a person's conscious worldview. It was first used by Swiss psychiatrist Carl Jung, though it became more popularized through analytical psychologists such as Donald Winnicott during the twentieth century. The silent child who is the Creatrix in shadow is known to be this side because she has been suppressed due to trauma with unexpressed emotions being held within her throat chakra. In her shadow side, the Creatrix can develop self-doubt and even question if she is really receiving inspirations from a higher power. She might also get trapped in a "starving artist" mentality or copy other people's ideas out of fear that hers are not good enough. If Imposter Syndrome were an archetype itself, it would be this one to own due to its common nature among women creators. This person may never finish any projects because they aren't perfect yet. They can end up feeling egotistical or self-sacrificing which makes them feel like there isn't enough of themselves to give out.

When to call on her: Now let's tap into a deep place of embodying inner knowing and juicy confidence. Your self-doubt comes from living in an environment where you were not nurtured as a child. You should give yourself permission to create, which will help heal your creative side and make it more vibrant. If possible, surround yourself with other artists who will inspire you through their work or passion for creativity itself. You'll find that these people are usually very open about sharing ideas and methods of inspiration they use themselves.

When creating new content be sure to focus on deep uninterrupted periods so the magic can flow better without any interruptions from outside forces such as social media etc... Connect to your soul/higher self. Embrace and learn to love who you are authentically. Let go of limiting beliefs that hold you back from being creative. Write a new story about yourself that empowers you.

"If you're not writing your own story, you're a character in someone else's." Being your true authentic self is about being who you are at the core of your soul. It's more than what you do for a job, it's not even about having certain material possessions or relationships with people - although those things can be an important part in helping to define that authenticity too. What does this mean? What exactly am I supposed to think when someone says 'authentic'? How would they act differently if their behavior was aligned with how they want themselves and others believe them to be? Is there any way we could measure authenticity objectively somehow, so everyone knows where each other stands on this scale based off actions instead of words only?

When the word "authentic" first entered my vocabulary, I was in my early twenties and used it for everything. I did not truly understand the meaning but loved saying it. Once someone asked if what they heard me say referred to a Mexican restaurant- embarrassing! Clearly, I was using the word out of context. I went home and wanted to know exactly what it meant to be your authentic self. *To be authentic is to be true to yourself through your thoughts, words and actions.* That was obviously not the case in my early twenties, and I had many lessons left that I needed learn about authenticity. I always had heard "fake it till you make it" – If there was ever a phrase that rubs me the wrong way, this is it. It wasn't faking it - putting in work became her; eventually becoming who you truly are as a person rather than pretending or trying too hard (which happens often at such an age where we just want things so quickly without learning valuable experiences.)

That whole spiritual bypassing thing just doesn't work out to well. We miss the alchemy of following our own desires, rather than falling in line with whatever everyone else thinks happiness requires. There's so much pressure to be authentic, but authenticity is a slippery thing. People feel most authentic when they conform to a particular set of socially approved qualities, this paradoxical truth seems self-evident—we edit our lives on social media and present only the edited highlights for one reason: because it makes us feel safe. It makes us feel interesting and wanted. When we are being ourselves, authenticity isn't about the ego or highlight reel. We are present in the here and now. Being authentic is also vulnerable; it requires showing all parts of us no matter what happens to others along our journey. It's not difficult for someone who lives authentically to maintain boundaries with ease because they follow their passions regardless of whether people get upset by them doing so.

> "Authenticity is the daily practice of letting go of who we think we are supposed to be and embracing who we actually are." – Brene Brown

Honoring the Cycles

During the pre-menstrual phase, women have a desire to be alone in order create and produce things from their hearts. This occurs about two weeks before menstruation starts. The Creatrix holds the energy of discernment that allows her to see what is working well or not with great clarity during this time period; it also affects tiny creatures such as ourselves: our blood, hormones and neurochemicals—every part of us including thoughts and moods become affected by moon phases which makes them waxing (attract) at times while waning (repelling/reflecting back). During this moon cycle one should focus on manifesting desires they might hold within themselves.

Journaling, reflecting on what works and doesn't work in life can prepare us for new opportunities that we want to manifest with the help of the moon phases. Now is a time where we let go and make necessary changes so that balance and clarity come more easily into our lives. This inwardly focused energy seeks its own resources to create without sharing it with anyone else first. Set yourself up for success with a plan that will help integrate these changes into your routine when the next chapter begins during full moon phase–which is an extroversive energy.

New Moon - this is when the earth blocks light so that only darkness can be seen. This phase of newness represents something fresh and untouched, like a seed waiting to grow into its full potential! During this time, you might want to start some personal projects or goals since your energy will easily expand them in strength and intensity. Set clear intentions on your goals and projects you wish to see manifesting with the utmost enthusiasm.

Waxing Crescent - is the second phase of a lunar cycle. It begins just after the new moon, when it has completely disappeared, and ends at first quarter moon or half-moon. As this stage progresses, an illuminated area on its surface appears to increase in size but remains less than 25% visible as seen with your naked eye. The gush of energy you can feel for growing plans are sprouting up now. You can utilize this time for growth by identifying your focus.

The energy expansion supports new ideas and even the meeting of new people in your life. This is a time to be positive, motivated and act.

First Quarter - This is the half-moon phase which consists of strength, determination and commitment to action. The seed starts growing roots at this stage too while you need to keep moving forward despite fears or doubts that might get in your way so use it as a creative energy instead.

The Waxing Gibbous – This phase is usually between the First Quarter and Full Moon. This moon phase indicates you are at a stage in life where your ideas, skills, beliefs are ready to be cultivated before blossoming into fruition.

Full Moon - During this period, the moon is opposite of the sun and aligned with Earth. The seed has reached its full bloom which represents abundance and completion. This is the time to let go of all no longer serving your highest good. An evening under the full moon can be the perfect time to recharge your energy. Sit outside and bask in the moon light - bring along crystals, oracle cards, meaningful jewelry, moon water or any other things which need cleansing under the magical full moon. The downside of this phase is intense thoughts and emotional behavior so make sure you keep yourself busy by writing out all those feelings on paper during waxing phases; it's also good practice to perform releasing ceremonies where you physically get rid of anything that no longer serves you - burn baby burn!

If you are not already part of a Goddess circle, now would be an amazing opportunity for introspection - if your curious enough... join one and explore this magical experience. I had no idea what I was getting myself into. The night before Halloween, I attended my first goddess circle gathering on a Blue Moon- the only way to describe it is through an emoji with heart eyes and fireworks! And even though at that time in my life--I'd turned into quite the hermit due to anxiety, but I still went despite my fear of being asked to dance naked under the full moon- The initial circle began with us all saging in and dancing around the outside of The Sacred Circle. I was chanting, drumming on my djembe, freaking out internally but it felt like I had reached a heightened state of consciousness -like nothing else mattered around me - this was awareness. I was surrounded by women who I'd never met yet felt like sisters. We called in the directions and sat down within the sacred circle. It was beautiful; there were marigolds, fruits, nuts and chocolates to place items to be blessed on an altar. I was in awe. We began sharing our stories whilst calling in our loved ones who had passed. While I didn't expect to have much of an experience with spirits, the room quickly became bone-chilling cold. Within ten minutes, it dropped 10 degrees and the leader said, "they're here." My face went blue as my options were freeze or try communicating, I chose stillness for observation. The moonlight glistened through the trees as I sat alongside my new sisters. We laughed, cried and released any pain we had been holding onto that night under its light. The air was filled with feminine energy - one of the most beautiful gatherings I have ever experienced which made me feel safe in releasing all I'd held inside for so long. Of course, I go monthly now, and it has been a huge part in my personal alchemy. Each month we choose new topics that flow with the seasons and phases. The moral of the story is to find yourself a goddess circle or start one for yourself.

Waxing Gibbous - All the excitement that comes with revealing secrets and telling all is heightened during this waning moon, especially if we're talking about ending a bad habit or breaking off something negative. During dissemination you want to keep your thoughts open for new opportunities as well as information coming in from other sources.

Third Quarter - In this third quarter, a sense of accomplishment and introspection is in the air. Seeds planted have been nurtured and allowed to grow into full plants with ripe harvests ready for picking. You stop, contemplate what has happened so far during your life journey which allows you to focus on new goals going forward. This phase gives creativity an opportunity as well as growth opportunities when it comes to planning towards future intentions. In the end there should be no negative thoughts or energy left over from past actions just simply looking forwards at all that can come next.

Waning Crescent - The Waning Crescent moon signals a transitional period before the start of another cycle and an opportunity to prepare. The Waning Crescent Moon marks the end of one phase in life, but also is a time for preparation for what's next.

The Story of Rhiannon

Rhiannon is a Lunar Welsh Goddess of inspiration whose name means "Great Queen" and serves as a muse for poets, artists, and royalty. She is also the goddesses of transformation who eases the dead into their afterlife by carrying them upon her white horse.

Rhiannon often appears in animal or bird form because she loves to shapeshift but will sometimes appear through song instead. When Rhiannon chooses Pwyll to be her husband, they encounter many problems before their big day. Although she is said to have beauty like Epona (Goddess of abundance), the two are smart and generous people who face trouble before getting married but still tie the knot.

Rhiannon, mother of the lost child, was accused by the people of killing her child and her husband agreed she needed to plead guilty because they didn't see another way of her surviving. She was sentenced to an unjust penance. The day after her son's birth she would have to go on a quest for someone who did not believe in her innocence; however, this is where fate intervened as he returned. She was unjustly accused of killing her infant son and as punishment, she had to carry visitors on her back as a horse for the royal court.

The Lord of Horses returns Rhiannon's son, she is free to marry again once Pwyll passes. She had more adventures involving enchantments with which she gained further notoriety due to Celtic folklore before marrying Manawydan once Pwyll died.

Rhiannon, being strong at heart and mind despite the unjust punishment she is enduring for a wrongful accusation, displays her strength as an exceptional steed or giantess when riding away from her future husband. She is said to be the mare and her son the foul.

Rhiannon is accompanied by three birds, (Birds of Rhiannon) who can wake the dead and lull the living to sleep with their harmonious tune. Taking this metaphorically we can see cycles of life and death gripping into each other.

The three birds symbolize a trinity for both male and female forms across nations as well as cultures: polytheism versus monotheism alike.

Now this is where it gets juicy and tied in with the archetypes. Rhiannon moves between the realms of life, death & imagination; possessing powerful magic that brings healing as well as granting access to parts of our psyche we may not want to visit on a regular basis. Three is seen throughout mythologies around the world: creation (maiden), motherhood/nurturing (mother) and wisdom gained through experience or age (crone). At their highest level these represent Love — creativity — making something out of nothing using only one's mind! A great theme for bringing about change while nurturing new growth, harvesting what has been sown so another cycle can begin again.

Throat Chakra

- Element: Sound or space
- Color: Blue

- Mantra: Ham (pronounced hum)
- Crystal Healing: Aquamarine, Turquoise, Lapis Lazuli, Sodalite, Quartz, Azurite, Kyanite, Labradorite, Larimar, Celestine or any other blue stone.

The fifth chakra, Vishuddha Charka, is located at the base of our throat and voice box. This center represents effective communication as well as inspiration and expression. The color of the throat chakra is blue, and this allows you to stand in who you are, speak your truth without fear or shame, and say what you mean. This chakra is related to the expression of yourself through your personal truth, dharma, creativity and individuality. It is connected to the second chakra or sacral center which itself contains a lot of emotions as well as being involved with your creative energy flow.

When in Balance –

When you're able to speak fearlessly and with compassion, it's easier for others to listen. When your throat chakra is open and balanced, getting all the facts on a situation will be effortless. You'll be able to articulate your ideas, feelings and opinions with clarity. When you can express thoughts clearly, people will have a better understanding of what you mean. You may also feel more heard when others understand where you stand on an issue or topic at hand. The pathway to enlightenment is not only verbal but what you say to yourself. Speaking your truth and consistently showing up for that truth, as hard as it may be sometimes, will open this chakra. When we feel in control of our lives and have an authentic voice, the result is a balanced Throat Chakra.

When Overactive –

When the throat chakra is overwhelmed with energy, it can lead to struggles in relationships because of what you say. You may be your own worst critic and speak too harshly about yourself or others which leads to conflict.

Throat Chakra Frequency –

192 Hz. The 741 Hertz frequency also helps people with blocked vocal cords and allows them to express themselves. It is known as the Tone 'Sol' which represents self-expression, a pure, stable life that promotes healthy living.

- I communicate confidently and with ease.
- I feel comfortable speaking my mind.
- I am balanced in speaking and listening.
- I am an active listener.
- I speak my true thoughts with clarity.
- I set clear boundaries.

When blocked –

When your throat chakra is blocked or misaligned, you will have issues with creativity and communication. A blocked throat chakra may occur if you're feeling too nervous to speak. Or, on the flip side, it could be from being a volcano and exploding when you reach your breaking point. These extremes in communication can lead to imbalance or a blockage. These issues can also lead to physical symptoms like thyroid imbalance, sore throat, and hearing difficulties. If your throat chakra is blocked during reiki, you might have trouble swallowing or feel as if something is stuck in your throat.

- Difficulty expressing your thoughts.
- Tight Shoulders.
- Hearing issues.
- TMJ issues.
- Feeling timid or shy.
- Talking without thinking.
- Dishonesty.
- Insensitivity.
- Insecurity.
- Social anxiety.
- Difficulty making sound decisions.
- Thyroid problems.

Nourishing the Throat Chakra -

Ever wonder why after a colorful meal from nourishment provided by Mother Earth you feel all sorts of amazing and energized rather than weighed down? All this has more to do with color than form - The foods that balance our chakras have more to do with the subtle energies of color rather than form itself. With the throat chakra you want to be eating blue but there are also some extras which are powerful to unblock this area.

Blueberries, blackberries, blue corn and borage; kelp; dragon fruit; wheatgrass (to promote energy), ginseng (for strength); honey (it's soothing); saline rinses, tea - and mushrooms.

Breath Work and Yoga –

If you're wondering how to unblock your throat chakra, look no further than regulating one of the most important aspects of our lives: Breath. I'll say it again and again, *breath is medicine*; not only will proper breathing improve physical health but also mental clarity and spiritual awareness. One way we can become more aware next time we breathe in and out is through equalizing our inhales with exhales while simultaneously lengthening them both so that they are at a perfect ratio (1:2). This means if we take 3 deep breaths every minute then each should last 60 seconds instead 30. Another great breathing technique to open the throat chakra is Lion's breath. To regulate this energy center by performing asanas you'll want to do poses such as shoulder stand, camel, plow, cat-cow or fish pose.

Oils –

I am a huge advocate for bringing all five senses while healing and our scent is not one to miss out on. To open the throat chakra, burn ether incense, essential oils, and candles like frankincense, geranium, jasmine, sage, cypress, peppermint, eucalyptus, clove, tree tea, and lavender.

Self-Realization –

How do I communicate in intimate conversations? How much do I listen, and how much do I speak? Is this ratio balanced?

_____
_____
_____
_____

How do I communicate in party settings? Do I tend to sit back and observe, or do I speak freely? How much do I listen compared to how much I speak? Is this ratio balanced?

_____
_____
_____
_____

Where am I unwilling to hear the truth about myself? When do I shut others down?

_____
_____
_____
_____

How do I feel when others break eye contact with me or look distracted when I am speaking?

_____
_____
_____
_____

WITHIN

How do I prefer to communicate? Text, phone, email? Why?

_____
_____
_____
_____

How can I clearly and effectively communicate my truth so that it's understood effectively?

_____
_____
_____
_____

Do my thoughts, actions and words all agree?

_____
_____
_____
_____

What does authenticity mean to you?

_____
_____
_____
_____

When we think about the past, there's often a moment that we wish we could change or do over. We wanted to gather our thoughts and say just the right thing, but the words never came out. Whether it be in a life situation or with a certain person, if you knew how to say something better and they would listen what would you say? Write an open letter to this person.

With Love,

In what situations do I hold back from speaking my truth? Is there a certain person I feel incapable of speaking my truth with? Are there any times in which I withdraw, even when I have something to say?

___

Do I use my words to hurt or to empower? How do I live in my authentic truth and stand in integrity?

___

Are there any people I surround myself with that cause me to feel like a chameleon?

___

How do I react when there is gossip happening around me? Do I jump on the train to make small talk, or do I remove myself from the situation? How do I feel if I hear someone is talking about me?

___

How often do I flake or break promises?

_____
_____
_____
_____
_____

How do I lose patience? What triggers send me over the edge? Why?

_____
_____
_____
_____
_____

If I was able to express myself without fear of judgement or rejection, what would I say? How would it feel to be unapologetically me?

_____
_____
_____
_____
_____

What do I express creatively? What outlets and practices do I use for creative expression?

Do you have any hidden talents that are uniquely yours, or maybe even something beyond your own capabilities with the right guidance to help tap into them? Maybe it's an unusual skill like having a good ear for music without being able to read sheet music or knowing how things work just by looking at diagrams of machinery in books. Being creative is often associated with painting pictures on canvases, but creativity isn't limited. There are infinite ways of expression.

_____
_____
_____
_____

_____

"I am the pure eternal consciousness and bliss."

"I'm not scared to speak my mind."

"My intent is always clear and noble when I speak."

"My voice is clear and powerful."

"I feel compassion toward others."

"I don't engage in gossips and criticism."

"I have access to my higher self for guidance and support."

"I am open to receiving messages from my angels."

"I don't interrupt others while they speak."

"What I do, I do it with full conviction and dedication."

"I am honest and authentic in my speech and actions."

"I am improving my relationships."

"I am calm and relaxed."

"I can feel that my immune system is improving."

"I avoid people who gossip and criticize."

The Enchantress

The Enchantress is one of the most stigmatized female archetypes. The Enchantress enters a very different phase of her life if her children are now grown or have left home, and she stands on the cusp of menopause. She represents women who own their sexuality and creative power, while at highest expression they embody forces to be reckoned with because they don't tolerate that which does not serve them. They also represent more than just motherhood - she is truly a magical woman who reaps rewards from harvest (autumn).

This archetype slides right in between the archetypal phases of the mother and crone. She expects and demands abundance, having confidence, wisdom and experience to cultivate it for herself. She understands the concept of energy and allows flow within her life.

Examples include:

- Advocates
- The Activist
- The Confident Entrepreneur or Leader
- The Harvest Woman
- Pre-menstrual woman or Waning Lunar Cycle Woman

- 40+ year old women who have time for themselves now that their children are grown up/The Warrior Women
- The Medicine Woman/Priestess

The definition of enchantress is a woman who uses magic or sorcery, especially to put someone or something under a spell. She is the aspect of the feminine that is other worldly and in tune with her darker sacred energies. The main difference between an ordinary witch and an enchantress would be their level self-awareness/consciousness about themselves as well as how they allow others around them into this realm. The Enchantress is introspected and at a phase in life where she wants to explore herself, her capabilities, her creativity. She operates from a place of love vs. fear.

Now that she is an empty nester, she will have more time to explore her hobbies and passions. They are likely mature with clarity on what they want out of life.

This phase can be viewed as "darker" since the Enchantress has no fear of expressing their shadow side without judgement; however, the enchantress energy is a healer's energy -- it brings forth all that needs to come to light while not being scared or judged for doing so because we give back by contributing our energies towards something greater than ourselves.

The Enchantress is our key to guidance when we feel a need to transition in life. She will guide you into your new journey with her deep sense of awakening within, no matter the age or stage that one may be in. You may embrace her as your transition before taking place on becoming the Wise Woman.

The Shadow: The enchantress has lost her sense of direction and purpose after becoming a newly empty nester. She may withdraw herself from opportunities or gatherings, feeling at a standstill in life. She will not recognize her newfound freedom and will withdraw from life itself until she finds her passions and new purpose. She may experience burn out and low libido and a feeling of blah.

Toxic Positivity

No matter how much you love and light your good vibes only way through life, there will always be darkness. If we don't acknowledge it in the world around us, then our dark side is not going to go away or get any lighter. It in fact can creep up or manifest at the most unexpected times. Positivity does sound bouncy and beautiful however when it's overgeneralized - like no one should experience anything but happiness or your "bad"- that can cause more harm than good because of denial towards our human emotions such as anger and sadness which are designed to allow us to grow, heal, and learn the lessons we came here to experience.

When you are going through a hard time, do not be bombarded with fake positivity. It can make people feel worse about themselves and their situation. Toxic positive attitude is the feeling of acting happy or cheerful when they're not trying to reach out for unconditional support from others but instead find that genuine emotions got ignored, dismissed or invalidated by someone else which makes them feel even more depressed than before.

When people invalidate your experiences, it creates a sense of self-doubt that makes you question yourself. This is like gaslighting because they're trying to manipulate and control how YOU feel about something or someone instead of just having an honest conversation. Being genuine.

We must be aware that positivity can often lead to shame, and this is completely unhealthy. Positivity should not silence the human experience; it gives us an avoidance mechanism - we're denying ourselves from facing challenging feelings which could bring about insight and growth.

Pushing a positive outlook on pain will encourage people to keep their struggles silent because of fear or embarrassment since there's no way you would want someone telling you what your feeling isn't valid due to them being so "positive". We need everyone around us to listen without judgement when we share how we feel during difficult situations in life while also making sure we aren't shamed for having "negative" thoughts.

When we deny our truth, like in hiding situations, it can be dangerous. The truth is that life sometimes hurts and if you don't acknowledge the angry feelings they get buried deep within your body - remember our previous chapter on the psoas muscle. Our anger and resentment get stored within at a cellular level when we do not allow ourselves permission to process and feel.

Now, I am not telling you to walk around acting like a Karen and creating chaos within your life. *Where the attention goes energy flows;* but we need to honor our sacred signs and signals when they come through certain situations. We're meant to be angry in an appropriate way, we are supposed cry over sadness, or get mad if something is against our truth--it's all about balance. Observing how you feel will allow for tapping into inner intuition rather than what others say should happen.

> Being a healthy human involves empathizing with
> our sisters and validating their expressions.

The Taboo

The enchantress archetype is not just about discernment, re-visioning and truth telling. These superpowers are used to align with her within her soul's purpose and divine calling.

Abundance: a very large quantity of something.

Confusion has led many people to believe that abundance and money are one in the same. However, this couldn't be further from the truth! Abundance is more than just a financial state of mind; it's an overall way of life. The definition of abundance has many components and ways for us to frame our lives around the idea. It doesn't have to purely revolve around finances or lack thereof but instead an overall mindset we should all adopt with whatever situation comes before us each day.

The universal truth we all desire, however, is money. It's not the actual dollar amount that matters; it's what you can do with your wealth to make memories or experiences happen. Money isn't meant for hoarding - instead, use it like fuel and live life mindfully! The most important thing about money is understanding its energy-like nature: nothing more than numbers on paper (or in a bank account). Our subconscious has ingrained ideas of how money should be treated since childhood...we must break free from these mental chains and limiting beliefs.

Your subconscious storage files may be screaming "No! We've been told otherwise!"

The real problem is not in the flow of money, but rather one's faith to receive more. Money comes and goes all around us daily; it only becomes an issue when we believe that our supply has run out. Money is meant to ebb and flow.

Be generous - Know that you already have everything you need and that the universe will see to the rest. Bruce Lipton (a cellular biologist) explains "We generally perceive we are running our lives with what matters most--our wishes and desires. But neuroscience reveals a startling fact...we only run our lives 95% percent of time with beliefs programmed in subconscious mind."

If you want to enjoy greater abundance, then practice appreciating the abundance already in your life. When we earn money and spend it consciously, this reflects what we value most in our lives. When we have an energy of scarcity, or think money is the root to all evil we need to understand that our ancestors lived in a much different world and hierarchical order of societies which rooted these limiting beliefs which were passed down through generations. I am sure at some point in your life you have experienced at least one of these thoughts or phrases.

> "MONEY IS THE ROOT OF ALL EVIL."
> "EITHER RICH OR HAPPY AND HEALTHY."
> "MONEY IS NOT THAT IMPORTANT. IT'S ONLY MONEY."
> "MUST BE NICE."
> "MY FAMILY HAS NEVER BEEN RICH."
> "THE RICH GET RICHER AND THE POOR GET POORER."
> "I'M JUST NOT GOOD WITH MONEY."

Right now, as a collective we are shifting to be more conscious. You've heard of 3d and 5d consciousnesses; in the simplest terms, we're becoming aware that our own thoughts can design anything for us. Everything is energy – nothing else matters but that one thing: vibes! When you think negatively about money or feel like it's too powerful against you, those feelings will keep occurring. But when money seems empowering and helpful towards your life goals (when thinking from your heart), there'll always be an abundance of wealth available to everyone.

The cells in your body are responsible for the current state of your finances. If you want to change this, then it is best that you start with healing yourself on a cellular level. This is also called your Money Blueprint. Many people focus too much on what they don't want instead of working towards their goals, which prevents them from ever seeing results.

Everyone experiences money differently. Some people have a hard time managing their bank accounts, while others are always on the lookout for ways to earn more cash or save some extra coins in times of emergency. No matter what your relationship is with money, it's important that you're aware of how certain thoughts and emotions can affect your finances! Money might be just another form energy - but understanding its different energies will help you move from feeling stuck about spending habits to living financially free without stress.

Since our life force energy flows upward, from the earth, it's important for your root chakra to be clear.

Born into a life of privilege, I grew up with everything money could buy. After my grandmother's passing and before moving to Illinois, the state of our family's finances changed drastically after a string of unfortunate turns left us living in poverty. I slowly watched my father lose everything piece by piece. As a teenager we lived in a horrible neighborhood, some weeks we scraped by on frozen burritos, I saw my mother with money and a new shiny life but unwilling to send child support or make sure we were okay. It made me subconsciously develop hatred towards money which gave rise to strong feelings of scarcity within myself. For example, when I was thirteen years old, I received one hundred dollars for birthday presents from loved ones- but instead of spending it immediately like most kids would have done; this bill stuck around in the wallet untouched because it was more precious than gold to me! Money has always been used as something that evokes control over others during my upbringing.

As an adult, I was constantly in fear or a state of feeling like I owed everyone everything because of this dynamic within my family. When I became old enough to make my own money, I became the "yes girl" who spends money frivolously to prove she has it. In fear of being the "poor girl," I would buy things to prove my worth and status quo. Hello ego. Being a Pisces, my shadow is that I naturally live with rose colored glasses and am 130% emotional when it comes to my decision process. I'll own that. This carried into my financial decisions. My bank account screamed scarcity, but my gram obnoxiously blared "glamorous" life. I could barely make ends meet until I changed my relationship with money. I confused conscious spending with hoarding money.

While being brought up with a religious upbringing, I will never forget sitting in the church pew next to my dad (I must have been about 15) while watching him put the last of our change out his pocket into an offering basket. Confused, I looked at him and he said, "there is always someone who needs it more." Devastated by this realization that people were selfish around money when there are others less fortunate than us, I began sobbing silently in that church aisle. I hated money. I hated people who had money. I hated that people were so selfish around money. Most of all I hated that I felt trapped by not having money.

Before realizing the energetic flow of money, I had no idea what savings was or how to invest. I wasn't even close to being able give back to charity. However, one of the most lasting and valuable gifts you can give yourself is learning about proper financial literacy skills, which includes knowing how to give too. How to operate finances from your heart center. Once my personal "money blueprint" changed abundance began flowing into my life - not just from certain sources but all over. Taking responsibility for myself allowed me only do things that bring results in return while letting go of those activities that don't add any value at all.

> "Do not try to become a person of success but
> to become the person of value."
> -Albert Einstein

The Money Meditation: Sit in a comfortable chair. Relax. Start to breathe with healing breaths: inhale through the nose, exhale through the mouth, make the sound of wind pushing air through lips as you say "O." Keep breathing this way throughout meditation. Inhale into your 1st Chakra (where you sit). When inhaling say out loud "I inhale money". And when exhaling whisper under breath 'I exhale lack of money' - Repeat this through all seven chakras. Before opening your eyes take a moment to observe your body - be careful to not attach - just notice and feel the abundance flowing through your body.

Your Money Blueprint: Your money mindset has been set since you were a small child. It came from the beliefs your parents have held about money and entered your psyche every time they talked about it around you when growing up. Think back, what is your story?

_____
_____
_____
_____
_____

1. Rich people believe "I create my life." Poor people believe "Life happens to me."
2. Rich people play the money game to win. Poor people play the money game to NOT lose.
3. Rich people are committed to being rich. Poor people want to be rich.
4. Rich people admire other rich and successful people. Poor people resent rich and successful people.
5. Rich people manage their money well. Poor people mismanage their money well.

(Reprinted from "Secrets of a Millionaire Mind" by T. Harv Eker)

What are your financial goals?

___

What are your spending habits? When you look around are you cultivating a life of value or are you spending on "stuff" that accumulates and feels cluttered?

___

"Nothing has meaning except for what you attach to it."

How do you respond when money is boughten up in a conversation?

___

What experiences do you want to create by having money?

___

What do you believe about debt? How do you feel about paying your debts?
_____
_____
_____
_____

Are you open to receive money? Does that feel safe?
_____
_____
_____
_____

Food for thought: How would you spend $1,000,000 dollars if you received it right now?

The History of Witches

Witches go back as far as we remember with tales across different cultures from the pointy nose woman with a hat to the boiled face hag. As we move through time, there were witch trials; Sabrina the teenage witch was popular too! Then came the witch who wiggled her nose and poof- Magic.

Where are our ancestors though? Our ancestors include women who called upon spirits to create change and cast spells - medicine women!

While there are all kinds of witches and practices, we have one thing in common. Witches are women whose embodiment of femininity pisses off society's boundaries and expectations of women—they are too old, too powerful, sexually aggressive or undesirable. Written accounts of woman who practice magic date back to recorded history and their appearance has inspired the infamous Halloween figure as evil beings due to its feminine characteristics that go against what's acceptable at the time.

The Puritans deemed women to be more likely than men to succumb the Devil's temptations, which was why 78% of all witches in New England were female. As such, male members of society enforced these rigid rules that dictated proper gender roles; for example, wealthy individuals would never have too much money because it meant they had made sinful gains and those with very little wealth demonstrated bad character. Furthermore, having an excessive number of children suggested deals with a devil on both ends. Too many - not enough. There was just no winning.

Witches used magic spells and called upon spirits for help or to bring about change. They were feared at the time because it was unknown.

Witches must have been doing "the devil's work." Most witches were natural born healers and wise women trying to make a positive impact in a chaotic world, but one of their earliest records can be found in The Bible from 931-721 B.C.

There are a lot of limitations, rules, and fear embedded into many religions - Witch hysteria really took hold in Europe during the mid-1400s when accused witches confessed to have committed various offenses. This was the start of witch trials where women were hung for being healers. "Witchcraft" encompasses mystical traditions that harmonize with nature which is gentle on empowerment and earth based. Not only did it become evident that men also suffered from these accusations, but they remain rampant today especially against female leaders who oppose patriarchy.

While growing up I was taught that Wiccans were of the devil, but they strive to live a peace-filled life in tune with nature and humanity. They avoid evil at all costs, their motto is "harm none." In Papua New Guinea, a young mother was burned alive in 2010 after being accused of using witchcraft. Several other men and women suspected of practicing the ancient art have been beaten or killed across the country since then.

A modern-day witchcraft potion is more likely to be an herbal remedy for the flu, instead of a hex that harms someone. But witches—whether actual or accused still face persecution and death.

A witch is not evil – she is an embodiment of her truth in all its power.

Calling on Your Enchantress

Witchcraft is a lifelong journey and it's always better to take your time than rushing through. The Enchantress energy knows that all will come in divine timing so we should enjoy every step of being open along the way. Take your time and do what feels right for you. It's okay to mess up and it's okay if your spells don't work right away. As the feminine energy flows so do you - this is how we learn; it isn't a "fail," simply an opportunity for growth in our practice (it was called a practice for a reason).

The best way to gain knowledge within this archetype or your craft is through practice and slowing down. Each witch is unique and what works for one person may not work as well for someone else. With social media, it's important to do your research first before you copy a post because there isn't anything like the "one-size fits all" method when it comes to your personal craft. The stigma of right and wrong - black and white should be broken within your practice. We are practicing magic every day, even when we don't realize it. It's the intentions behind our words and actions that cause this "magic". You do not have to be a Wiccan or any other religion - there are Christian witches, pagan witches, atheists' witches. You can believe in whatever higher power of your choice while still being able to use spells.

Just like anything else from cooking dinner for yourself instead of going out all the way down to speaking kindly about somebody rather than saying negative things; spell work is available across faiths and is personal to you and your beliefs.

The one rule I have found is to respect the boundaries of closed practices and do your research on other cultures' history with witchcraft.

Starting out with witchcraft can be very overwhelming. There is so much information out there and it feels expensive- it doesn't have to be expensive and many of your materials can even come from your backyard.

For example, a dandelion can be used in so many ways within your craft and is accessible to pretty much everyone. It may seem like there are lots of rules but remember that you don't have to follow them all the time - start small and keep things simple. If something doesn't work for you or your situation, simply find a substitution.

Each season your practice will shift. The word "Dandelion" comes from the French word dent-de-lion, meaning "tooth of lion." Dandelions begin to come up just as the winter fades completely, symbolizing hope and fresh starts, boil dandelion leaves and roots into tea and drink it before reading tarot or other divination practices for clarity and direction.

(The entire dandelion is edible).

Include dandelions in spells to jump start projects or break a creative block. Press between the pages of your journal to infuse positive solar energy. There are so many different options to use this magical root.

Another very simple starting point with embodiment of the Enchantress is crafting intentional tea spells.

What is your purpose for this tea craft? The first step is to set your intention. Select a main herb that best represents the goal of why you are creating this blend, then choose supporting herbs that enhance it in its taste or traditional practice. Doing your research is also very important before creating intuitive recipes to make sure you use the appropriate portion sizes, avoid allergens (if necessary), and understand dangers.

Seeds – Fennel, Coriander, Star Anise, Cardamom, Caraway and Cacao Nibs.

Seeds are the blueprints of the plant life, the messengers of the plant world. They represent our desires, potential, inspiration and ideas.

Fennel - Fennel seed has been used since ancient times as a natural remedy for many ailments. Fennel is very rich in antioxidants and anti-inflammatory properties, which can help strengthen the mind and memory with clarity and direction. It also helps fight cravings by repelling interference from other toxins.

Coriander - Coriander is a common ingredient in love spells and sachets. It can also be used to ease the pain of break-ups or divorces, as well as easing headaches and menstrual cramps. Coriander has been known since ancient times for its magical uses including love spells, overall healing, protection of gardeners and fire magic.

Star Anise - Star anise is shaped like a star and corresponds directly with energies of the micro- and macrocosm, stability and expansion, connection to divine information. This special herb increases psychic connections (for healing purposes), divine protection for health, success in lucky endeavors. Star Anise has many helpful uses: appetite stimulant; digestion aid; free radicals that can cause cancer or other ailments; gas relief; and influenza symptoms.

Cardamom - Cardamom is a stimulating herb that relaxes the body and clarifies the mind. It was used widely in Europe to treat digestive problems, but it can also be added to lust drawing sachets. Cardamom seeds are feminine in nature and correspond with element water.

Caraway - The tiny seeds from the caraway plant are used as a form of protection against negativity and evil spirits. Caraway is often added to sachets or charms to attract love & encourage fidelity.

Cacao Nibs - The source of happiness and concentration, Cacao beans invite optimism and magnesium is the most important mineral for a healthy heart. These delicious treats contain serotonin, dopamine, anandamide and phenylethylamine.

Roots – Dandelion, Ginger, Turmeric, Sarsaparilla, Licorice and Chicory.

Dandelion - This herb is a potent diuretic, good for vitamin A, C and K production, the root of many spells. Magically it's used in psychic work, wish fulfillment, creativity and sun magic.

Ginger - The magical properties of ginger are to boost the strength of any other ingredients you're working with. Ginger has an extremely long history as a healing herb and is used to treat nausea, pain, inflammation, colds, and more. Using ginger in abundance, success and prosperity spells is very powerful.

Turmeric - Turmeric is an amazing anti-inflammatory herb that helps fight existing inflammation, prevent inflammatory responses from occurring again, and has all sorts of other health benefits. It can help relieve stomach pains, support your immune system to bring down bad cholesterol levels while strengthening bones and joints. In spells it's passion inducing with commanding confidence & courage; exorcising evil spirits or magic - sensual strength spell breaking.

Sarsaparilla - Sarsaparilla is used to treat skin conditions, including eczema and psoriasis. It may also aid digestion. For spells you can use it for drawing money or to bless a house; it's even said that sarsaparilla has the power to increase sexual desire.

Licorice - Licorice root has been shown to be as good as codeine because it contains saponins, which are anti-inflammatory chemicals. It is also anti-allergic and antiviral. Licorice root has long been associated with lust, passion, love & fidelity and can often be found in spell or ritual work for these goals.

Chicory - To unlock the power of this humble herb, a witch should use the power of three. Chicory root has many holistic properties such as digestive problems and mild laxative; it was used throughout history to substitute for coffee. This root is documented throughout time with having magical properties including luck, strength, divination, favors and frugality; additionally opening locks can be done by using chicory and removing obstacles or curse removal are also possible when you consume/use chicory in your rituals.

Barks – Cinnamon and Sassafras.

Cinnamon - One of my personal favorite's cinnamon - can truly be used for almost everything, from blood sugar fluctuations to morning sickness. It has anti-fungal properties and slows digestion which is perfect if you have a slow metabolism or an upset stomach. Cinnamon, a common baking spice and dark, brown-colored powder associated with the sacral and root chakra. Cinnamon can be used for money spells as well as love or lust potions depending on what your intentions are. It also works to keep you safe from harm by repelling negative energies that might come in its path.

Sassafras - Sassafras was the original herb used in all "root" beers. It is also a great magical herb that can be used to both protect yourself or your space from malevolent spirits, as well as use it for craft projects like making furniture, objects etc. For example, you could make an altar cloth out of sassafras root bark so any negative energy directed towards you would not affect anything on this sheet. You may even want to burn these chips during bioregional incense rituals because they are known to rid places and living spaces of negative influence by entities, people etc.

Leaves – Black or Green Tea, Lemon Balm, Lemon Verbena, Lemon Grass, Chickweed, Stinging Nettle, Blackberry Leaf, Moringa, Holy Basil, Linden, Marjoram, Mug Wort, Sage, Ginkgo, Eucalyptus, Tarragon, Thyme, Rosemary, Peppermint, Red Clover, Spearmint, Yerba Mate and Rooibos.

Black Tea - Black Tea is the most oxidized kind of tea, and it' actually has more caffeine than green or white teas. It magically creates Courage to fight addictions; energy; stability in money spells and luck with studies/school.

Green Tea - Green tea is smooth and less oxidized than black tea. It's used in spells for health/healing, longevity, sex/love/passion spells, energy sorcery, cleansing /banishing negativity, money magic rituals & ceremonies that bring about financial prosperity or manifesting abundance.

Lemon Balm - Lemon balm has been used to treat a variety of ailments for centuries. This plant is also known as the "elixir of life" because it helps induce calmness and promotes longevity. The magical properties of lemon balm include love, success, longevity and healing.

Lemon Verbena - The little sprig of Lemon Verbena is believed to be capable of increasing the wearer's charm and attractiveness, as well as prevent them from dreaming. It can also function in addition with other charms or spells for added power.

Lemon Grass - The tropical plant Lemongrass is used in many Asian cuisines for its magical properties. It can help with communication and provide protection, along with helping people who are looking to find love or luck when it comes to their relationship status. On top of that, lemongrass helps reduce fevers while aiding digestion issues as well as providing antibacterial/antimicrobial benefits.

Chickweed - Chickweed is a detoxification agent and blood purifying herb with the botanical name Stellaria media, meaning "little stars" or commonly known as Chickweed. It affects physical and psychic health by opening cosmic energies, giving you strength to handle these energies. To attract new romance or maintain relationship mix Chickweed Roses & Orange Blossoms into your bath water daily for strength within your marriage or relationship add just a little bit of this herb to partner's food every day. Bring peace throughout home - sprinkle a tad around the home. Can also be used in teas.

Stinging Nettle - For a spring tonic, try drinking stinging nettle tea. Nettle is great for anyone recovering from an illness or who has chronic weakness, fatigue or anemia. It's also good for milk production in new mamas and can be used to drive out negativity - To get witchy with this magical leaf, burn it as incense to break curses and ground into a powder to use in spells.

Blackberry Leaf - Blackberry leaves are used for many things including returning evil back to sender, removing spirits and good luck. Both the berries and leaves can be offered as an offering or in invocation of goddess Brigit. They also have medicinal purposes such as healing throat ailments like sore throats or mouth ulcers, and gastric distress ailments.

Moringa - Moringa is known as the "phantom tree". This plant has more nutrition in its leaves than any other plant we know of, and it contains 2x more protein, 4x iron (iron!), 3x calcium and 2 x fiber compared to kale! Moringa also contains a lot of essential minerals; calcium, magnesium, potassium, and phosphorus which are necessary for supporting healthy bone structure, protecting the central nervous system and maintaining normal blood pressure.

Holy Basil - Holy Basil is a magical herb that can be used to increase your body's resistance to stress, enhance adrenal function and for physical endurance. Additionally, it balances the chakras and provides protection from insanity by bringing happiness, love, peace and money while also attracting luck in both astral projection and physically journeying. You could use basil spells on yourself, so you attract more love throughout life as well as placing the leaf inside your wallet with a cinnamon stick which attracts wealth.

WITHIN

Linden - A mixture of Linden flowers and Lavender are great for releasing the energies needed to keep both your body and spirit healthy. If you have insomnia, place a sachet with these two ingredients under your pillow at night! To relieve anxiety-related issues like stress or nervousness, mix equal parts Linden flowers and lavender together then set aside in an incense burner. Historically, linden has been used to soothe nerves as well as treat health problems associated with anxiety.

Marjoram - Marjoram has countless benefits including protection against anxiety and tension headaches as well as remedies for several stomach ailments such as digestion problems and bloating. Marjoram also contains an anti DPP4 which can be used in treating diabetes or other sleep disorders that affect the body's internal clock. Marjoram is a versatile herb that can be used for protection, health and wealth.

Mug Wort - The ancient, sacred plant called Mug wort has always been a powerful one. It is known to repel evil spirits and ghosts- as well as mosquitoes! The herb also brings about lucid dreams, divination of the future through intuition and psychic abilities; it's connected with Artemis (the moon goddess).

The intimate relationship between humans and plants runs deep – compelling us to both honor their power while taking care not to abuse this gift.

Sage - Sage, which has been used in traditional cleansing ceremonies since European traditions began. It is associated with wisdom, good luck and even mortality. Sage builds emotional strength and can help to heal grief. The Egyptians, Romans, Greeks used it for medicinal purposes curing snake bites or enhancing memory/cognition. Sage has incredible cleansing properties and was also recently discovered as having anti-inflammatory properties.

Ginkgo - Ginkgo Bilboa is the only surviving tree of its species that has been around since it was first on this planet. Its ability to survive and thrive makes Ginkgo a perfect herb for longevity tonics, vitality tonics, brain food spells/potions with magical benefits like aphrodisiacs or fertility. You can use gingko in healing sachets & love spells too.

Eucalyptus - Eucalyptus is known for its ability to remove negative influences from one's immediate surroundings. Eucalyptus helps to bring fresh energy into a situation, heal regret and worries, and relieve mental exhaustion. I love putting some in my shower so that it can help me feel rejuvenated every morning. Unlike other protective herbs, Eucalyptus doesn't attack or constrain others but instead gently creates a barrier without doing either.

Tarragon - Tarragon is a great herb for consecrating magical tools and banishing negative spirits. Tarragon can be sprinkled around the house to protect against malevolent entities, as well as used in healing situations such as those involving abuse or personal growth.

Thyme - The ancient Greek and Roman cultures believed thyme to be a source of courage, strength, and psychic power. Women who wore it in their hair were said to have made themselves irresistible with its use. The magical herb thyme, when burned and placed beneath the pillow, ensures a restful night's sleep free of nightmares. Used for health, healing, sleep, psychic powers, love, purification and courage.

Rosemary - To boost your test-taking performance, sniffing rosemary can give you an extra edge. Rosemary has been burned to purify a room or ritual space before magical workings since ancient times and was associated with Aphrodite/Venus in old folklore.

Peppermint - Peppermint is often used in spells, potions or other types of rituals that are intended to protect you from harm. It can be helpful for money-related goals and healing purposes too! If you burn peppermint as incense, it will help induce sleep. Peppermint has a long history being useful for digestion issues such as nausea, gas stomach cramps etc., which also makes it good treatment option for irritable bowel syndrome (IBS).

Red Clover - Red clover is used in baths to aid financial arrangements and love spells, as well as sachets for money, luck, fidelity and success. It also is a rich source of estrogen-like chemicals that have been found to prevent or relieve symptoms related to menopause such as breast pain associated with PMS.

Spearmint - Spearmint leaves are an excellent ingredient for use in spells of healing, protection and love. Spearmint is one strong herb for protection while sleeping; burn it with a hot flame so that its smoke can surround you as well as bring healing magic into action during sleep times. Carry spearmint in order to be constantly protected from harm or illness all around - stave any bodily ills away with ease by being always surrounded by this plant's protective powers! Use this special minty smell in ritual baths when working towards strength and vitality.

Yerba Mate - Yerba Mate, also known as "the drink of the gods," is a traditional South American beverage that provides an instant boost in energy and mental focus. It's loaded with nutrients and antioxidants which may even protect you from heart disease down the road! Magical properties: Fidelity, love and lust.

Rooibos - Rooibos is a magical elixir that carries vital energy! It's also packed with vitamins, iron, potassium and fluorine.

Flowers – Chamomile, Yarrow, Linden, Red Clover Blossoms, Cornflowers, Calendula, Rose Petals, Chrysanthemum, Elderflower, Hibiscus, Lavender, Safflower, Cloves and Bee Pollen.

Chamomile - Chamomile is more than just a flower that you put in your tea. It was associated with the sun gods of ancient Egypt and has many medicinal. Chamomile can be used for several different purposes, such as diarrhea or migraines - but it's best known for helping babies sleep soundly at night without any colic pains to keep them awake. Placed around your home, chamomile protects against psychic attacks, can be used to heighten meditation, assist in sleep and provide protection.

Yarrow - Yarrow is a powerful, all-purpose herb. It can be used to set boundaries and protect you from negative energy around your home. Yarrow also can attract good relationships into one's life both romantically and as friends! Yarrow is known for breaking bad habits and holistically is strongly tied with the five major organ systems in our body: circulatory, respiratory functions, digestive tract, urinary system.

Linden - The linden flower is known for its calming and heart-healing properties. It promotes sleep, soothes nerves, quells anxiety, eases spasms and cramps, promotes sweating and facilitates digestion. In addition to physical healing of the body it also opens spiritual energy centers by opening of the heart while soothing souls at a deep level which helps with cardiovascular function. Linden flowers are used for divination, love spells, tranquility and protection.

Red Clover Blossoms - Red clovers blossoms are often associated with fidelity, love, money protection, and blessing domestic animals.

Cornflowers - The Cornflower is known for its powerful abilities to awaken psychic awareness, enhance self-knowledge and access inner wisdom. It can be used in rituals involving magic or spirituality as well as with abundance work related projects like fertility, growth and creativity.

Calendula - The symbol of the Sun, Calendula flowers are also used in love spell divination. They signify sun energy and have many uses including healing, strength, love, marriage, stability, consecration, legal matters, dreamwork and spiritual growth. The chakra center for this flower is solar plexus.

Rose Petals - Roses are one of the most romantic flowers and can be used in many types of magical work. Use red roses to attract love, white for purity, pink for friendship or romance; even dried rose petals have their own uses. For beauty magic they're great in bath salts which you could add to a bubble bar recipe - try adding them with some lavender oil too. Rose syrup has lots of health benefits so make sure you keep any leftovers though because not only will it help ease sore throats but drinking regularly may aid digestion problems such as constipation.

Chrysanthemum - The dried flower heads of chrysanthemum can be burned during house blessing ceremonies. Chrysanthemum has been used for burial rituals and is a suitable decoration for Samhain and ancestral altars in Chinese medicine, the infusion of dried chrysanthemum petals has been used as an eyewash to relieve redness from eye strain brought on by stress. In addition, it's called Ju Hua and is also known to lower high blood pressure when drank as tea.

Elderflower Elder flowers are great for spiritual and emotional healing. They can help to break spells that have been cast against you, so add them in your tea or bath water! Incense blends with elder flower purify and protect homes from negative energy.

Hibiscus - Hibiscus, the flower of passion. Its other magical properties include love, divination and freedom from inhibitions. A common ceremonial tea in many cultures is also used medicinally to lower blood pressure and boost liver health.

Lavender - Lavender is a beautiful flower that can be used in many different spells. One of the most common uses for lavender are consecration and cleansing, happiness, healing love, peace and protection. Its scent relaxes individuals while simultaneously uplifting them making it great aromatherapy for stressed out or depressed people who are searching for relief. Another use of lavender includes sharpening your mind which will help you with concentration on what needs done at hand as well encouraging the purest forms of love.

Safflower - Safflower has been used for love and happiness rituals since ancient Mesopotamia. It's also an ingredient in making the iconic "saffron yellow" dye, which is why it was grown by humans as early as 4000 BC.

Cloves - The name "clove" originates from the Old French world clou and the Latin clavus meaning "nail" for its shape, like that of a nail. For this reason, cloves are often seen as protective. Cloves can be used in several spells including protection spells, banishing magic, money spells, healing rituals. Cloves can be used to soothe nausea, vomiting, and even flatulence as well as to stimulate the digestive system. They are also known for being an antiseptic and mild anesthetic.

Bee Pollen - Bee pollen may cause serious side effects in people with allergies, including shortness of breath and anaphylaxis. Use accordingly. Honey is used often in magic to sweeten a situation. The Honey Jar spell, for example: anointing your lips with honey will make your words sound sweeter and more persuasive.

Fruit – Elderberry, Lemon, Lemon Peel, Orange Peel, Rosehips, Peppercorn, Allspice, Nutmeg and Chili Pepper.

Elderberry - For hundreds of years, people from many different cultures have been using the elder plant to cure a wide range of ailments. The tree is believed to hold magic powers and has long been worshipped by various cultures for its connection with life, death, and rebirth. On the witchy side of things, it is used for healing, protection, and love.

Lemon - Lemons have been used for centuries and are prized for their health-giving benefits, including purification, happiness and beauty. They're one of my favorite things to work with! So much goodness. Medicinally lemons were historically used to prevent scurvy but nowadays they commonly flavor foods as well as treating medical ailments such as colds and flus.

Lemon Peels - Elemental Fire, for cleansing and rites of purification. Also used for clarity aura cleansing awareness. Lemon peels are a solar substance that can be used to cleanse the body or mind in order bring about an increase in energy levels as well as remove inhibiting factors from both your physical space and mental state.

Orange Peels - The high-energy scent of oranges is said to communicate the joy of angels to human beings. Orange peel is used in Yule celebrations, reminding us of the promise that Sun brings even during winter months; dried orange peels make a perfect addition for creativity sachets and are associated with abundant energy as well as monetary success spells.

Rosehips - The powerful and enchanting rosehip can be used for many purposes including love, protection, dreams or death. This fruit has a special connection with water so it is best to use in cleansing rituals as well as within witches' bottles or medicine pouches where healing will take place. Add them around your home to bring harmony and peace.

Peppercorn - Used in spells and charms that banish negativity, protection from evil, jealousy or if you're struggling help move past it. Peppercorn is an age-old spice popularly known not only for the unique taste of food but also their medicinal properties throughout history - particularly when keeping away demons or bad luck! In addition, mixing peppercorn alongside salt can be sprinkled into every corner on our house for powerful magic protective shield!

Allspice - Allspice is said to have the aroma of many spices including cinnamon, nutmeg, cloves and pepper. It was named "Allspice" because it has a mixed flavor profile. Allspice can be used in a paste to soothe toothache (much like cloves). The masculine tone should honor very virile and powerful male archetypes with its uplifting energy increasing determination making useful in various types of spells especially healing ones.

Nutmeg - Nutmeg can be added to beverages drank before meditation and divination. If you add it, this will ensure good luck in travel or business ventures through troubles. Nutmeg essential oil is an ingredient in Money Drawing Oil which can help with spell work when rubbed on candles and other items during the ritual process. However, use caution if adding nutmeg as people have reported hallucinations upon using too much of it because there are some cases where toxicity could occur depending on how many teaspoons were used at once so don't go overboard. (Recommended no more than 1 tsp).

Chili Pepper - The spell to break a curse/hex can be spiced up with the addition of chili peppers. Placed around your house, these red and green vegetables will help cure negative spells placed on you or those in the home. Chili peppers in love spells will give your relationship a kick and are used to keep things spicy!

Another excellent starting point is to create a book of shadows. A book of shadows is a diary, complete with drawings and insights into the witch's soul. But it doesn't just record your experiences as you become more powerful–a good one will teach you how to use spells properly- It can also help guide budding witches through their first steps towards becoming more skilled. It documents your craft and knowledge and develops who you are as a witch. This diary contains your story of information about witchcraft, including stepwise directions on casting different kinds of magic spells; what is required before spellcasting; lists traditional ingredients used in ritualistic practices such as making potions, candles, etc. and records, personal notes, like successes/or what may have not worked for you.

If you're starting your journey, knowledge is key. Start by reading all the books that feel relevant to you on witchcraft; it's where true power comes from for an Enchantress like yourself! A great spell to get your started would be a protection one (you can learn how in a simple google search). Once you've learned enough about spells and discovered what works best for YOU—you can begin to create your own.

> **"If you call yourself a witch you are taking on the mantel of hundreds of years of oppression and ostracism. It is your duty to stand beside those who suffer injustice. If you do not, your "spirituality" is aesthetic only."**
> -Holly Cassell

"I am a spiritual being in a physical body."

"I am following my path. It is right for me."

"I enable myself to learn and grow."

"I allow myself to let go of the past."

"I feel empathy and compassion for all life on Earth."

"I find joy in my magick and embrace my power."

"Witchcraft unleashes my strength."

"I achieve every goal I desire."

"I am transforming myself."

"I declare my intentions to the universe."

"I love myself, and my shadow self."

"My path is filled with knowledge, love, and prosperity."

"I follow my intuition."

"I release my mistakes and open myself to new opportunities."

"I see beyond the surface."

"I speak the language of the universe."

"My words and thoughts are powerful."

The Priestess

The Priestess archetype represents our unique soul path in this lifetime. She tunes into her intuition and womb wisdom, trusts Divine guidance as she walks the path to live a fulfilling life. The Priestess is a soulful and spiritually strong person. She's sensitive to the needs of others, but also very patient with them because she understands that everyone has their own journey through life. The Priestess finds peace in nature which helps her stay grounded while still being aware of higher knowledge all around us.

She has also been exalted, feared, revered and shamed. She's often desired for her secret knowledge and chastised for her power by those who are jealous or scared of it all. A Priestess is a woman with connections to the sacred and mundane worlds: both as an owner of that connection but also as a conduit between them; not only someone tuned into things but able to tune things in herself too-through meditation, ritual & manifestation work (however you might express this). The Priestess sits at the gate before great mystery like one side of its channeling switchboard-between darkness/light – tuning us back into Spirit when we've wandered off course. A Priestess at the core is someone who honors themselves with compassion, kindness and love yet also with strength and power. They are always authentic in being vulnerable to their surroundings while living life honorably. They cultivate a sense of inner peace by knowing the answer is always within regardless of outside circumstances.

The Challenge: For the Priestess, being open and protected are two conflicting things. She's challenged to have self-respect while also showing empathy towards others' opinions that don't align with her own beliefs. The archetypal Priestess has some challenges which her qualities present to her. She can find it difficult to stay grounded, with the contact she makes with the divine and spiritual realms making her feel above the world in which she exists.

They may become self-obsessed by having too much influence from their energetic dimension of life that isn't always visible or tangible.

The Shadow: The Priestess in shadow is a woman who has an incredible inner wisdom and sensitivity but does not trust it. If she became aware of this Archetype, she would serve as the receiver from other dimensions and become comfortable with having no idea what's going on around her. In her shadow side, the Priestess may struggle to differentiate between intuition and ego leading them to follow their own agendas instead of listening inwardly for guidance; they will push others away by controlling situations or becoming irritable when things don't go their way (which can lead others placing blame). She may have trouble setting boundaries and become a doormat. Another shadow expression is that she becomes egoic by identifying with spiritual energies and powers, using them to manipulate others rather than serve the Sacred.

A vivid example of the Priestess archetype is Pythia, who was a priestess in Ancient Greece. She held court at Delphi and communicated prophecies from Apollo while he spoke through her trance-like state. It takes some serious character to be chosen as one of these priests/priestesses; they had very high standards for morality that were expected when choosing someone new after their predecessor's death. The Pythia was required to give up all her familial ties and duties if she had a family. She would then be married into a life of fame in order to serve as the priestess at Delphi, who counseled kings with prophecy.

Womb Wisdom

Women are born with wisdom inside of them. We are magic. This includes the ability to create anything, whether it's a child, business venture, book— or even sexual pleasure. Even if you have never been pregnant before your womb still holds the life force energy. Many women want all these things, but they can't because something is blocking them. You are a woman. You have the power to create, yet somehow, you're still blocked by fear or trauma that has occurred in your life. Every drop of blood flowing through your veins comes from an ancestor who also experienced pleasure and pain - how wonderful is it that this gift runs deep within our souls? The womb is a women's unique connection to nature and can be used for not just procreation, but conscious co-creation with the Universe. Mother earth is called mother because it is from her womb that all life stems, it also is the place where everything returns. Celebrating milestones and transitions re-weaves the wisdom of our primordial birthright. We forget so often how important it is to celebrate each milestone, but we remember when we look at the ancient cauldron of the sacred feminine.

Womb Medicine seeks to re-wild our relationships with our primordial birthright and restore these connections. It is a place of sexuality and creativity, ruled by the sacral chakra where we connect with great Goddess power like Ix Chel who was one of their most important deities in Mayan culture. Ix Chel is the Mayan goddess of fertility, weaving and waters. She was generally considered to have power over floods. Her symbol often associated with the Moon because she had an importance in "weaving" within the Universe. She has a significant role as both midwife or physician during childbirth; Being one who gives life, this deity can be warlike at times too - usually depicted carrying weapons like spears and knives for protection against enemies and evil spirits. There are several deities or archetypes to call on when working through healing your womb. You must follow what feels sacred and right for you.

When we miss out on our thriving center, which is the womb area of our body, it's easy to feel powerless and disconnected. When our sacral center is blocked, we might fall into addictions or numb ourselves out in other ways like food cravings or meaningless sex that are meant to be pleasurable but instead cause us pain because they're being used as a distraction from what really matters - creating lasting happiness within ourselves.

> "When you are inspired by some great purpose, some extraordinary project, all your thoughts break their bonds: Your mind transcends limitations, your consciousness expands in every direction, and you find yourself in a new, great and wonderful world. Dormant forces, faculties and talents become alive, and you discover yourself to be a greater person by far than you ever dreamed yourself to be"
> - Patanjali

Co-creation is about understanding what your role in the universe and realizing that the best way to get things done isn't by doing it all yourself. You should work together with nature, since you're a part of it too. Don't try to do everything alone; instead let go of some control and trust that whatever happens will be perfect for everyone involved and serve the highest good.

Empath vs. Empathetic

Being an empath is different from being empathetic. I have heard an overwhelming amount of women claim to be empaths lately and I think it's important to understand the difference between empathetic and empath. While empathy involves feeling for another person's situation and extending compassion and love an empath can feel the emotions of the other person inside of their own body. They sense other people's happiness or sadness in the brain's mirror neuron system which is hyperactive within empaths. As a result of absorbing both positive and negative energies into their bodies at times it may even become difficult for them to tell if they are experiencing their own feelings or someone else's.

There are three different types of empaths: Physical, emotional, and food. If an individual is a physical empath, they can absorb other people's pain into their own bodies which may lead to them feeling sick or lethargic as well as experiencing muscle aches and pains. Emotional empathy means that individuals become so overwhelmed by emotions from others that it causes stress within the body leading to anxiety attacks, depression or manic episodes. Food empaths are those who feel energy around foods such as meats causing sensitivities for these individuals often resulting in exhaustion due to being overstimulated. With this type of sensitivity also comes challenges including becoming easily overwhelmed or absorbing negative energy from others along with having difficulty setting healthy boundaries.

It can feel vastly challenging.

Do you often get called overly sensitive?
_____

Do you easily get overwhelmed or have anxiety?
_____

When people scream do you feel sick inside or if there is conflict you go immediately into fight or flight mode?
_____

Do you feel like the black sheep?
_____

When you go to social outings do you need time after to recharge your batteries?
_____

Can you become easily over stimulated?
_____

Are you sensitive to chemicals? This can be anything from the tag on a shirt, to booze, to Tylenol?
_____

Do you prefer to be in control of situations?
_____

Do you over or under eat to cope with stressful situations?
_____

When faced with intimacy is it a struggle within your relationships?
_____

Are you jumpy or easily scared?
_____

Do you have an extremely low or extremely high pain threshold?
_____

Are you the girl in mean girls who claims to be "sick" on girls' night out?
_____

Do you take on others' emotions even if they have nothing to do with you?
_____

Does multi-tasking stress you out?
_____

Does nature make you feel rejuvenated?
_____

You require a substantial amount of time to recuperate after being with difficult people or energy vampires?
_____

Are you more comfortable in big cities or in the country or rural areas?
_____

Do you prefer 1 x 1 time vs. party settings?
_____

If you answered yes to one, you're at least partially an empath or highly empathetic and operating from your heart center.

If you answered between six and ten you are partially an empath.

If you answered between ten to fifteen you are a very strong empath.

Answering more than fifteen you are feeling all the feels and very aware of who you are as an empath.

Empaths can be highly sensitive individuals with an innate understanding of what makes those around them tick. This special connection allows them not only to understand but also experience how everyone else feels in any situation or circumstance. Empaths know when something isn't right for you just by looking at your face; it's as if they've had training allowing them access into another person's mind. It's a superpower within itself. A priestess is someone who goes within to create their vision. She represents the unlimited potential of creation that's waiting to be birthed in your hands when you embrace silence and tap into epiphanies, dreams, and spiritual imagery. The way to peace isn't always an easy one, but the Priestess archetype has something special in store for those who would like their life guided by passion. She teaches us how we can begin embodiment through devotion of our passions and find contentment at every turn; even when things seem dark or difficult outside your own personal spotlight shines bright enough that you don't need anything else beyond its brilliance. She places priority on her spirituality and allows nothing to interfere with her divine connection to source. The priestess is a practitioner of heartfelt ceremony and rituals. She teaches us how to connect with the divine through presence.

She helps teach you about your own personal gateway in this moment by teaching obligation-free devotion on what it means for your passions to guide you across life's path like an arrow leading towards its target -or perhaps more accurately: a goddess flame inflames.

> *They have a unique ability to not only find peace but also turn any discord into energy – into heart centered frequency – into love.*

Heart-centeredness is a destiny of peace in which life is aligned. It's not about suppressing feelings, but rather understanding them and how they connect to who we are as individuals so that our decisions line up with what matters most - decisions based on love and not fear. Being honest with ourselves allows us access into hearing the messages from our hearts more clearly - allowing for greater heart awareness leads us towards making healthier lifestyle choices rather than just what logic can dictate. As humans we are born with the ability and power-to heal ourselves and others. We can choose whether this healing will be from our conscious minds, which allows us greater control in decision making but at times may lead us into more confusion. We are given the choice of decision. We choose to become consciously aware, or we choose to continue the same pattern of operating our behaviors at a subconscious level. It comes back to awareness. The mind, like the heart and soul are all linked. We can't operate in a state of pure consciousness until much later in life because we are taught from such a young age to turn it off - which is why children have such an ability to sense and feel at such a deep level. They are still connected. We are operating out of theta and beta brain state until about the age of seven which means, we are operating purely from our subconscious. It is being wired. If children grow up around negative energy their empathic responses only become stronger over time because it becomes a part of their protection mechanism: for example, if you are around a toxic situation growing up, you learn to feel the energy in a room before entering out of a pure state of safety. You learn to read people's emotions to make sure it's okay to speak or communicate. Now as adults it can feel unsafe if you have experienced this to be vulnerable and operate from your heart center. It's important to remember that the danger isn't in being open, but rather having no defenses against what "may" happen. Boundaries. The heart is the director of communication, with its seat on our divine essence. When we allow fear to be our gatekeeper then all sorts of miracles and healing become unavailable because they're blocked from coming through this human experience. Awareness must remain present through self-love expressed authentically, nonjudgement, kindness, gratitude, and grace for your growth. It's called a practice for a reason. When you're looking for ways to make your life more fulfilling, it's natural that the first thing on mind will probably be "what do I want?". This is a good question and one without any easy answer because everyone wants something different from their lives: some may crave financial stability or travel while others might have an emotional need or desire; But despite all these individual differences between people-both inside we as individuals AND externally as a collective it comes down for the craving to feel loved and a sense of belonging. It comes down to the feelers – it comes down to the heart.

Re-live every adventure you had in the last 12 months or so. Think back to all those moments and how those experiences made you feel - did you celebrate?

_____
_____
_____
_____
_____
_____
_____
_____
_____
_____
_____

Tune into the vision and mission you have for your life. What makes you feel excited, even when times get tough? Tune into what inspires deep feeling within yourself that reflects an authentic sense of belonging.

_____
_____
_____
_____
_____
_____
_____
_____
_____
_____
_____

Dream big and imagine the world as your oyster, because that's exactly what you are. Digitize your dreams by engaging in divergent thinking.

> "Let me Love myself without judgement, because when I judge, I carry blame and guilt, I have the need for punishment, and I lose the perspective of Love."
> - Don Miguel Ruiz

Archangel Raphael

The Archangel Raphael is a highly influential healing angel and the main one who oversees individuals' health. Raphael controls etheric vitality and is who you call in when you need guidance or support within the healing realm here on earth. The angel of healing is symbolized through the crescent moon with the small star above it showing a connection to divine energies and medicine for those who need help in their journey on Earth. Archangels are here to help you step into your power. Raphael is known for green, which symbolizes the association of healing and protection. He often will wrap you in a green ray of light upon calling. The crystals emerald and malachite can be used so that you may connect better during meditation sessions. Raphael is called to assist individuals who want to heal themselves so they can be of service at a higher level. Raphael has such an incredible love forcefield around him which is capable of healing or for instant spiritual assistance. Often rather than instant healing Raphael will guide you while things happen around you. We must make sure our inner selves are aligned so higher frequencies can flow through and we can receive the guidance offered. Working with angels is a beautiful experience. One way to make the most of your time, though, is by being open and accepting about how they may appear when you call on them-release your expectations about what the experience "should" be like. When Raphael arrives, he'll always be there but remember that archangels won't influence our lives without permission or being asked.

Feeling strong sensations of energy, tingling warmth and seeing emerald green light are all indications that Saint Raphael is with you. You can think clearly or say aloud:

"I now call upon Archangel Raphael in the East".

Outline very clearly what you are needing help with and ask for assistance where you are needing guidance. This is sacred to you, don't overthink it, just speak from your heart.

The Priestess is the embodiment of peace and love. Her greatest source for power comes from aligning herself with Spirit in all aspects of life - be it through her sweet nature or fierce fierceness; she has no interest whatsoever competing against others on their own terms, but rather prefers that everyone share what they have as a gift so we may grow together into greater heights. The Priestess knows that she's here to birth life back into this world and continue evolution. In the time since human beings first walked upright, they have been seeking greater meaning in their lives. We are so often left searching for spirituality or truth without any concrete answers; it can be difficult not having faith when there isn't anything tangible around us - The Priestess provides this wisdom. She is a woman of power and magic; she knows that her mission in life is to bring empowerment for all beings. The priestess has learned from ancient traditions how we can take our lives into new heights with the use of sacred rituals which will help us reach enlightenment and connection to the Divine.

- Fresh air fuels the rose in my cheeks and the fire in my heart. Today I choose to do what I can, and I can do anything. I express myself verbally and creatively. I stand for self-determination and independence. I communicate my thoughts to others openly.
- Love flows into my life like a river. I am calm and centered, now and always.
- I trust my wisdom and insight. I am sacred, savvy, sassy and wise. I intuitively understand all my bodies – physical, emotional, mental

and spiritual. I relate to my highest truth. I am guided and protected by the Universe. Angels surround me, and I am always aware of them.
- I AM Goddess Wisdom in action. When I look in the mirror, I see a radiant goddess.
- I AM the spirit of enlightenment.
- Today and every day, I feel the healing power of the Goddess flowing through me.
- I am one with the world around me. The Universe is constantly sending me messages and direction.
- Now, is the time for my ascension. I return to light.
- I accept what I cannot change.
- With a twisted tongue, I speak both sides of the truth.

The power of the feminine has been undervalued for centuries. It's time we reclaimed this gift. This sisterhood. This strength. This receiving. By understanding our personal energy and using its various components, you can become more powerful than ever before.

It doesn't matter what archetype comes into your life or when - you will go through seasons when one archetype is more dominant than another and that's okay, give yourself permission to flow through archetypes as you feel drawn to them. If you just had children, for example, your more like to connect to the mother archetype. The archetypes do not always work in harmony so it's important to embody only what you feel called to at the stage within your life. You will know within your practice and path when it's time.

The key thing about feminine energy and archetype work isn't which ones come outwards but how they work together inside you; some combinations feel harmonious while others seem clashing within each other – listen to your body and tap into your intuition. A huge factor to keep in mind when practicing embodiment of the archetypes is where you're at in your menstrual cycle, what phase of the moon is happening and how far along someone feels with their journey- because each archetype carries a certain energy which attracts more dominant traits from these 3 categories (Mood/Emotion; Mindfulness Skills & Relationship Dynamics).

> "The deep Feminine, the mystery of consciousness, she who is life, is longing for our transformation as much as we are. She holds back, allowing us free reign to choose, nudging us occasionally with synchronicities, illness, births and deaths ... But when we make space for Her, she rushes into all the gaps, engulfing us with her desire for life and expression. This is what She longs for, this is what we are for: experiencing the Feminine through ourselves. We simply need to slow down and find where to put our conscious attention."
> – Lucy H. Pearce, Burning Woman

As we enter this new phase of life and begin to awaken the Goddess within, I think it's important to celebrate yourself along the way. Your work is vast - you deserve some self-love and celebration of your accomplishments because they will help guide you in ways that only make sense for YOU. Magick. Some signs to look for that feminine energy is awakening within you are feeling empathetic, compassionate and overall, gentler in situations, with people and things. Your intuition kicks up and you begin to trust yourself and just have that sense of knowing. Your creativity begins to soar, and you may feel urges and cravings to just cultivate and create new things. You will find yourself in a place where kindness is an expected thing, and you receive more acts of it. You're able to forgive quickly with no intentions on getting back at those who wronged, so communication becomes easier because people know how much love there really is behind your words and actions. You will be in a state of peace and harmony and learn ways to feel your emotions unapologetically and process accordingly.

You are a passionate person with an open heart. You don't miss out on experiences, no matter how strange or intimate they may be; in fact you find it fascinating.

When people close themselves off from others for their own safety - you understand why that is so difficult because of your empathy towards all living things. You have a calling to offer healing to those scars into beautiful artwork. You offer full acceptance for others just as they are.

You outstretch your heart enough to embrace anything life throws at you knowing this is part of your journey. You give your body and its phases the love they deserve.

COURTNEY HANSON

Courtney,

Wow, what a ride it's been! Did you ever think that we would be here? I know right now you feel empty, heartbroken and hopeless but I am here to tell you it gets better. Like better than what you can even imagine right now. We go back and finish school - you are a freaking spiritual bad ass. We continue to heal, we cut out toxic relationships, our children thrive, we stay married, we meet these people who change our lives within our career. We join a sisterhood and become proud of ourselves. I need you to hold on and to walk through all the pain, guilt and shame you feel inside. The only way we get better is to walk through it. You're going to cry a lot, you're going to get mad, you're going to forgive but most of all you are going to grow as a human and soul like you never thought possible. Your heart... Your heart is open, and this is where we live now. We do generational curse breaking girl, like did you ever think that was possible? You did that shit! The chaos stops and the pieces get put back together. It's not a quick process so I need you to practice patience with me. You don't know this yet, but you are so very loved. Everything you need is within you - we just need to get some crap out of the way first. All the things you wish you were but didn't believe you were worthy of you become. I used to hate you for all the choices you put us through, but I forgive and love you at such a deep level. I now know we just had some lessons to walk through. Your story, your life, your vulnerability is helping women. Your heart people see. Just keep going. I've got you.

"She came back a completely different person.

She had changed.

The girl that cared what everyone thought didn't seem to care at all.

Her mind was clear. She became free."

-Your Highest Self

About the Author

Courtney Hanson is an expert in transforming the lives of women all over the world. With a history of resilience in both the physical and spiritual realm, Courtney is equipped to get your mind, body and soul to a level of divine joy and a path with your personal practice in healing. She has the following licenses and certifications to help you remove limiting beliefs, heal from trauma, balance your chakras, renew your spirit and step into your dharma. NLP and Hypnotherapist, Meditation Expert, Energy Healing Therapist, Ayurveda Certified, Reiki Master, Yoga Instructor, Intuitive, and Motivational Speaker.

Courtney runs the podcast *The Sweetest Little Life* and has a constant stream of free resources for those on their personal path to grow from at www.thesweetestlittlelife.com Courtney is a wife, mother of three and successful entrepreneur. Her journey through life is the framework that has led her to passionately and fiercely help others. She hasn't just overcome darkness, trauma, and depression – she came inches away from death and she has used them as steppingstones to shape her into the woman she is today, helping others reach their goals physically, mentally and spiritually. Let her help you break through the barriers, step into your purpose and become the divine inner goddess you were destined to be.

With love and gratitude.

Made in United States
Orlando, FL
01 February 2022

14306728R00207